DATE DUE

DEMCO 38-296

Weaving Ourselves into the Land

SUNY Series in
Native American Religions

Kenneth M. Morrison, editor

Weaving Ourselves into the Land

Charles Godfrey Leland, "Indians,"
and the
Study of Native American Religions

Thomas C. Parkhill

State University of New York Press

Published by
State University of New York Press, Albany

© 1997 State University of New York

For information, address the State University of New York Press,
State University Plaza, Albany, NY 12246

Library of Congress Cataloging-in-Publication Data

Parkhill, Thomas.
    Weaving ourselves into the land : Charles Godfrey Leland, Indians,
and the study of Native American religions / Thomas Parkhill.
       p.   cm. — (SUNY series in Native American religions)
    Includes bibliographical references and index.
    ISBN 0-7914-3453-2 (hc : alk. paper). — ISBN 0-7914-3454-0 (pb :
alk. paper)
    1. Indians of North America—Religion. 2. Algonquian mythology.
3. Indians of North America—Public opinion. 4. Stereotype
(Psychology) 5. Leland, Charles Godfrey, 1824-1903. 6. Public
opinion—North America. I. Title. II. Series
E98.R3P245   1997
299'.7—dc20   96-41611
                                          CIP

10 9 8 7 6 5 4 3 2 1

Contents

PREFACE

Long before this book went to the editors at SUNY Press it was "work-shopped," not unlike a piece of drama might be. As I note in the Acknowledgments, I gave the draft manuscript to a number of trusted assessors and asked them to help me improve the work by making helpful responses as they read the text. My revisions were informed by these responses. Later, SUNY Press sent the manuscript to other assessors who, in addition to passing judgement on the text, provided suggestions for revision. A number of these people who read this book in draft and responded to it were adamant that I needed to make my "central thesis" more prominent in the introduction and first chapters. I needed, one assessor said, to stop "walking backwards through the text" and get things straightened around. I appreciate these concerns; I worried about this myself. Surely if this book is "really" about the negative impact flowing from the use of the "Indian" stereotype, why not foreground it? Why not at least begin with it?

Good questions.

First, this book is not about just one thing. I realized this when I tried to name it. My draft titles kept going on and on, following the turns the book itself takes. These turns may require some readers to practice patience.

The origins of these turns may help explain their presence. As I continued my inquiry into the minutiae of Charles Godfrey Leland and his work of a hundred years ago, my own thinking changed and grew. This process is common, I gather, to many who read and write by way of carrying out inquiries. Nonetheless, these changes resulted in some of the turns. Further, I made a conscious decision not to remove myself from this study. Since as academics our feelings and biases shape our work even to the very questions we ask of the "data," I feel compelled to admit who I am so readers might make better use of my thinking. My biggest presence in this book is not where I let my feelings show, or recount embarrassing incidents from my past, but rather in the way the book unfolds. The shape of the book replicates my story about how I came to see the work of Charles Godfrey Leland, about the stereotype of the "Indian," and about the study of Native American religions.

As I noted above, some readers find this approach frustrating. I sympathize. I had my moments of impatience myself. If, however, you are like one of my colleagues at St. Thomas University who admits he reads all academic papers and student essays back to front, starting with the bibliography, so he can see what the text is about without having to wait, you will find here reason to follow your custom, as well as miss something of the process of my own inquiry here reproduced.

It is my conviction that in Leland's case we learn more by confronting what at first seems like his "idiosyncratic academic twitches" before pushing on to our commonality with him. So, while I understand feelings of impatience, I hope most readers will bear with me through the whole of the story I tell here. I begin with a tale of twin brothers, Kluskap and Malsum, and from there consider in turn this story's history, the one involving Leland; my thinking about the stereotype of the "Indian" in its oscillating usage; the influence of that stereotype and its use on the study of Native American people generally, and their religions more particularly; and finally my efforts to understand the deep-seated need that causes many of us to invoke the stereotype of the "Indian" despite our awareness that it doesn't fit, and indeed may harm, living, breathing Native American people.

Acknowledgments

With this book I am "putting my oar" in the conversation about the study of Native American religions. Prior to this I have eavesdropped at the edges of that conversation; I've even cleared my throat tentatively a few times. Here, though, I "find my voice."

One of the problems with these images—putting in my oar, finding my voice—is that they suggest that writing this book has been a solitary endeavor. Nothing could be further from the truth. The artifact that now is this book results from and points back to a complicated series of interrelationships that usually, but not always, included me. This same social quality of the researching-thinking-writing means, looking ahead, that this book intends to engage others in this conversation. All this is a long-winded way of saying that this acknowledgments section—because it honors the social quality of my work—is most important to me.

There is a group of people, many unknown to each other, who became my "trusted assessors." Each of these trusted assessors read a draft of a version of this book and responded in the margins and by way of extended comments. Obviously these assessors each gave me an assessment of my work. Following my colleague, Douglas Vipond, I call them "trusted" because I believed these people would be honest without being hurtful; without exception they were. As I look over this list of trusted assessors I feel overwhelmed by my debt to them. They are a diverse group—colleagues both within and without religious studies, former students, friends—all with whom I shared my work in an unfinished form. I often felt vulnerable—I was sharing my halting wonky voice, not-yet-ready for lively conversation. Because writing is sometimes writing-to-think, I often learned from these trusted assessors what I really thought about the "Indian" stereotype and the study of Native American religions. When these assessors did not respond as

I had thought they might, their responses were especially helpful. The "angry" and "skittish" responses I write about in chapter 1 were particularly helpful. From them I began to get a sense of how powerful and dangerous some of the things about which I was writing were. Because each trusted assessor is a different reader, and because I tried to ask each for specific kinds of responses, and because each was kind and honest about my text, I was able to learn from each. These trusted assessors include Jeff Kay, Serena Francis, Douglas Vipond, James Reither, Russ Hunt, Sam Gill, Earle Waugh, Matt McDonald, Ken Morrison, Ruth Whitehead, Michael George, Larry Finkelman, Ron Grimes, David Kinsley, Lynn Caravan, Alison Belyea, Heather Todd, Patricia Dold, Anne Pearson, Dan Ennis, and Dorothy Turner.

One of the assessors engaged by SUNY and who later identified himself—Christopher Vecsey—deserves, by the quality and generosity of his comments, to be in this list of trusted assessors.

A number of the trusted assessors guided me at important points in my work, often by providing an important reference or references. These guides include Russ Hunt, Sam Gill, Earle Waugh, Ken Morrison, Ruth Whitehead, and Ron Grimes.

Archivists and librarians are vital to any extended research project. This one is no exception. Among the many librarians who have helped me, I want to single out the following: Linda Hansen, formerly of the Harriet Irving Library, Fredericton, N.B., Canada; Patricia Townsend, Acadia University Archivist, Wolfville, N.S., Canada; Benoît Thériault, and Geneviève Eustache of the Archives of the Canadian Museum of Civilization; Eric Swanick, New Brunswick Legislative Library; Charles Kelly, Manuscript Division, Library of Congress, Washington, D.C.; and Elizabeth Hamilton, Documents Librarian, the Harriet Irving Library.

Tom Sinclair-Faulkner read a draft of an article based on my earliest research and told me I had a book to write.

Thomas Abler, drawing on his extensive research on Silas Rand, provided me with a very useful reference; Serena Francis was kind enough to research this reference in the Archives of Acadia University.

David Seljak unexpectedly and generously gave me direction on two different occasions thereby enriching chapter 6 manyfold.

Laszlo Szabo kindly gave me permission to conduct research in the story collection he amassed for the Canadian Museum of Civilization.

Maureen Matthews and the Canadian Broadcasting Corporation

Ideas radio program gave permission to use excerpts from "*Isinamowin: The White Man's Indian.*"

Ralph Carlisle Smith and Angela-Marie Joanna Varesano in their Ph.D. dissertations did much of the groundwork on Charles Godfrey Leland, making my task much lighter.

In 1992, Peter Bernard, then band manager in the Lennox Island (Prince Edward Island, Canada) community welcomed me and provided me with a copy of *Micmac Legends of Prince Edward Island.*

From Andrea Bear Nicholas I received a number of timely references, as well as a model for careful scholarship, and although I am fairly certain she does not agree fully with my conclusions, she has always supported my work.

I began work on this project while on a sabbatical leave, granted by St. Thomas University, which also provided the kind of support only an institution can. One of my research trips to the Library of Congress was supported in part by a Social Sciences and Humanities Research Council General Research Grant. For this support I am grateful. A preliminary study of the Kluskap-Malsum story appeared in the *American Indian Culture and Research Journal,* whose editors and assessors helped me focus my work. Bev Thornton and Robert Evans helped with the photographs; Laura Glenn copy edited the text; Ruth Arseneault proofread it.

Noel Knockwood, George Paul, and John Martin generously shared with me what they knew of the Kluskap-Malsum story, and trusted me with their words. Margaret Paul, Peter Christmas, and Harry LaPorte, at different times and in different contexts spoke with me about the same story and puzzled with me about its absence in the communities they knew.

From Harry LaPorte I also received a reference about Leland's influence on contemporary wicca; from *elsoniwit skout* I learned much about myself and received a way of praying, for which I am most grateful.

Jessica Brookes-Parkhill and Charles Francis put up with late breakfasts and bouts of inattention as this project consumed four or five summers during their childhoods. The depth of my appreciation of their patience with me will not fully register, I predict, until they know firsthand how impatient some children can be.

Dorothy Turner found the right mix of prodding and encouragement to help me over the last inertia hurdle; for her wholehearted support and much more, I feel blessed.

Chapter 1

An Introduction to the Conversation
Charles G. Leland, and Naming

I am not very good at introductions. Two people meet; both are known to me but unknown to each other. I am there, and responsible for making connections sufficient for them to relate to one another. I often feel uncomfortable; I am never sure I have "done it right." Nevertheless, if you are going to be able to engage in this inquiry in a meaningful way, you will need to have a passing familiarity with some of the situations and people to which this study attends. You will need a series of introductions. The first of these is to the study of Native American religions itself.

Proper introductions are difficult at the best of times. These are difficult times for the academic study of Native American religions. It is a study haunted by a history of conquest and colonialism, whose present is marked by passionate intensity. Here is a story—featuring an Internet discussion—that illustrates what I mean:

In late April of 1993 a long message appeared virtually simultaneously on three academic electronic discussion groups.[1] Ron Grimes was making public a "highly charged stand-off" (1.1) that was simmering all over North America, but that boiled furiously at the University of Colorado where Native Studies scholars Sam Gill, Vine Deloria, Jr., Ward Churchill, and Deward Walker teach, and where Grimes was on sabbatical. Grimes was direct. He asked three questions contextualized in a long, thoughtful message:

1. Should or should not European Americans be teaching courses on Native American religions?

2. If we should not, why not, and what would be the results of
our refusal?
3. If we should, how best can we proceed? (1.1)

The questions were powerful, but the long message in which they were
embedded was what left me speechless. Grimes reported some of what
I already knew: the climate in Native American religions studies was
deteriorating. Some not-Native male scholars were leaving the study of
Native American religions. Against this phenomenon Grimes wrote,
"The notion of abandoning academic turf (as if it were bad land) and
giving it back to 'the natives' (as if it were a gift we previously owned)
seems to me a piece of bad choreography to which we have danced
several times before" (1.1). In response to those who claimed this situation was no different than non-Buddhists teaching about Buddhism,
Grimes replied that "this is a serious problem not to be written off by
assimilating it to the study of religion in general." And he added, "I
would just like some company, both Native and non-Native, in thinking through this specific dilemma" (1.3). I was not very good company.
I had little to say. All my easy answers had been gutted. Others were
not so easily deterred. The messages on the Religion discussion group
kept coming. Grimes weighed in again:

We who do fieldwork do so under both ethical and legal con-
straints regarding our consultants. Stealing sacred secrets would
not pass the ethics committee at my university. Is such knowledge, obtained under colonial conditions, legitimate for us to use?
Much (not all) of what we know about indigenous religions was
obtained under shady circumstances. Methodologically speaking,
how do we proceed—if our data is shady, our qualifications ques-
tionable, and our students and colleagues feeling ripped off by
acts of cultural imperialism?

I figure the only way to answer such questions is to become
identified with them. So far, much of what I hear sounds like
we're deflecting them. (1.10)

On a number of occasions Grimes underscored his fundamental assertion that "the primary issue is not whether only Native Americans can
study Native Americans but what it means when non-Natives determine most if not all of the terms of the debate" (1.17).

On into May the discussion churned. Deward Walker sent an out-line of a presentation he had given on the issue in another venue. My friend and mentor, Sam Gill, posted a long message explaining his "rubric shift" from Native American religions to religion and culture (1.22). I read hurt and anger, frustration and disappointment in his words. In his response to Gill, Grimes surveyed the academic land-scape: "At the moment negotiations are hard. There is shouting. There is sulking. There is conspiring. There is anger" (1.25). That was clear: one person suggested that there should be classes on Sam Gill at "Indian schools" (3.9); another that it was time for Gill to abandon the area completely (3.21). Grimes suggested a shift of metaphors from embattlement ("hold your ground") to human family ("we shouldn't walk away, I say to myself, they're family") (1.25). Reflecting on the depth of feeling in Sam Gill's posting, I found myself wondering what Grimes's family was like. I have been part of a number of families; I've often felt hurt, attacked . . . embattled. And walking away is never pos-sible: "There are continuing connections, obligations, relationships, snarls of all kinds," which, if one does find a way to amputate, result in a diminishing of what makes us human.[2]

Through May the discussion continued. There were what looked to me charges of racism leveled, later retracted . . . after a fashion. There were misunderstandings, some angry; these were "conversations hard and wild."[3] Improbably, the discussions had an extraordinarily long life. Electronic conversations rarely last more than a couple of weeks; this one lasted a month. If printed out, the conversation would run to over ninety single-spaced pages.

By late May the flurry of messages seemed to have finally subsided. Then, in early June, Vine Deloria, Jr., posted a message (3.36). After citing a number of instances where scholarly work had been or could be used either directly or indirectly in political arenas to harm Native Americans, Deloria concluded, "So we should admit that everything we do has political implications in the world outside our walls—the real world as it were." He went on to criticize the inappropriateness of many of the "basically insulting categories of analysis" often applied to Native American religions. He complained that "incredibly smug" scholars of Native American religions "rush non-Indian frameworks of analysis into the discussion as soon as possible in order to control the definitions of what is being said and thought about regarding Native religions. . . ." The notion that academic discourse might itself be a way of perpetuating the conquest of Native peoples had been raised earlier in the discussion by Grimes and others. Deloria here highlighted the point eloquently. He went on to criticize Gill specifically for his use of the word "goddess" in his study of the Mother Earth story. He stressed that the "Near Eastern concept" of "gods" had little to do with the "experience of personal energy within the physical universe," an experience with an important emotional component.[4]

Deloria finishes his message with a warning:

> I don't see why non-Indians cannot teach courses on Native religions, as long as they understand and accept the fact of modern American political life, and with the knowledge that they are intruding on the emotional commitments and experiences of a specific group of people who may not appreciate their efforts, and are willing to take the consequences.

Despite the provocativeness of Deloria's posting, the discussion veered off in another unrelated direction.[5]

Most of what follows was written before this discussion singed the edges of my electronic mailbox. I knew the outline and tenor of the discussion, however, prior to the sound of Ron Grimes's disconcerting whistle-blowing, Sam Gill's explanation of his "rubric shift," and Vine Deloria's challenge to the discipline.[6] I knew from the reaction of some "trusted assessors"—people to whom I sent drafts of this work for comment. As a study of the study of Native American religions, this inquiry intends to shed some light on the errors we students of these religions have made and continue to make in our work. I imagined myself a "good guy," trying to straighten out some harmful scholarly inclinations. I was perplexed, then, when some of my trusted assessors seemed angry or skittish in their responses. In this volatile atmosphere, I realized, even my awkward introductions were likely to generate friction sufficient for ignition; the larger study was likely to cause explosions.

As this realization dawned, my first reaction was fear. If trusted assessors responded this way, how would less sympathetic readers react? I was not sure I wanted to deal with what Deloria calls "the consequences." I toyed with leaving the manuscript unfinished, then thought about expunging all potentially controversial sections. I considered reducing this inquiry to a story of a 100-year-old scholarly transgression, the affront I felt by it, and leave it at that. Obviously I didn't act on my fear, but I thought about it. I relate my failure of nerve here both as an acknowledgment of the intensity of the conversation into which I send my voice, and as preparation for much of the remainder of this chapter with its awkward but thought-full labels and careful groundwork.

There are no good, all-inclusive labels for the original inhabitants of the American continents and their descendants.[7] In the early 1990s a number of labels vie for prominence—First Nations People, Amerindians, indigenous people, and Aboriginal people (even "Aboriginals"!). I have settled on the imperfect "Native American" largely because it has become the scholarly convention. As well, I prefer this label because it directs attention to what I will argue is at the heart of scholarly difficulties in the study of the religions of these peoples.

One label I never considered using was "Indian." The label floats in a solution of complex images, saturated with meanings. Fifteen years ago, in his *The White Man's Indian*, Robert Berkhofer demonstrated the complexity of those meaning-rich images, arguing that the term "Indian" should be reserved not for real human beings but for only the images themselves. Said Berkhofer, "I have employed the phrase *Native American(s)* to refer to the actual peoples designated by the term *Indian(s)*, which I reserve almost exclusively for the White image of those persons."[8] I have followed Berkhofer in this, and, noting our carelessness in the intervening years, I have placed shudder quotes around Indian to remind the reader and the author that "Indian" connotes not a person, but a set of images, a stereotype.[9] I will argue in what follows that the use of this stereotype is characterized by an oscillating duality. "Indian," then, refers to a stereotype used in two different ways.[10]

The brief quotation from Berkhofer above uses the label "White"; the title of his book uses "White Man." I have chosen to follow the convention that has arisen in the last decade of avoiding "White" or "White man." These too are more stereotype than helpful generalization. The problem, however, extends past these labels. "Whiteman," "White," "White Man," *as well as* their replacements, "non-Indian," and "non-Native" are, in most usages, stereotypical foils for images of the "Indian." Further, using this set of labels undergirds a central characteristic of the stereotype of the "Indian," one I shall describe in chapter 5 as the assumption of a nearly unbridgeable chasm between "Indian" and "Whiteman." I have therefore decided against using any of these terms.

What is needed is a label that can be used more descriptively. I have chosen "not-Native" in hopes that the jarring quality of the name will serve to remind reader and author that this is a descriptive term referring to a wide variety of peoples from disparate ethnic backgrounds. Where I have needed a more general label I have used "hegemonic culture" and "hegemonic popular culture" or "North American culture" if that seemed more appropriate. While I am aware on one hand that heaping U.S. and Canadian cultures along with their diverse populations into one lump is prone to the same abuse as the use of "Indian"; on the other hand, I find it useful and accurate to generalize about the mainstream anglophone North American cultural expressions in print and broadcast media.[11] With other scholars I acknowledge significant regional and national variations in the relationships between not-Native and Native Americans,[12] yet I see a consistency transcending time and place of the dual use of the "Indian" stereotype.

Inevitably in a conversation with this focus on stereotypes the question arises: Surely you are not saying that all generalizations about Native Americans are false? Not exactly. Generalizations about Native Americans are useful *where there are similarities*. More often than not, however, the "Indian" stereotype arises out of a not-Native necessity that forces similarities among Native American cultures (including religions) where none exist. We hope our generalizations have some connection to the reality of the people of whom we speak; we know our stereotypes do not. Generalizations are relatively flexible tools of understanding, not laden with emotional intensity; thus easily changed or retracted in the face of contrary evidence. Stereotypes, on the other hand, are far more rigid, held with an emotional intensity born of some need that makes alteration difficult and retraction agonizing.[13]

From one perspective, then, the difficulty of naming the original inhabitants of the Americas and their descendants—a difficulty at least as old as the first arrival of Europeans—stems from trying to generalize about different groups of people whose differences seem ready at any moment to overwhelm their commonality. Of course this difficulty arises not only with Native Americans, but with other peoples as well.[14] One would think, however, that if we were careful to be specific about particular Native American nations, this difficulty of naming would not arise. One would think.

This inquiry into the study of Native American religions touches on four Native American nations: the Maliseet, Micmac, Passamaquoddy, and Penobscot. These names are the ones currently in use, but they are neither the names that occur in the earliest European reports, nor are they the names that these people have historically had for themselves. The Maliseet called themselves *wulastuk kewiuk*, the beautiful-river-people; the Micmac, *lnu'k*, human beings; the Passamaquoddy, *pestemohkatiyek*, the people of the place where pollock are plentiful; and the Penobscot, *panawahpskek*, where the rocks widen or open out.[15]

There is no easy, neat way to refer to this particular group of Algonkian-speaking people of Northeastern North America. As a group Micmacs, Maliseets, Penobscots, and Passamaquoddies have no label that refers only to themselves. Some scholars have used the term "Wabanaki" to label these four Native American nations, but historically that term was used for a confederacy that included the Mohawks of Kanawake.[16] "Algonkian-speaking people of Northeastern North America," besides showing little economy of phrase, also includes more than these four nations.[17] Because it describes the historical kin relationship between the Maliseet, Passamaquoddy, and Penobscot, on the one hand, and the more distant cousins, the Micmac, on the other, many scholars have opted for the shorthand "Abenaki and Micmac."[18] I follow that labeling convention here, well aware of its imperfections.

Of the four, the Micmac used the easternmost territory, comprising what is now mainland Nova Scotia as well as Cape Breton, Prince Edward Island, and parts of what is now New Brunswick and Quebec. The Maliseet used the land along the St. John River from the St. Lawrence River to the Bay of Fundy, while the Passamaquoddy used land extending along the Bay of Fundy south from Maliseet territory and centering on the St. Croix River. The Penobscot used the land south of the Passamaquoddies, in a territory extending from the Bay of Fundy north into the interior of Maine, centering on the Penobscot River. Prior to European contact the Abenaki used land from the St. John River in what is now New Brunswick to Lake Champlain in what is now Vermont.

Currently Micmac people live on twenty-eight reserves in the Canadian provinces of New Brunswick, Prince Edward Island, Québec, Newfoundland, and Nova Scotia as well as one community in Maine and a large off-reserve population in Boston. The Micmac people who will figure in this inquiry are from communities in Big Cove, New Brunswick; Shubenacadie, Nova Scotia; Maria, Québec; and Lennox Island, Prince Edward Island. Maliseets live in eight communities with six reserves along the St. John River. There are two Passamaquoddy communities at three reservations in Maine, and one Penobscot community at Old Town reservation, also in Maine.[19] The significant Maliseet and Passamaquoddy consultants who appear in these pages—Gabriel Acquin, Tomah Joseph, Louis Mitchell—lived in the nineteenth-century versions of the communities of St. Mary's on the St. John River near Fredericton, New Brunswick and Sebayik (Pleasant Point) near Eastport, Maine.

While this inquiry touches directly on the religious history of these four Native American nations, its central concern is with the scholarly study of these and other Native American religions. I begin the inquiry with where my curiosity was first engaged—the story of Kluskap and Malsum, and the preeminent collector and reteller of that story, Charles Godfrey Leland.[20] Leland is himself worthy of a full-length study; the data from his life and folklore studies have already sustained two Ph.D. dissertations.[21] His personal religious history bears on this inquiry as much for what it does not contain as for what it does. Raised in the Unitarian Church of the Reverend W. H. Furness in Philadelphia, Leland spent his college years at Princeton attending the Episcopal Church, enamoured of its elitism, and, because it was required, the Presbyterian Church associated with the College.[22] While attending the latter, according to his own account, he read books during the sermons—which he characterized as mostly pouring water on a drowned mouse.[23] After he left Princeton, he was not a regular churchgoer, and he did not belong to any church.[24] Except the liberal Christian influence of the Unitarians and a life-long aversion to Roman Catholicism, little from his interaction with mainstream Christianity seems to have influenced his life work. Indeed, when he writes of his experiences of Christianity, as he does infrequently, he seems curiously unemphatic, especially in contrast to the extensive and enthusiastic work of his folklore studies. More than a mere observer but less than a full participant, Leland was attracted in his lifetime to Gypsy lore and language, the "Old Religion" of Italy, as well as the religions and stories of those he called the "Red Indians."

Although Charles Leland would, if he could have afforded it, have spent his whole life investigating liminal peoples and the religions at the margins of elite society, he could not and did not. He trained as a lawyer,[25] but worked as a magazine editor, journalist, and political writer. In this latter capacity he campaigned for abolition, using the argument that slavery was unnecessary because "white men" were capable of doing everything better than "negroes," including raising cotton. Furthermore, the dignity and prosperity of these "white men" were at stake.[26]

Part of Leland's journalistic duties took him to the "frontier" of the adolescent nation, which in 1866 was located in Kansas. There, as part of his tourist entertainment, he hunted buffalo and met a group of Kaw, a Siouan people.[27] Later, after a ten-year stay in England, he would meet the Passamaquoddy consultants who would provide the impetus for retelling, in 1884, a large collection of Abenaki and Micmac stories, *The Algonquin Legends of New England*, most recently reprinted in 1992.[28] In his autobiography Leland is intent on underscoring his close relationship with Native Americans, a theme picked up by his biographer.[29] In fact, Leland felt that there was something of the "Indian" in him, a character trait that was manifest in all manner of behavior from his habit of making small smudge fires alongside the road during rest breaks to what he saw as his "natural" rapport with Native Americans. This feature of Leland's self-understanding will prove illuminating in the chapters that follow. By way of this introduction, though, it is important to note that Leland is not alone in his sense that he shares something special with the "Indian." If the purely anecdotal evidence of the number of people who are eager to tell me of their "Indian" grandmother is a worthy indicator, this feeling is widespread among not-Natives.[30] I, too, have experienced the pull of this feeling. As a vantage point from which to reflect briefly on similar phenomena, I want to recount my most memorable formative encounter with the "Indian."

I spent my fifteenth summer as a staff member at a Boy Scout camp (called a "Reservation"[!]) in northern Vermont. Toward the end of the summer I was inducted into an esoteric organization within the Boy Scouts of America called the Order of the Arrow (see Figure 1.1).[31] The first part of the initiation was publicly to set apart the boys who, if they passed the Ordeal, would become members of the Order. It was dark but not quite chilly when the whole camp arranged itself in a number of concentric horseshoe-shaped lines before a large tipi in a field. Standing next to the tipi, a drummer in a loincloth and single feather kept a steady beat as we assembled. The boys in the lines stopped punching each other on the arms; there was anticipation. The drumming suddenly stopped. Even though I had seen this event before and knew all the guys—Jeff, Butch, Pud, and the rest—who would soon appear from the tipi, I found myself holding my breath.

Figure 1.1. "The Higher Vision" from *Order of the Arrow Handbook, 50 Years Anniversary Edition,* New Brunswick, N.J.: Boy Scouts of America, 1965. (Courtesy Boy Scouts of America)

We heard the bells first. With each step the ankle bells jangled. The drum began again. In all there were five "Indians" who emerged from the tipi: first a loincloth-clad torch carrier, followed by three powerful looking "Indians," then another torch carrier. The three central "Indians" commanded our attention. Over twenty-five years later I cannot remember exactly what they wore, but I do remember Plains dress: a full eagle-feather headdress on one, a complete buckskin outfit on another, buffalo horn head gear; one had his face painted half black and half red. They walked slowly, steadily, in time to the drum between the curving lines of boys. A sixth torch carrier had joined them, walking equally ceremoniously, but always behind the line facing the other five. Periodically this sixth, recognizing an initiate, would stop behind him, face the drum, and raise his torch slowly into the air. The drumming crescendoed, then stopped abruptly just as the three impressive figures stopped and turned to face the neophyte.

My own Scout troop was in camp; I had seen this ceremony three times already that summer. I knew, standing there in the dark, there was a good chance I would be chosen for initiation. I was nervous—scared even—and angry with myself for being so. I reasoned that two of the three prominent "Indians" (the "medicine man" and the "chief"?) were my bunkmates in the staff tent. When they stopped in front of me, I looked for some sign of recognition. There was none. I felt the adrenaline rush of fight-or-flight; my heart pounded; I forgot to breathe. One of them placed his hands on my shoulders, then slapped my left shoulder three times, hard.

I do not remember what happened next. I do remember all of the boys who were "tapped out" came together later that night at a central meeting area. There we underwent another part of the Ordeal. I remember my shoulder was black and blue for days after. I remember I was sworn to secrecy. Curiously, although I left the Scouts shortly thereafter (and not because of this initiation experience), I still feel bound by that vow. Suffice it to say that the "Indian" continued to play an important ceremonial role during the remaining twenty-three hours of the Ordeal. Further, my knowledge that the "Indians" were really Jeff and Butch and Pud and that the "torches" were really rolls of toilet paper soaked in kerosene, stuck in number-ten cans nailed to broom handles, did nothing to blunt my adolescent sense of epiphany when, after a typical initiatory trial that marched us blindfolded deep into the forest, an anonymous "brave" pulled down my blindfold and spun me around to reveal a breathtaking tableau of "real-live" torch-lit "Indians" arrayed on a bluff above me.

Reflecting on this sequence of events some time later, I came to see this whole experience, including the imitation of the "Indians," as pretty strange stuff. It turns out, however, that my experience of "Indians" is not all that unusual. The Scouts are not alone in their desire to play or even become "Indians." This "persistent theme in North American culture" has found expression in other children's camps, including those of the YMCA, as well as the Woodcraft League of Ernest Thompson Seton.[32] If these imitations of "Indians" by children were all there was, it would be enough to draw our attention; but adults, too, play "Indian."

The "Indian" Hobbyist Movement entails not-Natives learning

Figure 1.2. "Indian" hobbyist, Westerwald (near Koblentz) Germany. (Photograph by Dawn Goss)

"Indian" arts and crafts, songs, dances, ceremonies, and other aspects of (usually Plains) culture in order to gather periodically and share what they have learned with one another at "powwows." The result is what looks to be a Plains encampment in Cleveland, Ohio, or Detroit, Michigan; Dresden, Germany, or Stockholm, Sweden. Infrequently some political awareness of the situation of contemporary Native Americans is part of the hobbyist movement; usually it is not (see Figure 1.2).[33]

Beginning in the 1960s in North American popular counterculture, as Steward Brand indicates, "hippies" were also enamored of "Indians" but expressed their imitation in a much less systematic and rigorous way than the Hobbyists.[34] More recently, the Bear Tribe

Medicine Society provides an example with a more obvious and systematic religious dimension. These mostly not-Native followers of Sun Bear often express the transformative power of Sun Bear's words and Bear Tribe programs by their "Indian" names—Elizabeth "Turtle Heart" Robinson, Simon Henderson "Corn Man," Erika Thunderbird Woman Malitsky, David Whitehawk Moore.[35] At a 1983 Gathering of the Tribe, participants paid $100 for three days of camping, meals, and instruction in offering tobacco, the sweat lodge, pipe ceremony, Give-Away, and Medicine Wheel.[36]

Ten years later the Bear Tribe was recovering from the death of its charismatic leader. Sun Bear "passed into the Spirit" on June 19, 1992, from esophageal cancer, naming Marlise Wabun Wind as his successor to the position of Medicine Chief of the Bear Tribe. He left behind "some questions . . . that anyone claiming to channel me would have to be able to answer to prove the truth of their claim," and a heart that "kept beating for an hour after his life essence left his body, like the heart of the turtle, symbol of this continent."[37] Wabun Wind remembered her teacher as "the first true contemporary bridge between the Native and mainstream cultures and as the visionary who brought the Medicine Wheel back to his people."[38] Whether the Bear Tribe can remain a viable not-Native religious option following the death of this charismatic leader remains, in 1993, to be seen. It is making every effort, trying to replace the single teacher with a "tribe of teachers" organized into a network, a "web of light," complete with an organizational chart.[39] The *Bear Tribe Directory* lists a number of different programs. The ten-day Introductory Program, at which the participant will encounter topics like "techniques for connecting with your own energy and the energy of Mother Earth" and "working with the sweat lodge and pipe ceremonies," has a sliding fee schedule from $695 to $1,195 depending on income. Included in the program are "teaching, meals and camping space" (27). Another teaching topic is the "history, philosophy and life-ways of indigenous peoples as they relate to contemporary life." The appellations and phrases are here all correct; but the "Indians" and their special teachings are not far beneath the surface.

Finally there are, in this catalog of imitative encounters with the "Indian," not-Native individuals who, for a variety of reasons, have passed themselves off as Native Americans. In other words, they have become "Indians." Included in this group are Jamake Highwater,

Figure 1.3. Grey Owl at Niagara Falls, July, 1937. (Photo courtesy of the Archives of Ontario/S14482. Source: Grey Owl and Anahareo Collection, lent by Dawn Richardson)

author of the 1981 *The Primal Mind* which was made into a television film.[40] Buffalo Child Long Lance, author of the 1928 *Long Lance,* who went on to lecture on behalf of Native Americans all over North America;[41] and Grey Owl, a writer and lecturer who toured Canada, England, and the United States in the 1930s. Born Archie Belaney, an Englishman, Grey Owl was unique for his claim to have converted from a life of hunting and trapping to one of conservation. Grey Owl's work with wildlife led to his employment as "caretaker of park animals" at Riding Mountain National Park in Manitoba, a position he held until his death in 1938 (see Figure 1.3).[42]

The point of cataloging these manifestations of this persistent cultural theme—imitating "Indians"—is to underscore their incongruity. As I began my research into the study of Native American religions, I found the theme itself, let alone its persistence, baffling. It is also unsettling. Playing at being "Indian" offends many Native people. It is easy to confuse the imitation of a stereotype and the "appropriation of Native cultures."[43] It was a breathtaking experience reading the *Bear Tribe Directory* and Wendy Rose's "The Great Pretenders: Further Reflections on Whiteshamanism" in the same midwinter week. Rose, a Hopi, includes mention of Sun Bear in a section entitled "Cults and Culture Vultures." She reports the Chippewa had "never participated in or attended bona fide native activities" and labels his coauthor (and now Medicine Chief) Wabun "a bona fide whiteshaman."[44] From Rose's point of view "whiteshamanism" is pernicious:

> During performances, whiteshamans typically don a bastardized composite of pseudo-Indian "style" buckskins, beadwork, head-bands, moccasins, and sometimes paper masks intended to por-tray native spiritual beings such as Coyote or Raven. They often appear carrying gourd rattles, eagle feathers, "peace pipes," med-icine bags, and other items reflective of native ceremonial life. Their readings are frequently accompanied by the burning of sage, "pipe ceremonies," the conducting of chants and beating of drums of vaguely native type, and the like. One may be hard-pressed to identify a particular indigenous culture being por-trayed, but the obviously intended effect is American Indian. The point is that the whiteshaman reader/performer aspires to "embody the Indian," in effect "becoming" *the* "real" Indian even when actual native people are present. Native reality is thereby subsumed and negated by imposition of a "greater" or "more universal" contrivance.[45]

If "whiteshamanism" is the process whereby not-Natives try to incarnate their own images of the "Indian" stereotype—and it seems to be—then Rose's last comment here gives one pause. On one hand, if her perception that her "Native reality" is "subsumed and negated" by "whiteshamanism" is based on her experience, it is inviolable. On the other hand, her perception points to a layered set of incongruities at the heart of this phenomenon.[46]

What draws my attention is not so much that these imitations are offensive, although they may well be. It is that they just do not fit—they are anomalous. If, as Jonathan Z. Smith says, incongruity is an occasion for thought,[47] then this phenomenon—the determined not-

Native imitation of the image of the "Indian"—serves as a fine spring-board for this inquiry.

It is not an accident that our inquiry begins in the next chapter with a story. Native Americans, like people everywhere, tell stories as one way of engaging in the paradoxical process of simultaneously creating and responding to a world of meaning. Not surprisingly then, studies of Native American religions often rely on the explication of stories for insight. The story of Kluskap and Malsum—the linchpin as well as the beginning of our inquiry—has meant and continues to mean much to people both not-Native and Native. I cannot discuss either the history or significance of this story without the reader knowing something of the story itself. First, then, we will need a telling of the story of Kluskap and his twin brother, Malsum.

Chapter 2

The Story of Kluskap and Malsum

The study of Native American religions often turns on stories. This story, like most, has little absolutely new in it. There is pride and deception and treachery and fratricide and a sad ending. At the same time—and not only because I am retelling it now and in this context—this story speaks to us.

Listen.

It is long ago. There are two brothers. They are twins, still inside their mother. Kluskap is one; Malsumsis the other. They are talking there, inside their mother.

Malsumsis says, "How, my older brother, will you be born?"

"I will be born just like the People are born."

"That is the ordinary way. It is for commonplace births. My birth will be different. I will be remembered for this thing." So says Malsumsis, that Little Wolf.

Moons pass. Finally, Kluskap is born from his mother as most of the People are. Malsumsis chooses a different way. He comes out through his mother's side. He kills his mother.

The twins grow up together. They have Power. One day Malsumsis asks something. One day Malsumsis asks his brother what will kill him. This thing he asks him. Kluskap thinks about this. To be born differently his brother had killed their mother. To give him this thing, this secret of his death, this would not be wise. So Kluskap says, "An owl's feather. This will kill me. And what, my younger brother, what will cause your death?"

Malsumsis says, "Being hit by a fern root. This will kill me."

It is night; there is a moon. The brothers are in the lodge. Kluskap is sleeping there. Malsumsis gets up and goes out. He searches for Owl. Soon he finds him. "Owl, give me one of your feathers," says Malsumsis. Owl knows something. He knows why Malsumsis asks for a feather. "No," says Owl, "I will not give you one of my feathers. I know your purpose."

This one, this Malsumsis, is enraged. Without thinking he takes up his bow, fixes an arrow and shoots Owl. From the dead bird's tail he takes a white feather.

He returns to the lodge. Kluskap is sleeping there. He nears Kluskap with this feather. Just at the place between the eyes Malsumsis strikes his older brother with Owl's feather.

And then Kluskap wakes up. "My younger brother," he says, "a fly has awoken me." Malsumsis hides the feather. But Kluskap has Power. He knows his younger brother's purpose. So he says to him, "How is it you have done this thing?"

Malsumsis says this. "I knew you were lying to me about the owl's feather. Why did you say this to me? I told you the truth in this. I told you of the fern root. But you did not tell the truth. Why did you lie to me, older brother?"

Kluskap thinks on this. And then he says, "You are right. I have offended you. I will tell you this thing. It is a pine root that will cause my death," Kluskap says. And he smiles at his younger brother, but he trusts him even less.

The twins go hunting together. Farther into the forest Malsumsis leads his older brother. As they go Malsumsis sees a large pine tree blown down by the wind. He sees a thing. He sees its roots torn from the earth.

At night they rest. There is a moon. The brothers are in the lodge; Kluskap is sleeping there. Malsumsis gets up and goes out. Malsumsis goes to the pine tree he had seen and tears off a root. And then he goes back to the lodge and approaches his older brother. He strikes Kluskap with the pine root.

And then Kluskap wakes up. Angry he wakes up. And this time he screams at Malsumsis. This time he rushes at him in anger, ready to fight. The Little Wolf is afraid. He runs away. He runs from his older brother's anger.

Kluskap sits by a brook, alone. He talks to himself, staring at the water. He talks of all that has happened with his younger brother. And then he says, "Ah, it is really the head of a cattail only that can kill me." And he stares at the water flowing by.

Beaver hears Kluskap's words. He goes and finds Malsumsis. He knows Malsumsis has Power. There he says this thing. There Beaver says, "I know the secret of your brother's death. Give me what I ask and I will tell you." Malsumsis thinks about this. And then, "I will give you whatever you ask," he says.

So Beaver says, "The head of the cattail will cause Kluskap's death. This I heard him say." He goes on, "And it is wings I want. To fly, to soar above the trees and lakes, I want wings!" At this Malsumsis laughs. He laughs and teases, "With a tail like that, what are you going to do with wings? You won't get off the ground!" And laughing he goes away.

Beaver goes too. He goes muttering, looking for Kluskap's lodge. Beaver is mad at what Malsumsis has said. He tells Kluskap all that has happened. Hearing this, Kluskap is at first furious. And then he knows a thing that makes him sad. He knows he must find his younger brother. And he knows that finding him he must kill him.

At the bank of the river he finds the fern that in the spring feeds the People. The fern has Power. He digs its root and then looks for his brother.

Near his own lodge he finds his younger brother. Kluskap surprises him there and strikes him with the fern root. Malsumsis dies.

Kluskap arranges his younger brother's body and sings the death songs. With his Power Kluskap turns Malsumsis into a range of mountains. You can still see those mountains along the Gaspé.

Kluskap stays in this world awhile, making it right for the People. He does many things for the People. He teaches them many things.

Time passes. Kluskap promises the People he will return. And then he leaves this world for another.

I want to leave aside the significance of this story for a time in order to discuss briefly its history. While the missionaries who lived with the Micmac and Abenaki people in the seventeenth and eighteenth centuries do not record this story (or any other story that features Kluskap), it appears in a relatively early collection of stories that dates from 1863. In that year one of a group of Maliseets told it to Arthur

Hamilton Gordon, then the lieutenant governor of the then British colony of New Brunswick. Further evidence that the story was popular among the Micmac and Abenaki people might be gleaned from its presence in Silas T. Rand's monumental collection, *Legends of the Micmacs* (1894), and its prominence both in Charles Godfrey Leland's *The Algonquin Legends of New England* (1884) and *Kulóskap the Master and Other Algonkin Poems* (1902) which Leland wrote with John Dyneley Prince. It does not turn up again in written records from Abenaki and Micmac communities until 1962 when a member of a folklore class at the University of Maine recorded the story from Viola Solomon, a Maliseet of the Tobique community in New Brunswick, not far from where the Lieutenant Governor had recorded it a hundred years earlier.[1]

In the late 1960s, Big Cove Micmac, Michael William Francis, painted a series of murals for the Lennox Island community of Prince Edward Island. Included in one mural is Malsum's face turned into a stone cliff, being slapped by the waves washing up. Almost twenty years later, two other Micmac artists, both inspired by Francis, painted their versions of the same scene. Like Michael William Francis, George Paul of the Red Bank community was commissioned by the community at Lennox Island to paint some of the old stories. The painting by Francis's nephew, Roger Simon, hangs in the Big Cove administration building along with a number of his other works. In 1992, the sixth-grade class from the Indian Island school in the Penobscot community at Old Town, Maine made a video that featured a version of the Kluskap-Malsum story.[2]

Currently there are fewer oral renderings of the Kluskap-Malsum story than there are visual renderings. One of the aforementioned artists, George Paul, and Nova Scotia Micmac elder, Noel Knockwood, are the only people I could discover who tell the story in religious or spiritual contexts. It is the perception of most of the Micmacs, Maliseets, Passamaquoddies, and Penobscots I consulted that the story is not well known.

The story of the twins, Kluskap and Malsum,[3] has, however, found its way into the popular culture of the hegemonic North American society. The popularity it would achieve in the last part of the twentieth century was prefigured by its place in a tourist's guidebook in vogue in the last quarter of the nineteenth century. Osgood's *The Maritime Provinces: Handbook for Travellers* lists a version of the story for inquisitive travelers to read just as they enter the Kennebecasis Bay of the Saint John River. Apparently the editor, M. F. Sweetser, felt that the traveler's experience of "this noble sheet of water" would here be enhanced by a "quaint Indian tale." Sweetser admits in the preface that "the handbook is a guide to assist the traveller in gaining the greatest amount of pleasure and information while passing through the most interesting portions of Eastern British America . . . with economy of money, time, and temper." So that his readers might be cognizant of the relative insignificance of this "Indian tale" Sweetser sets it off from the rest of the text—about where to eat and sleep and what to see and do—by its smaller font and tight line spacing. It is easily skipped over. In its first appearance in hegemonic popular culture, then, the Kluskap-Malsum story appears as attractive informational embroidery to enhance the traveler's pleasure in the passing landscape.[4]

Leaving aside the story's presence in the two Leland volumes (1884, 1902) and in Rand (1894) for later more detailed treatment, its next appearance is in the 1914 collection of stories by Lewis Spence. Following two general overview chapters, Spence arranges his *The Myths of the North American Indians* more or less along linguistic lines. Moving from east to west, the first of these is "Algonquian Myths and Legends"; the first story featured is a retelling of Kluskap and Malsum.[5] Spence makes no claim to have worked directly with Native Americans,[6] thus we can assume his version of the story derives from a written source. Even if his bibliography listed no other possible source for this story than *The Algonquin Legends of New England*,[7] and even if Spence's analysis of the story did not acknowledge Leland by name, we might well discern his hand in Spence's retelling. The content of the story is virtually identical to Leland's, some of the phrasing is very close, and the remaining stories in the beginning of this chapter— "Glooskap's Gifts," "Glooskap and the Baby," and so on—are also stories from Leland's collection. Spence's *The Myths of the North American Indians* was originally published in Canada, the United States, and Great Britain. It has been reprinted eleven times since 1914, most recently by Dover in the United States (1989) and Senate in England (1994).

The Kluskap-Malsum story next appears in the 1918 *Canadian Wonder Tales* by Cyrus Macmillan. An introductory note to a recent edition of this volume describes it as "long one of the best sources of Canadian tradition in an easily accessible form" (see Figure 2.1).[8]

Figure 2.1. Kluskap killing Malsum from *Glooscap's Country and Other Indian Tales*. (The Illustration, by John A. Hall, first appeared in 1955)

Malsum is not named in the story, except as "Wolf the son of Wickedness"; Kluskap is here "the son of Goodness." The cause of their mother's death is not given; Squirrel, in addition to Beaver, is said to be jealous of Kluskap's Power; Kluskap hides himself near Wolf's "tent"; there is no voluntary exchange of fatal information and no death song.[9] Otherwise the story appears as I have told it at the beginning of this chapter.

From what Macmillan and the volume's "sponsor," Sir William Peterson, write in the prefatory material, we would expect this story with its variations to be authentic. Peterson compares Macmillan's

method with that of the Grimm brothers and with the pioneer
Canadian ethnologist, C. M. Barbeau: "He has taken down [the stories]
from the lips of living people, pretty much as they were given to
him."[10] Macmillan reinforces our expectation when he says, "The
writer's deepest thanks are here expressed to the nameless Indians . . .
from whose lips he heard these stories."[11] While we might wonder why
he chose not to record the names of the Native Americans as well as
their stories, Macmillan's authority on these matters seems impeccable.
He tells his audience that the stories in *Canadian Wonder Tales*, including
Kluskap and his wicked brother,

> have been gathered in various parts of Canada. They have been
> selected from a larger collection of folk-tales and folk-songs made
> by the writer for more academic and scientific purposes. They are
> not the product of the writer's imagination; they are the common
> possession of the "folk." Many of them are still reverently
> believed by the Canadian Indians, and all are still told with seri-
> ousness around camp-fires in forests. . . . The dress in which they
> now appear may be new, but the skeleton of each story has been
> left unchanged.[12]

Clearly *Canadian Wonder Tales* is the cream from "a larger collection of
folktales and folk songs made by the writer for more academic and scientific purposes."

Part of this "larger collection" has to be Cyrus Macmillan's extensive, typewritten manuscript, *The Micmacs: Their Life and Legends*,
housed in the archives of the Canadian Museum of Civilization. The
result of fieldwork done under Edward Sapir for the Geological Survey
of Canada—Division of Anthropology, the collection contains three
versions of the Kluskap-Malsum story. Macmillan says he did his collecting "among the Micmacs of the Maritime Provinces of Canada, during the summer of 1911, and part of the summers of 1912 and 1913.
During these periods the writer spent some time in every Micmac settlement, with possibly two or three exceptions."[13] Internal textual evidence suggests that he recorded the Kluskap-Malsum story in 1911
among the Micmac people of Northern New Brunswick or mainland
Nova Scotia.

In fact, Macmillan faked his research and lied about his method. His
three Kluskap-Malsum stories correspond almost exactly to published

versions in the collections of Silas Rand and Charles Leland. So does much of the rest of his manuscript. Macmillan's supervisor, Edward Sapir, "suspecting . . . that his material might not be entirely bona fide," asked C. M. Barbeau to examine the manuscript. In the fall of 1914, Sapir reports to his superior at the Geological Survey:

> Mr. Barbeau makes the general remark, "There may be something new in McMillan's manuscript on Glooscap. It seems, on the whole, to be a duplication of what is found in Rand and Leland. In fact it may all be secondhand material."

Sapir provides a number of examples of this duplication and concludes his report,

> One thing is certain. We will not be able to publish this material without making ourselves ridiculous. The only question remains as to whether it would be advisable to withhold payment of the $180 for manuscript that we recently figured as being Dr. McMillan's due. Would you advise that we refuse payment on the ground that the material submitted is not genuine, or would it be more politic to be rid of the whole affair by paying this amount and steering clear of Dr. McMillan in the future?[14]

They steered clear; but four years later Macmillan published *Canadian Wonder Tales*, complete with Peterson's comparison of Macmillan's method with Barbeau's.

Macmillan's text was reprinted at least eight times, and as recently as 1974 in Britain, Canada, and the United States.[15] Whatever its origins and despite its scandalous transmission, the popularity of the Kluskap-Malsum story in hegemonic society is firmly fixed by its place in Spence's and Macmillan's collection.

The popularity of this story received another well-crafted boost in the 1960s. Kay Hill, a writer working in radio and television, was asked in August of 1960 to work on a project for the local Halifax Canadian Broadcasting Corporation. Her task was to recast a number of "Indian" legends for a children's television program in which a local children's librarian, dressed in "Indian costume" would tell stories on camera. When, in response to the program, the station received over a thousand letters from both adults and children, Hill resolved to work further on this project.[16] Her first book, *Glooscap and His Magic: Legends of the Wabanaki People,* was published in 1963. The second, *Badger the Mischief Maker,* followed in 1965 and a third, *More Glooscap Stories,* was published in 1970. All three were popular enough to go into second editions later in the 1970s. The Kluskap-Malsum story is featured prominently in the first and last books, with a striking full-page illustration in *More Glooscap Stories* calling even more attention to it. In the illustration the two brothers, who have transformed into giants in Hill's version, square off over the territory between the Gaspé peninsula and Cape Breton Island. Both are dressed in leggings and breech cloth, but it is easy to tell them apart. Malsum's hirsute upper body is topped by a ferocious wolf's head, while Kluskap looks like a Superman with braids (see Figure 2.2).[17]

The importance of Hill's presentations of the Kluskap-Malsum story should not be underestimated. In that story's history in the popular culture, she takes up where Cyrus MacMillan left off, although without the deception that characterizes the latter's work. Her stories have been widely anthologized in readers for young children. The Kluskap-Malsum story appears in one such anthology, complete with an illustration of Kluskap killing his brother.[18] Further, the complete collection of *Glooscap and His Magic* has appeared in a British edition as well as a Japanese translation.[19] Moreover her collections have "done well in the States."[20]

Mainly concerned with telling a good story, Hill does not strive for consistency with the Rand and Leland versions she draws on.[21] In the introduction to *Glooscap and His Magic,* Hill tells her readers that she found "much of the original material recorded by Rand and Leland" to be "unsuitable for an audience of children." Omitting "some savage and erotic elements" and well as "a great deal of religious symbolism, meaningful only to the Indian," she "merely followed the example of the Indian storytellers themselves" who tailored their stories to the audiences and contexts in which they found themselves. She explains that her work "does not attempt to record every incident of Glooscap's mythical career in the scholarly manner, but to present unified and romantic dramas while endeavoring to retain the spirit and flavor of the original."[22] Hill leaves out the twin brothers' intrauterine discussion and Malsum's murder of their mother, for example, and she adds some other material such as the brothers' Power belts, their origin in the sky, Malsum's creation of the troublemaker Laks, Kluskap's admonition

Figure 2.2. Kluskap and Malsum fight from *More
Glooscap Stories*. (Illustration by John F. Hamberger)

about hunting,[23] as well as their gigantic size and the Maritime battle
zone noted above.

The more than thirty years that have passed since Kay Hill wrote the
television scripts that would become her "Indian" legends books have
sharpened our focus and narrowed our gaze about the "appropriation
of culture." No television producer would today carry out such a
scheme without vociferous objections. The scorn of the Wendy Roses,
Ward Churchills, and Vine Deloria, Jrs. would be withering. The children's librarian, dressed in what was supposed to be a Micmac "costume," memorized the stories that Hill wrote, and—to the accompani-
ment of harp music and a few illustrations that the camera panned to
provide some sense of action—recited them to the audience of children. It is the well-meaning not-Native imitation of the "Indian" again
in all its glory.

The story of Kay Hill's role in this project gave me a sense for how a whole array of forces came to bear on the creation of one particular "Indian" story. In 1960, the television producer had found a copy of Silas T. Rand's *Micmac Legends* among some old books in his garage. Intrigued, he invited three local professional writers to submit a television script, based on one of the Micmac stories. Kay Hill's version was chosen; she was offered the job of turning out a story every week. The task proved onerous, but, from Ms. Hill's notes and her well-worn copies of Leland and Rand, it is clear that she took her work very seriously. She found Rand "stolid and sturdy"; Leland "more entertaining," and consequently relied more on the latter's work when she worked up her own versions. She included the Kluskap-Malsum story in two of her books because it was "a vital creation story." She was keenly aware that her audience was made up of children and, thirty years later, remembered her decision to omit Malsum's destruction of his mother because "kids have enough to absorb, and that would be just one more thing." She was also keenly aware of the deadline: "The main thing was to turn out one [story] every week and to get them in on time." It is a tribute to her writing skill that the process of turning the television scripts into books was one of simply arranging the individual scripts. However, "there were places where the pictures had told some of the story, and where the music had suggested something, and so I had to be a little more descriptive than I was in the scripts."[24] It was within this context—a professional writer adapting freely from her sources to meet a deadline for a script for a children's television program—that the most well-known version of the Kluskap-Malsum story took shape.

If the role Kay Hill played in popularizing the Kluskap-Malsum story ended here, it would be remarkable enough. But it doesn't end here. When the sixth-grade class from the Indian Island school made their video in 1992, they used their own watercolor paintings inspired by the Kluskap-Malsum story. The animation relies on these paintings to show, for example, Kluskap and a wolf-headed Malsum descending feetfirst from the sky. Kluskap creates the animals of the world; Malsum, in a poor envy-driven imitation, creates Laks. Laks creates problems. The brothers fight. Kluskap kills Malsum.

The choice of which story would be the basis for the sixth-grade class's animation project was based on a number of factors. One was the need for a short legend, one that could be edited without losing its integrity. Another was that the children did not have enough time to write and complete the painting and animation in a single school year. Another was that the grant application under which this ambitious project was funded required that the focus of the projects be creation stories. Another was the students' input. Along with their sixth-grade home room teacher, they chose the Kluskap-Malsum story because they had been reading it and it was their favorite, in part because they liked the fight scene with Malsum.[25]

The source for the Indian Island School video is a curriculum guide and resource book, *The Wabanakis of Maine and the Maritimes*.[26] It is Kay Hill's retelling from *Glooscap and His Magic*, edited only slightly, that is included here. An Introduction to the Readings section explains how Kay Hill's version of the Kluskap-Malsum story found its way to the resource book:

> Most of the legends included here were recorded by Frank G. Speck and Charles G. Leland, both of whom studied Wabanaki cultures and who tried to preserve the legends as they were told to them. There are two exceptions. One is a Penobscot story written by a Penobscot, Molly Spotted Elk, in her youth. The other, a story written by Kay Hill, combines several different legends. We use it as an introduction or overview of Gluscap's life to help readers put other Gluscap stories into context.[27]

The Wabanakis of Maine and the Maritimes introduces Kay Hill's slightly edited Kluskap-Malsum story with a three-paragraph preface. It confronts the issue of good and evil in the story, cautioning that it may have been influenced by "the Christian account of creation." The preface concludes, "The Wabanakis did not, however, connect actions—or people—to an ultimate power of Good or Evil existing in the world."[28] This is an important point, well worth making, but subtle enough to escape notice, if the video, "Kluscap and His People," is any evidence. Throughout the summer of 1992 the video was played continuously at the Abbe Museum in Bar Harbor, Maine, thus further fostering the story's popularity in the hegemonic popular culture.

The Indian Island School sixth-grade class's video is not the only cinematic rendering based on Kay Hill's version of the Kluskap-Malsum story. In 1982 Daniel Bertolino and Diane (Renaud) Bertolino finished one of the films in the series entitled *Indian Legends of Canada*. Called "Glooscap Country," this is essentially the story of Kluskap and Malsum, again on film, this time rendered dramatically. In the film,

Micmac actors from the Gesgapegiag community near Maria, Québec, play Kluskap, Malsum, and Laks, as well as the animals. As in the Indian Island School version, Laks plays the role of the double-crossing beaver from Leland's version of the story. Similarly, in "Glooscap Country" Laks is portrayed as the distorted creation of Malsum who leads the other animals in a failed attempt to turn against Kluskap and harm his other creations—humans. In the end the two brothers fight and Kluskap kills Malsum with a fern.

The film begins with a shot of a cloudy night sky with the eerie majesty of the full moon. The narrator intones, "They came from Infinity; they came from Eternity." The camera cuts to Kluskap and Malsum, standing, moon behind them, dry ice mist swirling around. The narrator continues:

> These messengers from the light of the Great Spirit, Kluskap and Malsum, symbols of Right and Wrong, are coming to earth to do the transcendental work of creation: the creation of the first Indian people, the Wabanaki.

The camera tightens to a shot of the brothers' faces; the narrator goes on:

> They had been designated by the Great Spirit to instill in the first men the notion of what is good and what is evil so they might choose.

In keeping with the objectives of the film series, the producers, as part of their groundwork, engaged a Micmac researcher to provide an analysis. John Martin, a young man of the Gesgapegiag community, was commissioned to prepare a short report, which he called "Gloosgap the Great Chief." The screenplay for the film, including much of the narrator's introduction, was derived from Martin's report.[29]

John Martin was much more than simply a researcher for the Bertolinos' filmmaking project. Initially referred to the Bertolinos because he spoke French as well as English and Micmac, Martin became indispensable to the project: constructing traditional lodges of birchbark and cedar roots, helping to cast the roles, composing the Micmac dialogue, assisting with on-site direction, and suggesting three more Micmac stories to complement the Kluskap-Malsum story the Bertolinos came to the community with. Over the two years it took to make the four films, John Martin—like virtually everyone else in his community a Roman Catholic, but unlike most, college-educated—was at the center of the project.

Martin is currently the Education Director for the Gesgapegiag community. Deservingly proud both of the elementary school students, some of whom win prizes in regional competitions, and of the students leaving the community's Learning Center for postsecondary education, John Martin is clearly committed to educating the people of his community. In a sense, the filmmaking project shot on site in 1979 and 1980 marked the beginning of Martin's commitment. The film, "Glooscap Country," derives authority from the presence of Micmac actors speaking their lines in Micmac, and from the set of traditional lodges. Martin's hard work—his researching, his dialogue, his construction of the set—contributed greatly to the success of the project. "Glooscap Country," now a video, was, along with the rest of the *Indian Legends of Canada* series, still in distribution in the mid 1990s. According to its distributors, the series is intended primarily for use in the classroom.

In a wide-ranging conversation, Martin told me that while he was influenced as a youth by two Micmac storytellers, he learned of the Kluskap-Malsum story in "Rand's blue book," and Leland's story collection. In addition, he was familiar with Kay Hill's retellings of the stories. John Martin was clear: his written report on the story of Kluskap and Malsum was based on his research in Rand, Leland, and Hill.[30] The importance for Martin's work of Kay Hill's retelling can be ascertained by the substitution of Laks for the meddling beaver found in Leland's version.

It would be easy, I suppose, given the overwhelming reliance on Kay Hill's freely adapted version in texts and visual media, to blame her for the inaccurate story's wide distribution. In her written material and in my interview with her, though, Hill is clear: her work was writing children's stories by freely adapting her sources. That her collections get catalogued by libraries as folklore, used as the basis of extended cinematic renderings, and distributed in university classrooms as authentic "Indian" stories says more about how we read her stories than it does about the author's intentions. However we apportion responsibility, the popularity of the story is undeniable. Through the vehicle of the *Indian Legends of Canada* video series along with all the other examples mentioned, the Kluskap-Malsum story continues in the waning years of the twentieth century to reach a sizable audience in Canada and the United States.[31]

A larger international audience also has access to Kluskap and Malsum. The late Joseph Campbell ensured this when he included the story in his *Historical Atlas of World Mythology*. While Campbell "abridges and recasts" the Kluskap-Malsum story, his version follows closely that of Charles Godfrey Leland, published just over one hundred years earlier. Just as in Hill's *Glooscap's Magic* the story is accompanied by an illustration. Campbell chooses a smaller but more authentic looking birchbark etching labeled, "Glooscap killing his brother the Wolf."[32] Past their common source and use of illustrations, the comparison of Campbell with Hill is unfair. Kay Hill understood herself to be writing children's stories. Campbell, on the other hand, has shown he is a mythologist with the ability to ignite the popular imagination. The scope of his *Atlas* is breathtaking; the size and production values of even the paperback version are impressive. Campbell was a popularizer with tremendous stature. That he retells and comments on the story of Kluskap and Malsum is both a measure of its appeal in the popular hegemonic culture of late-twentieth-century North America, and a guarantee that its popularity will continue and perhaps increase.

Pausing to reflect at this point in our inquiry gives us a number of things we now know about this story of Kluskap and Malsum. For one, the story is known to both Native American cultures and the hegemonic popular and academic cultures. Micmacs have painted it; Penobscot school children have animated it in their video; and two Micmac elders tell versions of it. In the hegemonic popular culture, MacMillan's version, Kay Hill's retellings, the summer video showing at the Abbe Museum, the Bertolinos' video, and Joseph Campbell's incorporation of the story in his *World Atlas of Mythology* serve both to bolster and underscore its popularity. In my estimation its popularity and extent of influence in Native communities in Maine and the Atlantic region of Canada is paltry when compared to its popularity in the hegemonic popular culture. I shall return to this story as a Native American story in the last chapter. Next, in order better to show the Kluskap-Malsum story's importance to hegemonic popular culture and thus its significance to the study of Native American religions, I will trace the story's remarkable history back through its recorded versions to the Native American communities in which it was reputedly cherished.

Chapter 3

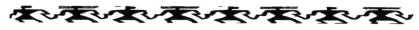

The Making of
"the Real Gospel of Manliness"

"**K**luskap and Malsum" is a popular story. As I noted in chapter 2, Joseph Campbell presented a version of the story that he "abridged and recast" from his sources.[1] Cyrus Macmillan popularized his version of the "wonder tale." Kay Hill also retold the story, concerned more for the sensibilities of her child readership and making good stories and deadlines than about her version's consistency with her sources. What of these sources? Where are the Native American antecedents of the popular Kluskap-Malsum story? What are they like? What is the history of this Abenaki and Micmac story? And, are the versions that have become popular close cousins of the Abenaki and Micmac versions, or their distant relations? If we are interested in the significance of this story and its study for the larger study of Native American religions, these are questions of some importance. Their answers, however, are not as straightforward as we might hope.

The first step, the one from Campbell, Hill, and Macmillan back to their sources is an easy one. All three relied heavily (two by their own admission) on the version of the Kluskap-Malsum story that appears in Charles Godfrey Leland's *Algonquin Legends of New England*, first published in 1884.[2] It is there that the investigation gets complex, and much more intriguing.

It is not surprising that the story's popularizers were drawn to Leland and his version of the story. Leland was himself an attractive figure, gazing out from the frontispiece of the book, a long beard, a rakish broad-brimmed hat (see Figure 3.1). Looking at him, I imagine he is about to tell a humorous story. In my imagination, I am sure I will laugh; so is he. In the last quarter of the nineteenth century Leland was

Figure 3.1. Charles Godfrey Leland, the frontispiece of his *Memoirs.* (London: William Heinemann, 1893)

an amateur folklorist before there were many professionals. He took his work seriously, although in his time he was much better known for his humorous ditties in German-American dialect, ditties that modern tastes might find offensive. Still, he valued his folklore studies among the English gypsies, Italian witches, and American "Red Indians" above all his other prodigious output.[3] As a Victorian gentleman, he kept his sense of his own difference from the people he studied, but he prided himself on his ability to know their ways at some deep level. He was, from our perspective, simultaneously an elitist and empathetic.

He seems to have genuinely liked the people he met and learned from. The stories Leland tells have a confidence and an easy turn of (now stilted) phrase developed before he came into an inheritance and could pursue folklore studies, a time when he made his living selling words as a journalist, editor, essayist, and pamphlet writer.[4]

Leland's personal charm and authority notwithstanding, we can safely surmise that Joseph Campbell, Kay Hill, and Cyrus Macmillan chose to retell the Kluskap-Malsum story primarily for other reasons. One reason may well have been the story's prominence in Leland's work. Leland himself told the story a number of times. It appears in two versions in *Algonquin Legends of New England* and once in *Kulóskap the Master.*[5] In both volumes, written over fifteen years apart, the Kluskap-Malsum story is the first story one reads. He clearly privileges the story, commenting on and annotating it extensively both in the body of the text and in discursive footnotes. Of the two volumes the later one is an attempt to render the stories into epic verse, and thus further from Leland's Abenaki and Micmac sources. There is little doubt that *Algonquin Legends* holds the more authentic version of the story. "Of Glooskap's Birth, and of His Brother Malsum, the Wolf" is the very first story Leland tells, and, allowing for differences in style, the story is much as I have told it in the last chapter.

Since so much of our inquiry here turns on Leland's version of the Kluskap-Malsum story, I think he should retell it:

> Now the great lord Glooskap, who was worshiped in after-days by all the Wabanaki, or children of the light, was a twin with a brother. As he was good, this brother, whose name was Malsumsis, or Wolf the younger, was bad. Before they were born, the babes consulted to consider how they had best enter the world. And Glooskap said, "I will be born as others are." But the evil Malsumsis thought himself too great to be brought forth in such a manner, and declared that he would burst through his mother's side. And as they planned it so it came to pass. Glooskap as first came quietly to light, while Malsumsis kept his word, killing his mother.
>
> The two grew up together, and one day the younger, who knew that both had charmed lives, asked the elder what would kill him, Glooskap. Now each had his own secret as to this, and Glooskap, remembering how wantonly Malsumsis had slain their mother, thought it would be misplaced confidence to trust his life to one so fond of death, while it might prove to be well to know the bane of

the other. So they agreed to exchange secrets, and Glooskap, to test his brother, told him that the only way in which he himself could be slain was by the stroke of an owl's feather, though this was not true. And Malsumsis said, "I can only die by a blow from a fern-root."

It came to pass in after-days that Kwah-beet-a-sis, the son of the Great Beaver, or, as others say, Miko the Squirrel, or else the evil which was in himself, tempted Malsumsis to kill Glooskap; for in those days all men were wicked. So taking his bow he shot Ko-ko-khas the Owl, and with one of his feathers he struck Glooskap while sleeping. Then he awoke in anger, yet craftily said that it was not by an owl's feather, but by a blow from a pine-root, that his life would end.

Then the false man led his brother another day far into the forest to hunt, and, while he again slept, smote him on the head with a pine-root. But Glooskap arose unharmed, drove Malsumsis away into the woods, sat down by the brook-side, and thinking over all that had happened, said, "Nothing but a flowering rush can kill me." But the Beaver, who was hidden among the reeds, heard this, and hastening to Malsumsis told him the secret of his brother's life. For this Malsumsis promised to bestow on Beaver whatever he should ask; but when the latter wished for wings like a pigeon, the warrior laughed, and scornfully said, "Get thee hence; thou with a tail like a file, what need hast thou of wings?"

Then the Beaver was angry, and went forth to the camp of Glooskap, to whom he told what he had done. Therefore Glooskap arose in sorrow and in anger, took a fern-root, sought Malsumsis in the deep, dark forest, and smote him so that he fell down dead. And Glooskap sang a song over him and lamented.

As I have shown elsewhere, Leland had four sources when he sat down to compose his version of the Kluskap-Malsum story, probably in the spring of 1884.[6] By that time he had spent two summers holidaying on Campobello Island where he met Passamaquoddies who also summered on the island, albeit in different circumstances. There is no question that there Leland collected both stories and physical objects from the Passamaquoddies.[7] Two of the people he met in the "Indian tents," Tomah Joseph and Lewy Mitchell, would become important consultants (see Figure 3.2). By early in 1883 Leland was corresponding with Joseph, receiving at least one story. By December of that year he contracted with Mitchell, then thirty years old, to collect and translate stories for him, then mail them to him.[8] It must have been just about the

Figure 3.2. Tomah Joseph, one of Leland's Passamaquoddy consultants. (Library of Congress, Charles G. Leland manuscripts, Box 373)

time he established more formal relationships with these consultants that Leland wrote an article, not published until September, 1884 in *The Century Illustrated Monthly Magazine* as "Legends of the Passamaquoddy." In the article he retells five stories and accompanies these with reproductions of three "drawings on birch bark by a Quädi Indian."[9] These were certainly the work of Tomah Joseph.[10] At the time he wrote this article Leland was still looking for more stories. In his concluding paragraph he writes,

It is to be desired that all who can do so will collect the Indian names of places from living Indians, and with them the accompanying stories. I should take it as a great kindness if those who do so would favor me with the results of their researches. There is not an old Indian living in New England or Canada who does not remember something well worth recording.[11]

The story we are concerned with, the Kluskap-Malsum story, is not one of the five Leland tells in this article. The story was so important to him, that if Leland had it, I believe he would have shared it. On this evidence, and his request for more material, I hypothesize this article was written in 1883. Soon Leland would have more stories than he would be able to fit into the book he was planning when he wrote the *Century* piece.

At the end of the *Algonquin Legends* version of that story, Leland acknowledges two sources for "Of Glooscap's Birth . . .": "the narrative of a Micmac Indian, taken down by Mr. Edward Jock; also to another version in the Rand MS" (17). Just under the surface of this acknowledgment is the first installment in our inquiry into the study of Native American religions.

Neither the "Micmac" narrative he mentions in this acknowledgment, nor the version collected by Silas Rand were the first traces of the Kluskap-Malsum story Leland found. Leland had read the version in *The Maritime Provinces: Handbook for Travellers,* before he received a letter from Edward Jack of Fredericton, dated January 13 1884;[12] and he knew of both story fragments by the time he wrote Rand about the story, probably in early February. What exactly did Leland know from the correspondence with Jack and from the tourist guidebook?

In the Jack letter he read, "'Glooscap had a brother who was very bad and caused him great trouble at last he became so wicked that he had to kill him, after death he was turned into the Shick-shock mountains.'" The story, writes Jack, was told to him by Peter Solis "over the campfire."[13] In the tourist guidebook he read a longer story which began,

In this vicinity [Kennebecasis Bay] dwelt the two Great Brothers, GLOOSKAP and MALSUNSIS, of unknown origin and invincible power. Glooscap knew that his brother was vulnerable only by the touch of a fern-root; and he had told Malsunsis (falsely) that the stroke of an owl's feather would kill him. It came to pass that Malsunsis determined to kill his brother (whether tempted thus by Mik-o, the Squirrel, or by Quah-beet-e-sis, the son of the Great Beaver, or by his own evil ambition); wherefore with his arrow he shot Koo-koo-shoos, the Owl, and with one of his feathers struck the sleeping Glooscap.

Kluskap was, of course, uninjured. There follows, in this version of the story, the attempt by Malsunsis on his brother's life with a pine root, then the intervention by the deceitful Beaver, who is scorned by the evil brother. As the guidebook has it: "'Get thee hence, thou with a tail like a file; what need has thou of pigeon's wings?'" The Beaver, who is here called Musquash, goes to Kluskap to confess his betrayal. The decidedly nineteenth-century, not-Native style—"it came to pass," "tempted thus," "wherefore with his arrows,"—pervades this part of the story right to the conclusion: ". . . by reason of these tidings, Glooscap arose and took a root of fern and sought Malsunsis in the wide and gloomy forest; and when he had found him he smote him so that he fell down dead. 'And Glooscap sang a song over him and lamented.'"[14]

Though an amateur, Leland was enough of a folklorist to know he could not trust a tourist guidebook as the source of a "Red Indian" story, but tantalized by the fragment from Jack, he pressed Rand for more information. Apparently he pressed hard. On February 19, 1884, Rand wrote to protest Leland's accusations: "I can assure you that I am innocent of any *secret* in the matter of Glooscap [Rand's emphasis]." He had, he wrote, never seen the guidebook Leland spoke of: "I do not know the author of whom you speak and do know the work to which you refer "Osgood's Maritime Provinces." Is it a school book? or what is it?"[15]

Not long after this, Leland took Rand up on his offer to use his manuscript, mentioned earlier. Silas T. Rand's manuscript was substantial; the loan of it ensured Leland's book would be an important contribution to folklore studies.[16] Leland had been corresponding with the Baptist missionary since autumn, 1883. In addition to his religious calling, Rand was also a linguist of considerable talent who had spent years learning to speak Micmac and collecting stories. Since he did not see his story collecting as central to his main work of evangelizing (largely convincing the Micmacs and Maliseets of "the error" of their Roman Catholic beliefs), he sent his 900 page manuscript to the persistent folklorist with permission to use what he could, asking only for help with postage and for the manuscript's return.[17]

The Rand manuscript yielded a brief abstractlike story. Unlike

Sweetser's tourist guidebook version, though, the Rand story, "Glooscap's Origin," knows of Kluskap's beginnings: Kluskap is a twin who talks with his brother before birth about how they wanted to be born. The younger decides to break through his mother's side, and does, thereby killing her. From this point "Glooscap's Origin" parallels the Sweetser version. The brothers exchange information about deadly weapons (this time a cattail flag and a handful of bird's down); the younger tries to kill the older but is unsuccessful; Kluskap kills his brother instead. Between the title and the body of the story, Rand wrote, "The following information respecting Glooscap was given me by Gabriel Thomas of Frederickton. I question, however, whether it does not refer to some other fabulous person."[18] Given Rand's experience, his annotation might give a cautious scholar reason to question the authenticity of the story. Hot on a trail of his own blazing, Leland pushed on.

At the same time as he was pressing Rand for more information, Leland was canvassing his other consultants. Shortly after February 16, he heard from Lewy Mitchell in Maine. The tone of Mitchell's letter indicates that he was feeling some pressure from "Friend Leland." Apparently Leland ignored the signals from his consultant and increased the pressure on Mitchell to find evidence of the Kluskap-Malsum story. In a March 12 letter Mitchell's first words are that he is "very sorry" that Leland was dissatisfied with his stories. Obviously Leland, feeling Mitchell was letting him down, had written him of his dissatisfaction.[19] Meanwhile Leland was asking Edward Jack in Fredericton for more information.[20] Jack had earlier provided Peter Solis's allusion to Kluskap's problems with his brother. Leland wanted more. Unfortunately, Edward Jack's consultant, Gabriel Acquin, was unavailable, most likely guiding some clients on a hunting trip (see Figure 3.3). Jack begins his letter, dated March 18, with an apology: "Your last letter has remained unanswered until I could get hold of my Indian." In a postscript Jack tells Leland the whereabouts of the "Shick-shock" Mountains (Monts Chic-choc of the Gaspé). From this we can deduce that Jack's March 18 letter was in response to a letter from Leland asking for more information. This time Leland's persistence was rewarded. Jack includes with this letter the record of a story told by Gabe Acquin, a story that gives legitimation and authority to the story Leland had, up till now, found in its fullest version in a tourist guidebook.

Figure 3.3. Gabe Acquin, Fredericton, N.B., Canada, c. 1866–1869. (Photo courtesy of the British Museum, #MM024082)

In Acquin's story Kluskap and his unnamed brother are twins whose prebirth discussion led to the death of their mother. So, like Rand's version, it knows of the twins and their origin. Again, as in the Rand version, in the exchange of information about death-dealing weapons, Kluskap told his brother that bird's down would kill him when in fact it would only stun him. The brother tells him the truth—cattails would kill him. The Acquin story details the battle (the down only stunned Kluskap; the cattail killed his brother), but then, unlike the Rand version, it goes on to tell of Kluskap's uncle, Turtle, who "got so big in his own opinion" that he tried to destroy his nephew. The story ends with a reference to Wolf, but not the evil twin Wolf of the Leland version: "Glooskap had two dogs one was the Loon (paqueem) and the Wolf (mol-som). . . . The Loon and the Wolf were so fond of Glooscap that they are still lamenting for him." Not only did Jack deliver what was the linchpin of Leland's Kluskap-Malsum story, but he went to some lengths to guarantee the story's authenticity: "I give it to you just as it came from his own lips as he sat in front of the fire in my room this evening smoking his tobacco mixed with willow bark, he has any quantity of Indian lore."[21]

Thus by the end of March 1884 Leland had all four sources for his version of the story of Kluskap and Malsum. From the version in the Rand manuscript he took the first part, paraphrasing Rand's record of the original up to Malsumsis' first attempt on Kluskap's life.[22] At this point in "Of Glooskap's Birth . . ." Leland began paraphrasing the Sweetser story, which he does to Kluskap's lament at the end. It is worth noting that Leland retains Sweetser's discordant, "'Get thee hence, thou with a tail like a file; what need hast thou of pigeon's wings,'" omitting only the pigeon from his version.[23] From the Solis version, the fragment Jack first sent, he took the validation line about the Monts Chic-choc of the Gaspé.[24] The fourth source—Jack/Acquin version—he does not quote from directly for his rendering, using it instead to give authority to his story. It is, after all, the most complete version with a Native American source. I will return to this point in the next chapter.

What can we now say about the authenticity of the Leland Kluskap-Malsum story? We know that one of his four sources, the one he borrows the most phrasing from, was a tourist guidebook whose editor made no pretense about the accuracy of the "Indian" stories he retold. He had to worry about steamship departure times and coach schedules.

Another source, Peter Solis, provided a brief sketch and a validation line. But was the sketch necessarily of the Kluskap-Malsum story? In 1910 Truman Michelson collected a story from Mrs. Catpat, then eighty-eight, in the Micmac community of Restigouche, just across the New Brunswick border in Québec. In that story Kluskap returns from many adventures to find his brother Amkotpigtu has been abusing other members of the family. They fight. Kluskap kills Amkotpigtu who is turned into the "Six Shot Mountain."[25] Given the similarities between Mrs. Catpat's 1910 version and Peter Solis's from roughly thirty years earlier, it seems more likely that the Solis fragment describes the Kluskap-Amkotpigtu story, not the Kluskap-Malsum story. Only a scholar who needed one story tradition concerning fratricide in Kluskap's family would roll the two story lines into one.

The last two sources come, significantly, from the same place—Fredericton, New Brunswick. At this time the Native population of Fredericton was not large. When in 1794 their main settlement, Aucpaque ("Savage Island") on the Saint John River upstream from Fredericton, was fraudulently taken from them, the community dispersed to a number of sites up and down the river. One was St. Mary's, across the river from Fredericton.[26] It was there, on August 27, 1870 that Silas Rand collected a version of the twin story from Gabriel Thomas, a Maliseet.[27] Finally, there is a the fuller version Edward Jack collected in Fredericton from a Maliseet from the same community, Gabe Acquin.

In some important features the Maliseet stories from Fredericton agree. In both, twin brothers have an intrauterine discussion and in both one brother kills his mother by breaking through her side. In both the brothers exchange the secrets of their death, and in both the secret elements are only two—bird's down and a cattail, but they are reversed from one story to the other. In both Kluskap's brother tries to kill him, and when he fails, Kluskap kills him. In both the murderous brother tells the truth while Kluskap does not. Gabe Acquin's story is much richer, noting, for example, that their mother was a Turtle person. There is the long passage about Kluskap's maternal uncle, Turtle, that ends with Kluskap foiling a plot to do away with him.[28] Both stories, though, end the same way. Kluskap had two "dogs," one a loon and one a wolf. The cries of these animals, both stories conclude, show the grief they feel now that Kluskap has gone.

The two Maliseet stories from Fredericton are silent on some important features that Leland takes from the Sweetser version. Neither include the sequences involving multiple death-wielding elements, nor the sequence involving the tattle-tale, double-crossing Beaver, the one with a "tale like a file." Neither of the Fredericton stories are concerned with the motive of Kluskap's twin when the latter tries to kill him. Neither calls the twin "wicked" or "evil." Neither story makes Kluskap's twin into Malsum the Wolf, in fact neither names the brother. Both portray the wolf as a sympathetic character, mourning Kluskap's departure. From this catalog of features it is clear that the tourist guidebook version of the story of Kluskap and Malsum had quite an impact on Leland.

Had he not wanted to rush the results of his newest folklore investigation into print,[29] Leland might have wondered where Moses Foster Sweetser, the editor of *The Maritime Provinces*, found the Kluskap-Malsum story. Perhaps he did wonder. Perhaps he found the list of sources Sweetser gives at the back of his guide. There, after the index, Leland would have found seventy-seven "Authorities Consulted in the Preparation of this Volume." But he would not have found Sweetser's source there; it is not listed. Instead, he would have had to look to the travelogue recorded by Arthur Hamilton Gordon, the then lieutenant governor of New Brunswick.[30] It is Gordon's version of the Kluskap-Malsum story that Sweetser filched for his guidebook.

Recorded in August of 1863, this is the oldest print version of the story I have found. Comparing the Gordon version to the later ones is instructive. One significant feature is missing from the Gordon version: it does not know about the origin so important to Leland. For Leland the brothers are twins, but Gordon is clear, "'Now, whence came the brethren, or what their origin, no man nor beast knew, nor ever shall know;—nay they knew it not themselves.'" Sweetser collapses this passage saying they were of "unknown origin." Sweetser also follows Gordon's version by locating the great beaver's lodge on the Kennebecasis River on which the tourists glide, at least in theory, as they read the Kluskap-Malsum story in their guidebooks. Sweetser departs from Gordon at one noteworthy point: he turns Gordon's double-crossing muskrat into a double-crossing beaver, *named* "Musquash" or muskrat. Sweetser is also responsible for cutting the story down in size and for making it a Micmac story when Gordon is clear that his consultants were Maliseets. Curiously Leland follows Sweetser on *both* these inaccuracies. He understandably repeats Sweetser's error about the beaver; he had no other source with this incident in it. But why he insists Jack's consultant is a Micmac when Jack unquestionably identifies Gabe Acquin as a Maliseet defies explanation.[31]

When we examine the language of Arthur Hamilton Gordon's version, we find some familiar phrasing. For example this from the Gordon version: "'But how these thoughts arose no man nor beast knoweth, nor shall know. Some say that Mik-o the squirrel taught him thus to think, and some say Quah-Beet-E-Siss, the son of the great beaver. But some say he had no tempter save himself.'" Or this memorable passage: "'Get thee hence, thou with a tail like a file; what need hast thou of pigeon's wings?'" And lastly this: "'And he smote him with a fern-root, and Malsunsis fell down dead. And Clote Scarp [Kluskap] sang a song over him and lamented.'"[32] It is the phrasing of the lieutenant governor that finds it way through Sweetser into Leland and through him into contemporary popular renditions.

More than phrasing appears first in the Gordon version. The concern for Kluskap's brother's motive, as well as the name Malsunsis (later Malsumsis) and its identification with Wolf occurs here first. I cannot speculate on the concern for motive in the Gordon version without considering the origins of the story, but the author himself gives us some evidence about Malsunsis, the little Wolf. In a footnote following the first occurrence of the appellation, Gordon writes, "Malsunsis, 'the Little Wolf,' was not the name of the second brother which has escaped my recollection."[33]

So much for Malsum. Kluskap's twin, whatever his name might be, is not a wolf. This footnote explains, I think, why Sweetser abandons the "Little Wolf" translation of Malsunsis in his version. Ironically, Leland puzzled out the meaning of Malsumsis for himself. Evidence from the Leland's handwritten manuscript of *Algonquin Legends* shows that he comes to his translation of Malsunsis very late, adding "Wolf-the-younger" and ("correctly") changing the spelling of Malsunsis to Malsumsis in the draft that went to the typesetter.[34] I imagine Sweetser, uneasy with Gordon's admission that he concocted Kluskap's brother's name, left out the English, "Little Wolf," safe in the knowledge that his tourist readers, ignorant of Maliseet, would be none the wiser. He did not figure on Charles Leland who was, as we shall see, delighted to find that Kluskap's "evil" twin brother was a wolf.

I began this chapter wondering about the history of the Kluskap-Malsum story. At this point it is the issue of the origin of the Gordon version of that story which looms as vitally important for our investigation. As I mentioned in the last chapter, Gordon learned the story while traveling with a group of Maliseets. It is on the last of three "wilderness journeys" that he first mentions hearing stories: "I sat long over the fire after the rest had gone to sleep, listening to Indian legends told in low mysterious tones."[35] "The rest" here refers to the rest of the not-Natives in Gordon's party. Of the five Maliseets traveling with him three knew very little English (although one knew some Micmac). Gordon could not understand Maliseet. So the low tones were for the most part Maliseet low tones that Gordon did not understand. In any case, he does not set the stories in this context. Rather he waits until he is relating the end of his journey, after taking "an affecting leave of our Tobique Indian friends," when he, a friend and his main guide are taking a side trip up Mount Teneriffe. This is the context for his story telling. Gordon writes,

After devouring our supper of trout, I sat long over the fire, listening to Indian legends. Some of these are very picturesque and
curious. They are more or less connected with each other, and
form part of one great legend, very nearly resembling that of
Hiawatha—that is to say, a hero, not a God, but more than a man,
is supposed to have existed, who ruled all things living, and in
whose time animals and men spoke to each other freely. A few
specimens of the nature of these stories will not, I think, prove
uninteresting.[36]

And with that he launches into "The Story of the Great Brothers," the
story we have been tracking.

If we believe Gordon that he heard the story when he says he did,
then it was his guide who told it to him. He introduces his readers to
this guide early in the book:

a Melicete Indian from the camp opposite Fredericton, Gabriel by
name, the pet guide and huntsman of the garrison—a clever fellow, speaking good English, which, however, as he had learnt it
chiefly from officers, abounded in odd expressions of military
slang.[37]

Twenty years before Edward Jack secured a version of the Kluskap-
Malsum story from Gabe Acquin in Fredericton, Arthur Hamilton
Gordon heard the same story from the same man, who may or may not
have heard it from his Tobique colleagues a few days earlier. In trying
to determine the relationship of the Leland (and subsequent popular)
versions of the story to its Abenaki and Micmac antecedents we have
ended up doubling back on our own trail. It turns out that Leland used
Jack's recording of Gabe Acquin's story to verify and add authority to a
tourist guidebook story that stemmed from Lieutenant Governor
Gordon's written version of the story recorded twenty years earlier
from the same Gabe Acquin. Clearly Gabe Acquin is a figure to be reckoned with in our investigation.

Probably in his early seventies in 1884, Gabe Acquin was remarkable
in many ways. Renowned as a hunter, guide, and interpreter, he is
remembered as the founder of the St. Mary's Reserve in Fredericton.
Never taught to read or write English, Acquin was often cited by not-
Natives for his honesty, wit, and intelligence. In 1883 Gabe had gone on

the first of two or perhaps three voyages to England, on this one representing Canada at the International Fisheries Exhibition. To prepare for his exhibit, "he took with him his wigwam, spruce boughs for a bed, his canoe and paddles, moccasins, snowshoes, baskets, in fact samples of about everything the Indians made."[38] All of the beadwork he took, and perhaps most of the crafts, had been made by his wife, an extraordinary craftswoman.[39] Although he was, from the organizer's perspective, part of the exhibit, he was far from passive. Acquin is reported to have made a distinction on this visit between two types of women who he took on canoe rides on the South Kensington Ponds. There were, he reported on his return, the "real ladies" like Princess Beatrice and the daughters of the Prince of Wales who sat quietly in the bottom of the canoe; and there were the "make-believe ladies" who insisted on sitting on the cross bar, exclaiming loudly, and often upsetting the canoe—no great tragedy in the shallow water, but no doubt an annoyance to Acquin.[40] From this distinction one can begin to get a sense for how Acquin assessed the Europeans and EuroCanadians he encountered. While in England, Gabe Acquin was invited to the homes of high-ranking army officers whom he had befriended thirty years earlier in the British garrison town of Fredericton.[41] From these friendships he had apparently acquired an appreciation for things British and a corresponding disdain for things colonial.[42] This explains why, when ordering provisions for the hunting parties of significant gentlemen, Acquin insisted on Cross and Blackwell's pickles and Lea and Perrin's sauces.[43] No doubt his collaboration with Lieutenant Governor Gordon in the early 1860s helped form his attitudes about not-Native people.[44] On this evidence it is most likely that Acquin in 1884 found Edward Jack a likable provincial, a man who was tolerable because, while a local, at least knew how to behave like an English gentleman.

At this point it is worth pausing to remember that Gabe Acquin is "the Indian" whose lips and willow-laced pipe tobacco certified the suspect tourist guidebook twin story as authentically aboriginal. When Edward Jack was listing Acquin's qualities, he neglected to note he was well-traveled and well-connected. Acquin was indeed an "aboriginal authority" but a sophisticated, cosmopolitan one, recently returned from a lengthy journey during which he hobnobbed in some of the finest homes of London and regularly met with royalty.[45]

Without considering either Gabe Acquin or Charles Godfrey Leland further, we know that a few of the features of the later versions of the story have been altered. First, Kluskap's brother is not a wolf named Malsunsis or Malsumsis. Second, if there is a conniving disloyal creature in the story, it is a muskrat, not a beaver. And third, the rococo phrasing so often repeated ("Get thee hence, thou with a tail like a file") is much more likely that of Lieutenant Governor Gordon than that of Gabe Acquin. Finally, whether the Native American story dealt with Kluskap's brother's motive or not, all the Maliseet versions are silent about the brother's inner nature.[46] None describe him as "wicked" or "evil," and certainly none claim, as Leland does, that "in those days all men were wicked."

The version of the story of Kluskap and Malsum that Leland composed and that through him has entered the hegemonic popular culture rests on very little that is Abenaki, Micmac, or both. To make a claim that the story was even a minor story tradition among Micmac and Abenaki people is risky. What we have is a story apparently popular among a few Maliseet people, recounted by only two Maliseet men, in the late 1800s. This story, distorted and promoted by a few not-Native men, reached its definitive and most distorted form in a collection that Charles Godfrey Leland asserted was a scholarly collection of stories. This is the Kluskap-Malsum story that has entered popular culture.

Chapter 4

Raw Data and Cooked
Rendering "Indians" into Aryans

T hat the Kluskap-Malsum story was probably at best a minor Maliseet story tradition seems, at first, the end of our investigation. After all, now we have discovered the origin of the story, and thus its importance for the study of Native American religions, have we not?

When I began this inquiry, I thought we would be through by now. Instead this knowledge propels us into the second installment in our story about the study of Native American religions. Consider that knowing this story was not as popular in Abenaki and Micmac societies as it has become in hegemonic culture means the latter has some claim to it. Whether or not there was an "authentic" aboriginal version of the Kluskap twin story, the version by Leland has been appropriated by his culture. This is why I argue that Leland's story belongs to the hegemonic popular culture and is "authentic" to it. The Kluskap-Malsum story means something to those of us who identify in some sense with that culture, or our storytellers would not still remember it. And it means something to us that this is an "Indian" story. What the story and its history mean for us is becoming more central to our investigation. Perhaps if we can understand what moved the story's editor and its primary benefactor, Charles Godfrey Leland, we can begin to understand the hegemonic culture's reaction to this story. Extrapolating from this understanding, we can then attempt a new perspective on the dominant North American culture's relationship to Native American religions in general.

This orientation prompts some intriguing questions. It is true that Charles G. Leland was careless and sometimes reckless in his story-gathering techniques. Yet how is it that the Kluskap-Malsum story could break from its Native American roots in so many places? What motivated Charles Leland? Why was he so persistent in his quest for this particular story? Why did he showcase the story, drawing attention to it by its placement and his extensive annotation? In short, why did he do what he did?

A first response to this line of questioning is the simplest: Leland did not care about "Indians" or even actively disliked them. Perhaps he was a racist.

While this response is far too simplistic, it is worth considering. At times, especially early in his career, Leland made use of the stereotype of the "Indian" in negative ways. His description of his encounter with the Kaw tribe, written in November 1866 for Eastern newspaper readers, cast the members of this Plains nation in a very bad light. For Leland the Kaw were part of the "wild tribes" and thus still a threat to the U.S. conquest of that territory. At one point he compares them with another nation who had settled in Kansas and were farming and hunting on land they "possessed." The Kaw, still trying to follow an older life-way, Leland describes as "miserable, shirking, thievish-looking specimens."[1] These remarks are compounded by his many casual references to the "Injun"—by which he means something unpredictable and wild. It is this "Injun" quality that Leland often identifies as part of his and his colleagues' personalities.[2] Leland remarks that a "very eccentric Canadian Frenchman named Louis" was "subject to attacks of Indian rage at mere trifles, when he would go aside, swear, and destroy something like a lunatic in a fury, and then return quite happy and serene." Leland also says he himself is "by nature as vindictive as an unconverted Indian."[3] Such remarks deserve further comment, but for now I need only point out that the blatant disparaging use of the "Indian" stereotype has almost disappeared by the time of the *Algonquin Legends* twenty years later. By the time he wrote *Algonquin Legends* Leland was anxious for his audience to see the stories of his "Indians" as infused with all that was noble, trustworthy, with lofty moral values. To accomplish this Leland made approving use of the "Indian" stereotype.

Leland's identification with the "Indian" was not limited to those "wild" parts of this personality. His was a deeper identification.[4] To effect this, Leland made a more approving use of the "Indian" stereotype that turned on the notion of an almost unbridgeable gulf between the "Indian" and not-"Indian." This was a gulf Leland felt he mediated. When, in his writings, he made explicit his identification with the "Indian," he offered as evidence of his "Indian" nature various examples that showed how Native Americans recognized "the Injun" in him. He quotes a seasoned teamster whom he portrays as knowing the ways of the frontier. This man tells Leland that the latter has "Injun ways." Leland describes himself as surprised. Transparently pleased, he asks the teamster why he says this.

> 'Cause I've watched you. You've got Injun ways that you don't know of. Didn't I notice the other day, when the gentlemen were buying the whips from the Kaws, that every Injun took a squint [a coin], and then came straight to you. Why didn't they go to one of the other gentlemen? Because they've got an instinct like a dog for their friends, and for such as *we*.[5]

Notice that Leland's teamster does not say that men such as Leland and he were the "Indian's" friends. Instead he meant that there are certain people who have "Injun ways"—ways which in Leland's case were unconscious. Real "Indians" recognize in a few others this shared human quality, which in most not-Natives has been hidden by civilization. The desire to tap an inner, natural source unsullied by the alienation and pollution that seem inherent in an industrialized society, and the tendency to identify that source with the "Indian" are shared by Leland and contemporary imitators of the "Indians" like the Boy Scouts and Bear Tribe Medicine Society. Premised on two of the skewed characteristics of the "Indian" stereotype, this kind of identification indicates a positive or approving use of that stereotype.

From this evidence I would argue two things. First, that Leland used the "Indian" stereotype in both approving and disparaging ways, often in the same piece of writing. Second, Leland's attitudes toward "Indians" underwent some change in the course of his life. Earlier negative, racist attitudes were tempered, but not expunged, when he met and entered into relationships with Passamaquoddy people on Campobello Island in the early 1880s. Our inquiry will return to a discussion of this "Indian" stereotype in the next chapter, but for now we will have to look deeper for answers to the questions posed earlier about Leland's motives for pursuing and then championing the Kluskap-Malsum story.

We already know that Leland constructed "Of Glooskap's Birth . . ." if not out of whole cloth, at least out of pieces of material that should have caused him to hesitate. We also know he was persistent to the point of showing disrespect to his consultants. This characteristic of his story-gathering technique calls attention to his overall folklore collecting methods. Exploring his methods further may give insight into his motives.

The consultants Leland had personal contact with were the Passamaquoddy men he met in the summers of 1882 and 1883. It was from them that he began his story gathering. In his comments about the work of recording these stories, he is careful to establish his versions as accurate and authoritative: "I have taken very great pains . . . in all the tales written down from verbal narration, to be accurate in details, and to convey as well as I could the quaint manner and dry humor which characterized the style of the narrator" (119). The authority of these stories came in large measure, according to Leland, from the unique relationship he had with the "Indians." He writes, "if Tomahquah [Tomah Joseph] and others fully expressed their feelings to me, it was because they had never before met with a white man who listened to them with such sympathy."[6] This refrain suggests Leland's approving use of the "Indian" stereotype noted earlier.

Elizabeth Robins Pennell, Leland's niece (by marriage) and biographer, witnessed some of the exchanges between her uncle and Tomah Joseph. She gives us some insight into her uncle's methods. She writes,

> I was allowed to sit there while Tomah told his stories, and the Rye [Leland] made his notes, interrupting every now and then, with that emphatic outstretched hand of his, to settle some difficulty or get the uttermost meaning of the last 'By Jolly!' . . . of Tomah [an exclamation he used] when the drama grew too intense even for the traditional stolidity of the race.[7]

It is worth noting here that though Leland's language skills were formidable, they did not include Passamaquoddy, at least not enough of the language to hear and understand Tomah Joseph's stories.[8] Joseph told the stories in English.

Leland elaborated on his story-gathering method in a March 22, 1902 letter to his collaborator, John Dyneley Prince, in which he discusses the similarities between working among the secretive Shelta-speaking Gypsies and the taciturn Passamaquoddies.

In both Shelta and Wabanaki there was only a few years ago *extraordinary* secrecy and reticence, just as there was 20 years ago among the Gypsies, as regarded letting anybody learn Rommany. But as I had gone through and through the Gyps with success, I was to a degree qualified for Injuns. I wonder how many *drinks* I took first and last in the pursuit of Rommany and Indian philology and traditions! . . . I solemnly believe that those among the learned who despaired of getting at Rommany and Passamaquoddy did not go to their tents with a bottle of beer in either pocket and a half-pound of tobacco, and sit over the fire in the real loafer attitude by the hour![9] [The emphases are Leland's.]

From the letters he received from his Passamaquoddy consultants, it seems Leland's story-gathering methods involved more than gifts of alcohol and tobacco. Leland engaged Tomah Joseph in finding silver trade brooches and other articles of material culture.[10] In late summer 1883 Joseph wrote Leland thanking him for the dollar he had sent with his last letter.[11] Another consultant, John Gabriel, who like Joseph is listed in the "Authorities" section of *Algonquin Legends*, had written Leland earlier in the same year explaining that the winter had been hard, that he had not been well, that baskets were not selling in Eastport, and, because he had bills to pay, he would like a loan of ten dollars "till you come to Campobello next summer." He concludes with this appeal: "I would ask you more if I think I get. I need about—$25.00. If you would do so you will greatly oblige."[12] Leland did not return to Campobello that or any other summer. In 1884, his manuscript off to the publisher, he left for England. This correspondence from the men who told him stories begins to clarify Leland's comment in *Algonquin Legends* regarding the loss of "the early and grand mythology" of "the Indians": "a few hundred dollars expended annually in each State would result in the collection of all that is extant of this folklore" (308).

If the letters from the Passamaquoddies who shared with Leland hospitality and stories in their tents begins to clarify this comment, the letters from Lewy Mitchell, who provided Leland with a multitude of written stories, draw it into sharp focus. When Leland wrote in late 1883 asking for assistance, Mitchell responded:

Please Answer this letter as soon as possible and let me know how often you want me send the stories or how By mail or by express. and how you going to allow me to assist you this work. I am willing to assist you But of course I want something for it. My family is large. What ever you going to allow I want part of it now. Rightaway.[13]

The Mitchell correspondence reveals just how much money Leland spent obtaining Passamaquoddy stories. The rate he established early on in the relationship was one dollar for every eight pages of manuscript: "You say," writes Mitchell, "you will allow Dollar for Every 8 Pages. Some of the Paper is little Smaller than the other But I make a allowance in writting my writting is very fine you will get good many words in my Stories."[14] Mitchell was himself the middle man who recorded stories from *his* consultants, consultants that *he* sometimes had to pay: "I wished you Can advance me $12.00 in Cash. These Stories I am getting I have to pay out Some money to get them. If you Can furnished the money I can get you good Stories and get you valuable information Relating to the Passammaquoddy indians."[15] At the heart of Leland's story-gathering method, then, was the exchange of money for information.[16]

Not surprisingly, once Leland was employing Mitchell to procure stories for him, he brought his own storytelling standards to bear on Mitchell's work. In a penciled letter dated March 12, 1884, Mitchell writes, "I did not understand you only want 8 Pages Stories the way I understood you if the Story is very long you allow more than Dollar. Of Course that means more than Eight Pages. That is the Reason why I Send you two long Stories instead of four as you ordered."[17] By ordering stories of a certain length, no doubt to conform to his reader's expectations and perhaps to keep his project within budget, Leland was no longer merely gathering stories, he was shaping their form.[18]

It was not just the form he shaped; he changed the text as well. Once he received the stories from his consultants, whether Mitchell, Rand, Jack, or Louise Brown, Leland would recast them into the sort of stories he knew his readers would appreciate. The second Acquin version of the Kluskap twin story—the one recorded by Edward Jack—is a case in point. While Leland used it for authenticating the other versions of the story he already had, he did not borrow extensively from it. For one thing there was no Malsum the Wolf in it. For another, the secret death-wielding elements disagreed with his preferred versions both in number and kind. Finally, the Acquin/Jack version has Kluskap's brother born first (destroying their mother because he could not wait to be born); however he is described as the younger brother in the story. Yet it was a good story, and its presence in *Algonquin Legends* would add prestige to the showcased version, "Of Glooskap's Birth. . . ." Ironically when Leland told it again later in the book he told it as, "The Tale of Glooskap as told by another Indian. . . ."[19] The "other Indian" was, of course, the same Maliseet who originated most, if not all, of the story versions Leland worked with. When he retells Acquin's story, Leland alters the text considerably. Acquin's story is a long one, and Jack's record gives almost no punctuation, but it begins like this,

> Glooscap & his brother were twins they talked to one and other before they were born, the youngest said to the oldest they must be born right away, they must get out into this world, the oldest said we must wait he could not stop him the other however he must get into the world. So he went out of his mother's side, this killed the mother, they agreed to go then after this; after a few years the younger brother asked the older what would kill him (the older) he thought a long time, he did not tell him what would kill him dead but only what would stun him, he then told him that down (feathers) would kill him. The older then asked the younger the same question, the younger told the truth as to what would kill him (the younger) which was cattails (bull rushes).[20]

And here is Leland's version of the same section:

> In the old time. Far before men knew themselves, in the light before the sun, Glooskap and his brother were as yet unborn; they waited for the day to appear. Then they talked together, and the youngest said, "Why should I wait? I will go into the world and begin my life at once." Then the elder said, "not so, for this were a great evil." But the younger gave no heed to any wisdom: in his wickedness he broke through his mother's side, he rent the wall; his beginning of life was his mother's death. Now in after years, the younger brother would learn in what lay the secret of the elder's death. And Glooskap, being crafty, told the truth and yet lied; for his name was Liar, yet did he never lie for evil or aught to harm. So he told his brother that the blow of a ball or handful of the down of feathers, would take away his life; and this was true,

Figure 4.1. Mikamwes by Tomah Joseph from *The Century Illustrated Monthly Magazine.*

for it would stun him, but it would not prevent his returning to life. Then Glooskap asked the younger for his own secret. And he, being determined to give the elder no time, answered truly and fearlessly, "I can only be slain by the stroke of a cat-tail or bulrush." (106)

A comparison of the remainder of the two texts show similar differences throughout.[21]

Despite these abuses, Leland was not, I think, deliberately trying to deceive his readers. If he was, he did a bad job of it. Many of the reviewers of the day picked up on his heavy editing hand.[22] Leland himself is often quick to admit where his blue pencil lands. He is willing, he writes, to omit part of a story because it is repeated elsewhere; to change "guns" to "arrows" in a story which he states is "evidently very ancient." Elsewhere he chooses between variant endings, rejecting one as a "senseless termination"; and he is often willing to reduce many versions of a story into one.[23]

It is curious that Leland saw no incongruity between tampering with the text in any number of ways and his claim that the *Algonquin Legends* stories are authentically "Indian." In the book's preface, for example, he says he can "give the name of the aboriginal authority for every tale except one" (iv). Our study of the Kluskap-Malsum story gives contrary evidence. On the same page he crows that future students of the "Indians" "will be much more obliged to me for collecting raw material than for cooking it" (iv). This is patently false as well as bad prophecy.[24]

There is evidence of further meddling. Not content to alter just the text of the stories, Leland set about "improving" the illustrations in *Algonquin Legends* as well. His early piece on Passamaquoddy legends in *The Century Illustrated Monthly Magazine* was illustrated by birch bark drawings. A comparison of the first drawing here (see Figure 4.1), that of "Mikamwes" (an other-than-human person), with the comparable drawing in *Algonquin Legends* (see Figure 4.2) reveals they are different. In *Algonquin Legends* the drawing is the frontispiece, a full-page reproduction, with more vegetation, a more intricate frame and a figure sporting two pointy ears. The *Century Illustrated* Mikumwesu has none of these. The body and the face of the figure in the two drawings are remarkably different. Leland tells us which was done by a Passamaquoddy. The *Century Illustrated* piece is subtitled, "with drawings on birch bark by a Quādi Indian." The caption for the illustration in *Algonquin Legends* reads, "From a scraping on birch bark by Tomah Josephs, Indian Governor at Peter Dana's Point, Maine." The *Century Illustrated* drawing is by the talented Tomah Joseph; the *Algonquin Legends* version "from" that "scraping" is by someone else (see Figure 4.3).[25] At this point it is not hard to guess who. If proof were wanted, we have Leland's 1902 letter to his collaborator Prince, written as they were preparing *Kulóskap the Master* for publication.[26]

The more I think of it, the more convinced am I that our illustrations ought to be often birch-bark pictures. I can hold my own with any Indian at the work (in fact I *am* the author of one or two

MIK UM WESS,
THE INDIAN PUCK, OR ROBIN GOODFELLOW.
*From a scraping on birch bark by Tomah Josephs, Indian
Governor at Peter Dana's Point, Maine. The Mik um wess
always wears a red cap like a Norse Goblin.*

Figure 4.2. Mikamwes by Charles Leland, the frontispiece of *The Algonquin Legends of New England,* ©
1884 by Houghton Mifflin Company.

in my book [*Algonkin Legends*]), but for honesty's sake we must
get them from an aborigine.[27]

Not satisfied with changing the stories he received to suit his tastes,
Leland reworked the birch bark drawings he included in *Algonquin
Legends.* It is Leland's version of Mikumwesu that Joseph Campbell

Figure 4.3. Mikamwes in the center of a birchbark wall pocket by Tomah Joseph. The Mikamwes of *The Century Illustrated* reappeared in Joseph's other work; the Mikamwes of the *Algonquin Legends* does not. (From the collection of Charles Adams; photograph by Rip Gerry)

unwittingly chose to grace the Table of Contents of his *Atlas,* thus ensuring "the eclectic folklorist's" work would endure for generations.[28]

In his time Leland's folklore studies garnered mixed reviews. As we have seen, Leland's heavy hand was as discernible up close as from the distance afforded by time.[29] Evidence turns up in, of all places, an obituary notice of Leland. In it F. York Powell notes both the negative critics of Leland's work and his response to them:

> He could and did make careful and exact notes, but when he put the results before the public, he liked to give them the seal of his own personality and to allow his fancy to play about the stories and poems he was publishing, so that those who were not able quickly to distinguish what was folk-lore and what was Leland

were shocked and grumbled (much to his astonishment and even disgust), and belittled his real achievements.[30]

This admission comes from an eulogizer. One can only imagine what Leland's detractors were saying on the occasion of his death.

It is easy to criticize Leland's work, especially from our vantage point. His meddling scholarly skulduggery is reprehensible; his arrogance inexcusable; his self-aggrandizement tiresome. And yet, his notions prompt the questions—What did Leland think he was doing? And what was he about, really? If we want to learn from him, not about "Algonquin legends," but about the study of Native American religions, we had better attend to his motives, or, better, to his story. That scholars engage in storytelling is hard to dispute. We often construct narratives reflecting more our own needs than those "Others" we purport to study.[31] In this Leland was no different.

Leland was willing to go to great lengths to tell *his* story—altering text and illustrations as well as shaping the stories to his own specifications. Fundamental to *his* story was that his readers take seriously the stories in *Algonquin Legends.* Why, besides his admittedly large ego, would Leland be so concerned?[32] The frontispiece of *Algonquin Legends,* the one to which he added a pointy-eared cap to Mikumwesu, gives the first clue. The caption reads, "The Mik um wess always wears a red cap like the Norse Goblin."

Leland was keen to show that "Algonquin" mythology derived from Norse mythology, which he knew from translations of the epic Edda. His fascination with the idea is unmistakable.[33] Besides the twenty-seven references he makes to the Norse-"Algonquin" connection in the body and notes of his 1884 book, Leland published an essay in *Atlantic Monthly* that same year called, "The Edda among the Algonquin Indians." Two years later in June 1886, he presented a lecture to the Royal Society of Literature in London in which he reiterated his thesis. The essence of Leland's idea is that "Indian" tradition, especially what he called "Algonquin" tradition, was "steeped and penetrated with the old Norse spirit."[34]

Following this thesis, Leland identifies Kluskap with both Odin and Thor.[35] This identification leads back to the Kluskap-Malsum story of our investigation. It helps with the enigma of why Leland made Kluskap's brother a wolf, and then was delighted to find him so. In the Norse stories Leland was reading, the conflict between Odin and

Fenris, the Wolf, was central. Commenting on a Passamaquoddy story in which Kluskap makes arrows in preparation for the end times, Leland writes,

> Glooskap is now living in a Norse-like Asa-heim; but there is to come a day when the arrows will be ready, and he will go forth and slay all the wicked. Malsum the Wolf, his twin brother, the typical colossal type of all Evil, will come to life, with all the giant cannibals, witches, and wild devils slain of old; but the champion will gird on his magic belt, and the arrows will fly in a rain as at Ragnarok.

Characterizing this particular "Indian" story as "very heathen" and "grimly archaic," Leland goes on to drive his point home (and this reader to distraction): "It may be assumed at once that this Indian Last Battle of the Giants, or of the good hero giants against the Evil, led by the Malsum-Fenris Wolf, was not derived from the Canadian French."[36]

Matching detail for detail, Leland forces this "Indian"-Norse connection at every turn. He compares, for example, an "Algonquin" story with a Norse. In the former Plawej ("Pulowech"), a Power-user and a Partridge, at the end of series of wondrous adventures, overcomes his Porcupine foes with the very heat they initially use on him. In the latter a king attempts in vain to roast Odin and dies for his trouble. Following this breathtaking juxtaposition, Leland exults,

> The grandeur of Odin and the behavior of the Indian are set forth in a strikingly similar manner in both narratives. If any modern poet had depicted this incident in so like a style, every critic would have cried out plagiarism![37]

If anyone should know about plagiarism it is Leland. Unfortunately for him, his bombast does not carry the argument.

At the heart of the "Indian"-Norse connection is, for Leland, "the world's first religion."[38] Regrettably the folklorist is vague on the characteristics and traditions of this religion. It is possible he means "the terrible black sorcery which preceded Shamanism, and compared to which the latter was like an advanced religion." It is more likely, though, he wants to equate this first religion, with what he calls "Shamanism," defined as "a vague fear of invisible evils and the sorcerer." In Leland's diffusionist view, the essence of this religion spread in a series of steps, . . . from the Eskimo to the Wabanaki, of Labrador, New Brunswick, and Maine, from the Wabanaki to the Iroquois, and from the Iroquois to the more Western Indians.[39]

The possibility that "Eskimo" intervention in the transmission might have sullied the "first religion" concerned Leland. He reassured his readers that the proportion of Norse elements in the stories was "simply surprising." "There are," he wrote, "actually more incidents taken from the Edda than there are from lower sources."[40] In the *Atlantic Monthly* essay he goes so far as to contend that the Finnish epic, the *Kalevala,* shares less with the Edda than do the legends he has presented to the public.[41] By the time he delivers his London lecture on the topic two years later, he has resolved the issue of origins, at least for himself:

> I could go on much longer with these points of resemblance between the Edda and the Algonkin mythology. The only way in which I can at all account for them is, firstly, that the Norsemen, who dwelt for centuries in Greenland, communicated them to the ancestors of these Indians.[42]

Leland consistently overstates the "Indian"-Norse connection. For example, in this prefatory passage to a catalog of the points of similarity:

> This American mythology of the North, [the "Algonquin"] which has been the very last to become known to American readers, is literally so nearly like the Edda itself that, as this work fully proves, there is hardly a song in the Norse collection which does not contain an incident found in the Indian poem-legends, while in several there are many such coincidences.[43]

He then proceeds to list the similarities. He begins like this:

> Thus, in the Edda we are told that the first birth on earth was that of a giant girl and boy, begotten by the feet of a giant and born from his armpit. In the Wabanaki legends, the first birth was of Glooskap, the Good principle, and Malsum the Wolf, or Evil principle. The Wolf was born from his mother's armpit.

The Wolf as Evil principle is in Leland's version of the Kluskap-

Malsum story because he put it there. The detail of birth from the mother's armpit is not in the story at all. Vital for Leland's thesis is the substance of the story whose history we have been investigating, "Of Glooskap's Birth. . . ." It provides the essential points of comparison: the battle of cosmic Good and Evil with the latter represented by a wolf. In fact, we know these are precisely the points most likely of Leland's creation.[44]

Most scholars have not warmed to Leland's thesis about this "Indian"-Norse connection. During Leland's time his own coauthor, John Dyneley Prince, distanced himself from the theory. While he praises Leland for his inspiration, his diligence in collecting, his able treatment of Kluskap (who he calls, without irony, a "purely American creation"[45]), he is careful to skirt any association with the "Norse connection."

In 1937 Alfred Bailey argued conclusively that Leland's theory was untenable "in light of the wider knowledge of North American mythology" of the day.[46] Nowhere in his painstaking analysis, however, does Bailey indicate that he suspects the Kluskap-Malsum story.[47] Instead he criticizes Leland for forcing the comparison of elements in Algonkian and Norse stories. His first example is the Kluskap-Malsum story. Bailey points out that the intrauterine quarreling of two brothers, and the resulting matricide occur in an Ojibwa story of the culture hero Nanabozho. There is no need, he says, "to build up a case for its Norse origin." After quoting large portions of Leland's Kluskap-Malsum story, Bailey concludes,

> Apart from the fact that in both accounts death is caused by the application or the thrust of a fragment of an organism, none of the incidents narrated in the Prose Edda corresponds in any way to those of the Indian tale just quoted. In one case the instrument of death is a twig of mistletoe, in the other it varies between an owl's feather, a cat-tail, a fern-root, and a pine-root. Moreover, Balder is not Odin, and it is the latter who figures in Leland's mind as the Norse counterpart of Gluskap. Malsumsis fails to kill Gluskap and is himself slain; whereas Loki, through the action of a third person, the blind god Hother, with whom there is not corresponding character in the American tale, actually succeeds in effecting Balder's death. And the general contexts have nothing in common.[48]

Bailey goes on for ten pages to demolish Leland's argument point by point.

Apparently Stith Thompson, when he set out to critique Leland's Norse-Algonkian theory, did not know of Bailey's meticulous work of thirty years earlier, nonetheless the result is the same. Like Bailey, he does not doubt the authenticity of the Kluskap-Malsum story. He writes that "as far as the main, basic myth of the culture hero Glooscap is concerned, a careful examination of this later literature does not modify in any substantial way the legends as Leland has recorded them."[49] With a cataloger's care he identifies twelve points of compari- son in Leland's *Algonquin Legends.* Of these, three—"Birth of the Culture Hero and His Adversary," "Unique Vulnerability," and "The End of the World"—refer to the story of Kluskap and Malsum. Thompson is characteristically thorough in his investigation. A foot- note indicates that Thompson had a colleague go over all the passages Leland cites from Icelandic sources and retranslate them. He found "no errors that would affect Leland's argument, though often there was some change of emphasis."[50] He concludes that,

> The problems presented by Leland seem to have been more apparent than real. A careful reading of his sources and of paral- lels in Norse mythological literature discourage the belief that we have here a case of direct borrowing.[51]

Thus, even before this investigation of the Kluskap-Malsum story, Bailey and Thompson had, independently, reduced Leland's Norse- Algonkian edifice to rubble.

Only Joseph Campbell has had the temerity to embrace Leland's Norse hypothesis. Since Campbell is the lone exception, it is worth returning to his use of the Kluskap-Malsum story for a moment. Campbell chooses fourteen stories from the Abenaki and Micmac cor- pus, each one evidently selected to demonstrate his central point that "the" mythic experience is the same worldwide.[52] One story is, of course, the suspect Kluskap-Malsum story. Not only does Campbell use Leland's stories, he follows his Norse theory. He interrupts his own recasting of the Kluskap-Malsum story three times, once to add:

> Leland . . . points out that in Norse mythology, as represented in the Icelandic Eddic literature of the ninth to thirteenth centuries,

the god-man Baldr is killed by an apparently harmless twig of mistletoe hurled by the blind god Hoth, whose hand is guided by Loki; and that Baldr, like Glooscap, comes to life again. Commenting on this feature of the Wabanaki tale, he remarks: "In this story, as in that of Baldr and Loki, it is the very apparent harmlessness of the bane which points the incident. . . . In the Edda the mistletoe, the softest and apparently the least injurious of plants, kills Baldr; in the Wabanaki tale it is a ball of down or a rush.[53]

In striving to demonstrate the diffusion of these stories from the Vikings of Greenland to the Abenaki and Micmac peoples of what is now Northeast North America, Campbell is engaged in telling his own story. Showing the diffusion of a particular myth from one geographical area to another—like the one he relies on Leland to provide—further validates his own central thesis.[54] Sadly, Campbell depends on Leland to be an authority when scholars unanimously agree he is not; and he relies on a story, the centerpiece of Leland's work, that Leland had forged to his own specifications.

These specifications command our attention. It is one thing to demonstrate Leland's theory wanting; it is another to ask why Leland was so determined to prove his ideas that, when evidence was lacking, he would improvise it. Why was he so keen to show this connection between "Algonquin" and Norse mythologies?[55] Or asked another way—what part of Leland's story demanded these specifications?

As improbable as it seems to contemporary sensibilities, Leland wanted to show these "Indians" to be in some sense Aryan. According to his story, if the "Algonquin's" mythology derives from the Norse, then their myths, like the Norse's, are related to Vedic mythology and are thus "Aryan." If Leland's "Indians" are Aryans, or even Aryan-like, they would be seen as strong, aggressive, virile—showing manly virtue. It is the Aryan component of Leland's story that, more than any other, shaped his specifications for "Algonquin" stories.

In the later 1800s Indologists were making much of the Aryan quality of the Vedic texts of Hinduism. This both shaped and fueled Leland's story, and helps make sense of the otherwise mystifying correspondences between "Hindoo" and "Indian" mythologies with which he salts the notes and text of *Algonquin Legends*. For example, he notes that in the Vedas the Milky Way is called "the Gods' Path" while "the American Indians" believe it is the "Spirits' Road." He states, without evidence, that this is "one of their very earliest traditions."[56] Further, referring to a story he calls "Three Strong Men," Leland says,

> There can be no doubt as to the Hindoo origin of this and many more plots found among the red Indians. But a careful study of the Norse story convinces me that the tale did not come to the Wabanaki through any other than a Norse source.[57]

Clearly Leland intends these comments to reinforce the Aryan quality of the "Algonquin" stories for his readers.

In case his readers might miss the "Hindoo" to Norse to "Indian" connection, Leland spells it out. Kluskap, he says, "is by far the grandest and most Aryan-like character ever evolved from a savage mind."[58] It follows, then, that his stories are the remnant of the "world's first religion," passed from Aryan "Hindoos" to the Norse to the "Indian" stories of *Algonquin Legends.* At the very least Leland is signaling to his readers that the stories in his book are worthy of their attention.

It is easy to see that Leland's theories about the relationships between Norse mythology and Abenaki and Micmac story traditions have, with the exception of Joseph Campbell, fallen out of favor with scholars, and out of the memory of hegemonic popular culture. Thus, most of us would not accept Leland's story about the "Indians" as part of our story. But Leland's story does not end here. All of us tell our stories in a context, a context that is conversational. That is, we often exchange our stories with others. To appreciate more fully Leland's story and to explore over one hundred years later its relationship to our stories—especially our stories about Native American religions—we must look more suspiciously at "the others" Leland was talking to and what he was saying. Perhaps then we can gain some insight into why Leland was so intent on making "Indians" into Aryans.

Chapter 5

Of Conversations

Savagism, Primitivism, and the
Use of the "Indian" Stereotype

W hen Charles Godfrey Leland set out to demonstrate to his readers that "Indians" were Aryan-like, he was not expressing a brand new idea. One of Leland's mentors,[1] the German-born British philologist Max Müller, was a preeminent European "Aryanist." Since the early 1860s, when Müller delivered two important lecture series in London, he had been arguing that the primitive ancestors of modern Europeans were the crop-growing, road-building, law-abiding, order-loving, God- (or at least gods-) fearing Aryans. When Leland made his case for the Aryan-like quality of "his Algonquin Indians," then, he was adding his voice to Müller's in a "conversation" that was ongoing.[2] This conversation is one of the contexts in which Leland told his story through *Algonquin Legends*.

Assuming a social perspective on the exchange between scholars like Müller and Leland (or on the electronic exchange between Grimes, Gill, Deloria, and others in chapter 1) leads us to think of them, after James A. Reither, as belonging to "academic discourse communities."[3] Reither uses Kenneth Burke's parable of a conversation in a parlor to illuminate the workings of an academic discourse community:

> Imagine that you enter a parlor. You come in late. When you arrive, others have long preceded you, and they are engaged in a heated discussion, a discussion too heated for them to pause and tell you exactly what it is about. In fact, the discussion had already begun long before any of them got there, so that no one present is qualified to retrace for you all the steps that had gone

before. You listen for a while, until you decide that you have caught the tenor of the argument; then you put in your oar. Someone answers; you answer him; another comes to your defense; another aligns himself against you. . . . However, the discussion is interminable. The hour grows late, you must depart. And you do depart, with the discussion still vigorously in progress.[4]

Burke's parable draws our attention both to aspects of the social context of *Algonquin Legends*—the "parlor" of the parable—and to those moments when Leland's discussion becomes "heated." We know, for example, that in the European parlor where Leland listened most intently, Müller's was a significant voice. Further, we sense that at those moments of heated discussion Leland is most engaged with his academic discourse community; at those moments he is closest to telling his own story.

Reither notes that academic discourse communities "are conversations among `knowledgeable peers' who, through their characteristic ways of making meaning, construct the knowing and the modes of knowing that identify disciplines and distinguish them from others."[5] Two things are immediately obvious. One is that Leland is engaged in what would now be called cross-disciplinary conversations. Müller is a philologist, Leland a folklorist, another we will meet below is a proto-ethnologist, yet another a mystical botanist. The second is that the disciplines themselves were processes more in flux than they are today. In 1884 when Leland was writing *Algonquin Legends*, he and his colleagues were still negotiating both the knowledge and the making of that knowledge—especially knowledge about "Indians"—in their still amorphous academic disciplines.

Still, despite the disciplinary flux, Charles Leland must have known his "Indian"-Norse theory would not receive easy acceptance. In *Algonquin Legends* he is aware of a voice already raised in opposition. Before "putting in his own oar," Leland quotes Henry Rowe Schoolcraft at some length.

A failed glass blower, an Indian agent for thirty years, and a self-trained ethnologist, Schoolcraft had contributed a number of works to the conversation of the time. Of these his *Algic Researches* (1839) would have been most important to Leland. The revised edition of this book was issued in 1856 as *The Myth of Hiawatha and Other Oral Legends . . .*

apparently to take advantage of the success of Longfellow's poem based on the earlier edition.[6] It is from the introduction to this book that Leland quotes Schoolcraft:

> Where the analogies are so general, there is a constant liability to mistakes. Of these foreign analogies of myth-lore, the least tangible, it is believed, is that which has been suggested with the Scandinavian mythology. That mythology is of so marked and peculiar a character, that it has not been distinctly traced out of the great circle of tribes of the Indo-Germanic family. Odin, and his terrific pantheon of war-gods and social deities, could only exist in the dreary latitudes of storms and fire, which produce a Heela and a Maelstrom. These latitudes have invariably produced nations, whose influence has been felt in an elevating power over the world. From such a source the Indian could have derived none of his vague symbolisms and mental idiosyncrasies, which have left him, as he is found to-day, without a government and without a god.[7]

A more categorical dismissal of the possibility of an "Indian"-Norse connection is hard to imagine. "Indian" stories cannot have Scandinavian sources because northern latitudes have always spawned powerful nations. The "Indians," not part of the "Indo-Germanic family" of what would for a time be called Aryans, were characterized by powerlessness, strange stories, and mental disabilities. For Schoolcraft, "Indians" and the Teutonic Norse were "antagonistical" "types of the human race"; examples of the "alpha and omega of the ethnological chain."[8]

The disparaging use of the "Indian" stereotype saturates Schoolcraft's prose. It would, however, limit our investigation simply to label Schoolcraft a racist and dismiss him. Our investigation at this point turns on understanding the conversational context for Leland's scholarly misbehavior, and through that, his story. Since Leland does not dismiss Schoolcraft's views, neither can we.

The passage Leland quotes places Schoolcraft on a particular thread in a particular conversation. That thread hung on a dispute between monogenists who argued that all humankind stemmed from one source and the polygenists who argued for many sources. This conversation about the beginnings of humankind was heating up in the 1840s and '50s.[9] For Schoolcraft, a monogenist, the issue was not merely scholarly. It was essentially religious. An entry from his journal dated February 7, 1831, indicates that Schoolcraft had had a profound religious experience, probably during one of the religious revivals that punctuated life on the Michigan frontier.

> This day is very memorable in my private history, for my having assumed, after long delay the moral intrepidity to acknowledge, *publicly*, a truth . . . the divine atonement for human sin made by the long foretold, the rejected, the persecuted, the crucified Messiah.[10]

Before he was born again Schoolcraft was already a monogenist, but his conversion experience deepened his animosity to the polygenist position. That position was contrary to revealed Biblical truth. Thus, for Schoolcraft, working out of a fundamental Protestant context, it was vital to show that "Indians" could claim Adam as an ancestor. He found philological and mythological evidence to support his position. Robert Bieder states that:

> Along with physical anthropology, Schoolcraft utilized data from Indian religion, language, and mythology to further confirm the theory that Indians were the descendants of Shem and therefore could be fitted into the Mosaic account of man and share in the first creation. Schoolcraft cautioned that data on Indian diffusion out of Asia could be pushed only so far. It could not be made to yield the exact people or tribe from which the Indians were descended, but in the absence of historical proof "the mere conjecture that these tribes are off-shoots of the Shemitic race of Asia, is important and becomes deeply interesting when it appears probable, as many of learning and genius have asserted, that their history, fate, and fortunes, can be connected with that of the Hebrew race."[11]

Stories were especially important for, according to Schoolcraft, they "illuminated `the dark cave of the Indian mind.'"[12] This illumination was a prerequisite for Christianizing the "Indian." Schoolcraft's voice in the conversation, then, took much of its resonance and direction from his religious convictions that what the "Indian" needed most was to be led to Christianity.[13]

By the time of *Algonquin Legends* Schoolcraft had been dead for twenty years and the monogenist-polygenist conversation was not as deafening as it had been. Nonetheless, when Leland "put his oar in," he was not oblivious to this conversation about the origins of humankind. He tries to sidle past the discussion by stating that it is premature to decide in favor of one or the other position:

> It will be long ere the scholar definitely determines whether Shamanism as it now exists originated spontaneously in different countries where the same causes were to be found, or whether it is *historical*; that is, derived from a single source.[14]

Notice that Leland wants to talk about "Shamanism," not, like Schoolcraft, the connections between "Indians" and "the Hebrew race." Not associated with any of the mainline Christian religions and feeling an affinity with what he called "magic," Leland was more interested in that "first religion," "Shamanism," than with Christianity.

> If we, declining all question as to the origin of monotheism, limit ourselves definitely to what is known of Shamanism alone, we shall still have before us an immense field for investigation. Shamanism is the belief that *all* the events and accidents of life are caused or influenced by spirits, . . . [especially] *evil* invisible beings.[15]

Further, the shaman in Leland's understanding of this "first religion" is the one who claims to be able to counteract or neutralize the power of evil spirits. For him this first religion, sculpted by an icy climate, is readily apparent in the Aryan-like stories of the Norse and "Indian."

Schoolcraft's problem, according to Leland, was that, besides being "not generally over particular or accurate,"[16] he was ignorant of the more northern "Algonquin" story corpus.

> it was not known to [Schoolcraft] that there already existed in Northeastern America a stupendous mythology, derived from a land of storms and fire more terrible and wonderful than Iceland; nay so terrible that Icelanders themselves were appalled by it. . . . Here then was the latitude of storm and fire required by Schoolcraft to produce something wilder and grander that he had ever found among Indians.[17]

As a result of this ignorance, Schoolcraft misses the power and significance of "Indian" stories. The comparison of the little-known "northern
Algonquin" and the well-known "western Chippewa" becomes a
recurring theme in *Algonquin Legends*. It is also a rhetorical strategy.
Leland notes, for example, that Kluskap has none of the "silly, cruel, or
fantastic" qualities of "Manobozho-Hiawatha." He adds,

> it cannot be denied that in the red Indian mythology of New
> England, and of Canada and New Brunswick, we have a collec-
> tion of vigorous, icy, powerful legends, like those of a strong
> northern race, while those of the middle continent, or Chippewa,
> are far feebler and gentler. Hiawatha-Manobozho is to Glooskap
> as a flute to a war trumpet.[18]

Two years later he continues this theme, this time to a London audience:

> Glooskap, the Lord of Men and Beasts, the sublime American
> Thor and Odin, who towers above Hiawatha and Manobozho like
> a colossus above pigmies, the master of the mighty mountains,
> has still a wonderfully tender heart.[19]

Using this strategy, Leland can allow Schoolcraft his views, even his
negative use of the "Indian" stereotype, and still counter his voice by
promoting "his Indians." Thus he lobbies for the significance of the
"Algonquin" stories based on their Aryan-like quality. This quality, in
Leland's pre-Darwinian understanding, depends in equal measure on
the cold climate and their Norse ancestry. Schoolcraft, according to
Leland, was wrong on these points simply because he did not know
what Leland knows—the existence of the "Algonquin" story corpus.

   Henry Rowe Schoolcraft was not the only prominent, dead
American Leland chose to engage in conversation. There was also
Henry David Thoreau. Leland's conversation with Thoreau is brief—a
discursive footnote running on to three pages—but it is noteworthy
because it is so vituperative.[20] It is unlike Leland to berate any other
writer, especially a famous one, and especially one who, like himself,
seemed to hold "the Indian" in high regard. For him to engage Thoreau
in a "heated discussion" of this nature, Leland must have cared deeply
about its content; and his own story's retelling must be near.

   Thoreau drew Leland's wrath for underestimating the importance of

Abenaki stories. After the time Thoreau had spent with Passama-quoddies and Penobscots, he should have known better, at least according to Leland. The latter enters the conversation much as he did with Schoolcraft, by quoting from the author. In this case Leland begins by quoting from Thoreau's *The Maine Woods,* a book popular when Leland wrote *Algonquin Legends.*[21]

> While we were crossing this bay, where Mount Kineo rose dark before us, within two or three miles, the Indian repeated the tradition respecting this mountain's having anciently been a cow moose,—how a mighty Indian hunter, whose name I forget, succeeded in killing this queen of the moose tribe with great difficulty, while her calf was killed somewhere among the islands in Penobscot Bay, and, to his eyes, this mountain had still the form of the moose in a reclining posture, its precipitous side presenting the outline of her head. He told this at some length, though it did not amount to much, and with apparent good faith, and asked us how we supposed the hunter could have killed such a mighty moose as that,—how we could do it. Whereupon a man-of-war to fire broadsides into her was suggested, etc. An Indian tells such a story as if he thought it deserved to have a good deal said about it, only he has not got it to say, and so he makes up for the deficiency by a drawling tone, long-windedness, and a dumb wonder which he hopes will be contagious.[22]

Leland's response is stinging: "This concluding criticism is indeed singularly characteristic of Mr. Thoreau's own nasal stories about Nature, but it is utterly untrue as ridiculous when applied to any Indian storytelling to which I have ever listened."[23] He has listened, he reminds his readers, to many of the "near relatives" of the Penobscots and Passamaquoddies Thoreau talked to. He is, he is saying, an authority on the matter. Furthermore, by page sixty-five of *Algonquin Legends* where he enters this conversational fray with Thoreau, Leland's readers have been able to read for themselves his (edited, recast) versions of "Indian" stories. They would have concluded that on the point of deficient, long-winded stories Thoreau is simply wrong.

Leland continues his attack on Thoreau. We will have occasion to return to Leland's footnote in the next chapter, but for now it is enough to point out that Leland's concern is that his "Indian" stories receive the attention he is certain they deserve. The voices of Schoolcraft and Thoreau proded Leland to "put in his oar" in order to counter what he saw as their belittling of a great "Indian" epic. That this "Indian" epic was one that he had done much to shape only added the pique of bruised ego to his argument.

There is in Leland's conversations with Schoolcraft and Thoreau a distinctive feature that warrants further inquiry. While not immediately obvious, this motif—the disparaging and approving use of the "Indian" stereotype—permeates the conversation and perhaps even the very walls of the parlor.

Roy Harvey Pearce labels the disparaging use of the "Indian," "the idea of savagism," and finds in the work of Henry Rowe Schoolcraft the culmination of the idea.[24] Pearce argues that Euro-American society created the idea of savagism in order to play it off against an idea that described themselves—civilization. The tension between the two ideas allowed Euro-Americans to understand their often brutal conquest of real human beings as an inevitable working out of human history, of the victory of the civilized over the "savage."[25] Examining Schoolcraft's work, especially his "masterwork," *Historical and Statistical Information Respecting the History, Condition, and Prospects of the Indian Tribes of the United States* (1851–1857), Pearce finds evidence of savagism everywhere.

> The received idea of savage society, though [Schoolcraft] did not know it, supplied him, just as it had supplied others before him, with categories into which to fit data. The questions he had his informants ask virtually supplied their own answers. The informants were to find out *how* the Indians whom they knew hunted and warred; *how* loosely their society was organized; *how* brave, simple, cruel, incapable of systematic thinking they were; *how much* they clung to the immediacies of life about them; *how little* sense of progress they had.[26]

Savagism was, according to Pearce, an all-pervasive notion, blinding those who held it from seeing what was before them. Noting that Schoolcraft's multivolume "masterwork" was an organizational nightmare, Pearce observes that "the chaos of the work is perhaps a product of a tension between recalcitrant human data which will simply not be brought into proper focus and a mind which is sure that it has brought them into focus."[27]

Two attitudes were most common in savagist Euro-Americans—pity and censure. Pity, says Pearce, arises from a feeling of identity with the "savage" life, especially, from the savagist point of view, its simple closeness to nature. Censure arises from a feeling of revulsion from what the savagist sees as the excesses of the "savage" life. Censure comes because the "savage" is not and will never be civilized.[28] Pearce found both pity and censure in Schoolcraft. Early in his work, pity predominates. Later, as he became more and more discouraged about the possibilities of civilizing the "Indian," Schoolcraft became a censurer.

> In Schoolcraft's last thinking savagism has become so abhorrent as to be abolished from human history. . . . For Schoolcraft, savagism has become simply noncivilization. If pity will do no good, then little but censure is left. And the Indian must die, since noncivilization is not life.[29]

There is another idea—"primitivism"—which is used to image Native Americans. Pearce makes brief reference to this idea, for example, when he discusses Thoreau. In 1953 Pearce believed that primitivism, an imported notion, had failed in North America because it was formed in isolation from actual nonliterate people, and was thus inaccurate.[30] I do not follow Pearce's argument here. Savagism's fundamental inaccuracy seems not to have affected its popularity. It is hard to see why primitivism's inaccuracy should either.

If only because of its venerableness, primitivism deserves more than a mere aside. Part of the conversation about "primitive people" since "the earliest documents of Western thought,"[31] primitivism's central tenet concerns the relationship of the imaged "primitive" and nature. According to Lovejoy and Boas who reckoned with the idea in 1935,

> The history of primitivism is in great part a phase of a larger historic tendency which is one of the strangest, most potent and most persistent factors in Western thought—the use of the term `nature' to express the standard of human values, the identification of the good with that which is `natural' or `according to nature.' The . . . life of `savage' peoples has usually been extolled because it has been supposed to constitute `the state of nature.'[32]

Primitivism, like savagism, is not descriptive of real human beings. Rather, the idea reflects "the discontent of the civilized with civilization."[33] It serves to provide a place from which to critique the culture of the person enamoured of the primitivist ideal. Central to primitivism is the idea of the noble savage, a strong, heroic, stoic human being in his or her natural state. Exemplary in every way, the noble savage usually appears as a foil for the civilized person. The positive valence is ascribed in this tension between savage and civilized not, as in savagism, to the civilized, but rather to the savage.

Primitivism's inversion of the savagist judgment of the "savage" does nothing to reduce its reliance on stereotypes. Further, the stereotypes inherent in primitivism are similar in kind if not in emphasis to those in savagism. Thus while savagism stresses the barbaric, stolid, or terrifying quality of the "savage," primitivism, more attentive to the etymological roots of the "forest dweller," stresses the close relationship of the "savage" to nature. In both primitivism and savagism, though, the "savage" is often counted as part of the fauna of the forest. Here is a descriptive example from Thoreau's *The Maine Woods*:

> It is a country full of evergreen trees, of mossy silver birches and watery maples, . . . the forest resounding at rare intervals with the note of the chicadee, the blue-jay, and the woodpecker, the scream of the fish-hawk and the eagle, the laugh of the loon, and the whistle of ducks along the solitary streams; and at night, with the hooting of owls and howling of wolves; in summer swarming with myriads of black flies and mosquitoes, more formidable than wolves to the white man. Such is the home of the moose, the bear, the caribou, the wolf, the beaver, and the Indian.[34]

So it is that the "savage," whether noble or ignoble, whether super- or subhuman, has essentially the same characteristics.[35]

Robert F. Sayre, in his thorough study of Thoreau and the "Indian," seems to recognize this essential sameness of characteristics. Sayre uses Pearce's insights in his investigation, but for the most part he folds primitivism into the idea of savagism, using the latter to stand for both positive and negative images of the "Indian."[36] Following Pearce, Sayre identifies five stereotypic characteristics of savagism:

> Indians were 1) solitary hunters, rather than farmers; 2) tradition-bound and not susceptible to improvement; 3) child-like innocents who were corrupted by civilization; 4) superstitious pagans

who would not accept the highest offerings of civilization like Christianity; and therefore, 5) doomed to extinction.[37]

To this I would add, again following Pearce, a sixth characteristic, not only of savagism, but of any use of the "Indian" stereotype: that "Indians" are essentially all the same. The remarkable diversity of tribal nations, languages and cultures can be distilled into one generic "Indian" who can stand for all the others.[38] Robert F. Berkhofer, contrasting, as he often does, "Indian" and "White," underscores this dimension of the stereotype and identifies another—the other or alien quality of the "Indians":

> As with images of other races and minorities, the essence of the White image of the Indian has been the definition of Native Americans in fact and fancy as a separate and single other. Whether evaluated as noble or ignoble, whether seen as exotic or degraded, the Indian as an image was always alien to the White.[39]

Jean-Jacques Simard deepens this characteristic otherness. Noting that both "Indian" and "Whiteman" are stereotypes, he finds one constant in their history—they are "logically obverse":

> Whatever features are defined as typical of *The Native*, they display a simulation that is the absolute reverse of *The Whiteman's* moral ideal for self and community (at any one time!). This rule applies whether *The Native* is seen as morally better or worse than the *Whiteman*, whether the icon represents a *Noble* or a *Wild Savage*.[40]

When this characteristic of the "Indian" stereotype is stressed, there appears to be an unbridgeable gulf between these two collections of images, between *Them* and *Us*. Whether it is used in disparaging (and often racist) ways or approving ways, this characteristic is so powerful it is well to remember that these are *images*, not real people sharing human problems and joys. As we have seen in both Schoolcraft and Thoreau, an often central fissuring agent in the "unbridgeable gulf" is the eighth underlying stereotypic characteristic: the "Indian" is inextricably linked with nature.

Returning to Sayre and his investigation of Thoreau, I want to illustrate the power of the "Indian" stereotype to grip even the most creative imagination. Focusing on Thoreau's relationship to two Penobscots, Joe Aitteon and Joe Polis, as well as to the "Indians," Sayre argues that Thoreau pushed at the boundaries of savagism, but never freed himself completely. Sayre's main texts are *The Maine Woods,* the book Leland quotes from, and Thoreau's "Indian Books," notebooks in which he recorded his study of the "Indian." Although Thoreau's trips to Maine in September 1853 and July–August 1857 provided him with virtually his only extended contact with living Native Americans, his work and indeed his life was influenced by "the Indian" of savagist imagination.[41]

Sayre exposes what he calls the "peculiar logic" of savagism in part of *The Maine Woods.* In this passage Thoreau is describing the Penobscot community at Old Town:

> Generally [the houses] have a very shabby, forlorn, and cheerless look, being all back side and woodshed, not homesteads, even Indian homesteads, . . . The church is the only trim-looking building, but that is not Abenaki, that was Rome's doings. Good Canadian it may be, but it is poor Indian. These were once a powerful tribe. Politics are all the rage with them now. I even thought that a row of wigwams, with a dance of pow-wows, and a prisoner tortured at the stake, would be more respectable than this.[42]

Sayre points out the savagist sentiments of Thoreau's prose:

> Such clichés and stock responses come . . . from the most hackneyed commentary on the Indian plight. They seem sympathetic, but there is no understanding. They shift the burden of guilt to the Indians themselves or the French missionaries, and they set up the peculiar logic of savagism and civilization. Drunken or Catholic Indians are bad because they are improperly civilized; dancing or torturing ones are bad because they are too savage. To say that the latter are "more respectable" is idle.[43]

Engaging with the physical community at Old Town and with the Penobscot men, Aitteon and Polis, even for the short time he did, Thoreau for the first time came up against the incongruity between his savagist images of "the Indian" and the human reality of Penobscot life.

There is evidence that Thoreau grappled at some level with this incongruity. Discussing his reasons for not publishing his essay on his last trip to Maine, the one guided by Joe Polis, he wrote in a letter,

> The more fatal objection to printing my last Maine-wood experience, is that my Indian guide, whose words & deeds I report very faithfully,—and they are the most interesting part of the story,—knows how to read, and takes a newspaper, so that I could not face him again.[44]

Sayre argues that Thoreau realized that to print his work "would infringe on Polis's privacy and their friendship." Sayre is being charitable. Just the number of times Thoreau pokes fun at Polis's accent in *The Maine Woods* gives substantial reason for his uneasiness at seeing the account in print. In fact, the account was published for the first time as part of *The Maine Woods* six years later, after Thoreau's death.[45] We may quibble about Thoreau's reasons for not being able to face Polis again if his travelogue was published, but whatever they were, they demonstrate that he had begun to feel and struggle with the discrepancy between the stereotypes he used and his experiences with the Penobscot human beings he met.

There is little evidence Charles Godfrey Leland felt or struggled with a similar discrepancy. Thus far in our investigation of Leland's scholarly misconduct, we have found evidence that he used "Indian" stereotypes both approvingly and disparagingly. In the last chapter we read of his description of the people of the Kaw nation, and his admission that he was sometimes "as vindictive as an unconverted Indian." At the same time he claimed a deep-seated affinity with "the Indian," an affinity he was proud of.

Disparaging and approving uses of the "Indian" stereotype run through all of Leland's writing career, but, as I indicated, the disparaging usage slackens by the time of *Algonquin Legends*. Still, there are moments of disparagement even in that text. For example, Leland notes in the "Introduction," that "the most ancient and mythic of these legends have been taken down from the trembling memories of old squaws who never understood their inner meaning, or from ordinary *senaps* who had not thought of them since boyhood."[46] Embedded in Leland's self-serving insult to Abenaki and Micmac elders is that aspect of the "Indian" stereotype that sees Native Americans as locked in their traditional past as if in amber. According to the stereotype, the timeless "Indians" are incapable of change, especially to accept "the highest offerings of civilization," most notably the teachings of Christianity.[47] Thus, within the "peculiar logic" of the stereotype, if "the Indian" does change, for example to become Christian like the ancestors of Leland's Abenaki and Micmac consultants, then he or she is no longer "Indian."[48] Unpacking Leland's disparaging use of the stereotype, then, leads to this rendering: in order to discover these "Algonquin" legends Leland has to penetrate the layers of alien Christian veneer to touch the true, pure "Indian" core of his consultants. It is almost too late. There are only a few of the "real Indians" left. They will soon be extinct.[49] But by calling on that "Injun" part of himself Leland has been able, just in the nick of time, to ferret out and then wrest from his "informants" their "Indian" treasures. Our investigation of Leland's story-collecting techniques puts the lie to most of this fiction. The existence over one hundred years later of human beings who self-define as Passamaquoddy or Penobscot, Maliseet or Micmac contravenes the rest.[50]

If Leland ever worried about how his Passamaquoddy consultants might react to his writing, I have found no evidence of it. Lewy Mitchell wrote him continually as he prepared his manuscript, and continued to write him in London. Tomah Joseph and John Gabriel wrote as well. Perhaps knowing he was traveling to Europe for an extended period—it turned out to be the last nineteen years of his life—dulled some of the concern Leland ought to have felt.

Easily the most common example of Leland's approving use of the "Indian" stereotype in *Algonquin Legends* is his ongoing discussion of the relationship of the "Indian" and nature. According to Leland, this relationship is essentially religious, and in his scheme, it belongs to "the world's first religion"—Shamanism—the essence of which is magic:

> It is absurd to laugh at or pity the Indian for believing in his magic. Living as he does in the woods, becoming familiar with animals, and learning how much more intelligent and allied to man they are than civilized man supposes, he believes they have souls, and were perhaps originally human. Balaam's ass spoke once for every Christian; every animal spoke once for the Indian.[51]

Here Leland draws on the power of those characteristics of "the Indians" that conveys them as solitary hunters of the forest, and virtually part of the forest's fauna.

In fact, Abenaki and Micmac people of precontact time lived in communities near rivers or ocean, as well as "in the forest." In season many communities engaged in limited agriculture. More important, by 1880, when Leland is writing, most Abenaki and Micmac people lived on the margins of the hegemonic economy, engaged in a variety of activities to sustain themselves. These included fishing (including for porpoise), coopering, lumbering, quillwork, making baskets or ax handles, providing domestic help.[52] The most economically successful often were, like Gabe Acquin, guides for hunters. Such employment, however, did not mesh well with the older Abenaki and Micmac understanding that the other-than-human Persons that manifest animal and other forms deserve respect. Maliseet historian, Andrea Bear Nicholas, notes that Acquin boasted of shooting sixty red deer in a two-week period. According to Thoreau, Joe Polis's record was ten moose in a day.[53] However we come to understand the behavior of these admittedly Christian guides, it is clear that the solitary forest-hunting "Indian" Leland is approving of has more to do with his and his audience's needs than with a description of real human beings.

Leland continues his discussion of the religious relationship between "Indians" and nature by comparing them with his predominantly not-Native audience. This is consistent with both disparaging and approving uses of the stereotype, "Indian." It is also vintage Leland.

> The greatest cause for a faith in magic is one which the white man talks about without feeling, and which the Indian feels without talking about it. I mean the poetry of nature, with all its quaint and beautiful superstitions. To every Algonquin a rotten log by the road, covered with moss, suggests the wild legend of the log-demon; The Indian corn and sweet flag in the swamp are descendants of beautiful spirits who still live in them; . . . And how much of this feeling of the real poetry of nature does the white man or woman possess, who pities the poor ignorant Indian? A few second-hand scraps of Byron and Tupper, Tennyson and Longfellow, the jingle of a few rhymes and a few similes, and a little second-hand supernaturalism, more "accepted" than felt, and that derived from far foreign sources, does not give the white man what the Indian *feels*. Joe, or Noel, or Sabattis may seem to the American Philistine to be a ragged, miserable, ignorant Indian; but to the *scholar* he is by far the Philistine's superior in that which life is *best* worth living for.[54]

It is hard to argue with Leland's call to openness, his attempt to deflate the sense of religious superiority of hegemonic popular culture. Nonetheless, it is important to realize that in his laudable efforts Leland employs—in an admittedly approving manner—the stereotype, "Indian." Although he gives real Abenaki and Micmac men's names, his comparison between "the white man or woman" and "Indian" requires a unitary "Indian" to stand for all apparently nature-sensitive Abenaki and Micmac. Note, too, that Leland relies on the perception of an unbridgeable gulf between nature-sensitive "Indians" and the "white man or woman," between *Them* and *Us.*

Luckily for his readers there were, Leland proclaimed, the rare scholar-mediators who could bridge the gap. I noted earlier that Leland was proud of what he saw as the "Injun" in him. His identification with the "Indian" stressed two characteristics of that stereotype: (1) they are tradition-bound (or better, according to the approving use, "respectful of timeless tradition"); (2) they are connected to nature.[55] Thus Leland understood himself as gaining two important and unique qualities from the "Indian." From the first aspect of the stereotype Leland gained access to the mystery and power of humankind's "first religion, Shamanism." From the second aspect—the "Indian's" deep and enduring connection to nature—Leland received his affinity for the natural world. Notice that Leland's nature is pure, the primitivist's repository of human virtue.[56] Both qualities, which he imagined he accessed by means of his inner "Indian" part of himself, set him apart from the rest of his culture. These same imaginings may be at work in more contemporary imitators of the "Indian."

Leland's self-image, premised on the approving use of the "Indian" stereotype seems relatively harmless. After all, in *Algonquin Legends* he is, a few disparaging comments aside, supportive of the "Indian." I will argue that this approving use of the "Indian" stereotype is, contrary to first appearances, wrong.[57] It is wrong both in terms of ethics and accuracy.

Leland trades heavily on the "Indian's" closeness to nature. In the 1880s, just as now, this simply was not true for many Micmacs, Maliseets, Passamaquoddies, and Penobscots. Thoreau's guide, Joe Polis, lived in a neat, clapboard house; Leland collected some of his stories from "Passamaquoddy tents" set up near the big hotel on Campobello Island to take advantage of the tourist trade; Leland's niece was distressed by the poverty of a Passamaquoddy community;[58]

Abler argues many Micmacs were peripatetic merchants; Gabe Acquin traveled to Europe at least twice hobnobbing there with royalty. Many Micmac and Abenaki people were, even in the 1880s, comfortable in "human-invented environments" no more or less close to nature than their not-Native neighbors. Today, Gabe Acquin's and Joe Polis's old communities have become parts of urban landscapes, while Tomah Joseph's descendants have access to all the features of life in small-town Maine, provided they have sufficient funds. As Jean-Jacques Simard puts it, "These real Indians today do not scour the countryside for small game and roots. Like other North Americans they hunt money, jobs, social services, grants, and media attention."[59]

Simard singles out the "'living close to nature' fable" for close analysis.

Consider the image of The Indian as the world's original environmentalist, "living in perfect harmony with nature." In the far reaches of prehistory, where we would surely expect to find the purest of True Indians, real ancestors of Indians by over-hunting contributed greatly to the extinction of many species of Pleistocene megafauna. More recently, not too long before the first European transatlantic voyages, the sedentary, town dwelling, farming, pyramid building Mound Builders of Ohio and Illinois created their own versions of civilizations that peaked and disappeared—brought on by their own destruction of the ecological base on which they were raised.[60]

This is a sensitive point. So as to be clear, I want to state the obvious: some individual Native Americans today and in the past no doubt have had a close, harmonious relationship to the earth. Some Native American nations today have, and in the past no doubt have had, as a religious ideal, a close, harmonious relationship with the earth. Some, but not, as the "Indian" stereotype would have it, all.

So the "Indian" stereotype is inaccurate. Still, if it is used in an approving manner, can it do any harm? In short, yes. Here is what Simard says about the hurt caused by the approving use of the characteristic of the stereotype we have been discussing—the "Indian's" deep, abiding closeness to nature:

Naive platitudes about inbred environmentalism reduce all the many varieties of real Indians to one cliché, the False Indian. And such stereotypes make many modern Indians seem like traitors to their kind, for preferring bungalows to wigwams as habitations, television viewing to ritual dancing, Kentucky fried-chicken to Indian fried bread, employment as an attorney rather than deer hunting.[61]

The fixed, rigid nature of stereotypes, when they are tenacious, can block real human beings, in this case real Micmacs and Maliseets, Penobscots and Passamaquoddies, from identifying with others of their nations without feelings of inadequacy or inauthenticity.[62]

But wait. As Jean-Jacques Simard points out as part of his inquiry, he was raised a French Canadian and became a Québécois.[63] I was raised a Vermonter and became a Canadian. Neither of us makes any claim to having Native American "blood." What right do we have to talk about the effects of the hegemonic popular culture's approving use of the "Indian" stereotype on native Americans?

That question, it seems to me, is predicated on that other characteristic of the "Indian" stereotype—the unbridgeable gulf between *Them* and *Us.* It also harkens back to the feisty electronic discussion I described in the first chapter. However we contextualize the question, it is certain that good scholarship requires that our conclusions about the harmfulness of the approving use of the "Indian" stereotype be based on expressions of those feelings by real human beings who self-identify as Native American. Michael Dorris of the Modoc nation speaks directly to the harm of the *Them* and *Us* characteristic of the stereotype:

> Native rights, motives, customs, languages, and aspirations are misunderstood out of an ignorance that is both self-serving and self-righteous. Part of the problem may well stem from the long-standing tendency of European and Euro-American thinkers to regard Indians as so "Other," so fundamentally and profoundly different, that they fail to extend to native peoples certain traits commonly regarded as human.[64]

From a radio interview is a second assessment of the power of the stereotype. Rayna Green is curator of ethnology at the Smithsonian Institution. She is Cherokee.

> What's the harm in it? Well, the roles people assume have nothing to do with real Indians, they've nothing to do with reality. But

they think it does have to do with reality. And they invest those myths with reality and then expect the rest of us to pay the bill for them. I cannot tell you how many times I've gone into a classroom or lectured in front of a group of little children, who are deeply unhappy because I don't wear a costume every day, who think that what the Boy Scouts do is real stuff, real Indian life, and then they want us to live that life. And, when we don't live that life for them, they're brokenhearted.

They don't believe in us . . . they don't believe we're alive, because we've changed. They don't believe we can carry briefcases, because the Indians they play are an invention, a figment. And they want us to live up to the Indians they play and the price for that is almost . . . it's a mythological and sometimes real death for real Indians. I'm convinced that, in order for them to really successfully play Indian, we need to be dead.

She concludes,

As long as it's based on image and myth, it's smoke and mirrors, and it doesn't help real Indian people survive and thrive. And I'm more concerned about what it does to Indian people in the long run than how good it makes non-Indians feel, because I don't think we get the pay-off, I don't think the positive images help us.[65]

Vine Deloria, Jr. is convinced the discontinuity between the image of the "Indians of America—those ghostly figures that America loved and cherished"—and the image of the Native American activist on the television news has blocked solutions to problems experienced by Native Americans.

When a comparison is made between events of the Civil Rights movement and the activities of the Indian movement one thing stands out in clear relief: Americans simply refuse to give up their longstanding conceptions of what an Indian is. It was this fact more than any other that inhibited any solution of Indian problems and projected the impossibility of their solution anytime into the future. People simply could not connect what they believed Indians to be with what they were seeing on their television sets.[66]

Hopi poet and anthropologist, Wendy Rose, is even angrier:

Organizers of readings continually ask me to wear beadwork and turquois, to dress in buckskin (my people don't wear much buckskin; we've cultivated cotton for thousands of years), and to read poems conveying pastoral or "natural" images. I am often asked to "tell a story" and "place things in a spiritual framework."

Simply being Indian—a real, live, breathing, up-to-date Indian person—is not enough. In fact, other than my genetics, this is the precise opposite of what is desired. The expectation is that I adopt, and thereby validate, the "persona" of some mythic "Indian being" who never was. The requirement is that I act to negate the reality of my—and my people's—existence in favor of a script developed within the fantasies of our oppressors.[67]

Many of the pioneering investigators of the stereotype of the "Indian" like Pearce and Sayre, Lovejoy and Boas write from a kind of "enlightened present."[68] That is, they are remarking on a pattern of behavior they identify as old, worn out, almost exhausted—one that has all but passed from use. Finally, they say, we have progressed! We have done away with the old negative image of the "Indian!"[69] Most often this optimism in fact heralds another pendulum swing to the approving use of the stereotype rather than a new era of understanding.[70] What is most remarkable about the "Indian" stereotype, according to Berkhofer and others, is its "persistence and perpetuation." "The basic images of the good and bad Indian," says Berkhofer, "persist from the era of Columbus up to the present without substantial modification or variation.[71]

As is by now obvious, I find it more helpful to talk about the approving and disparaging use of the stereotype of the "Indian" than about good and bad images. There are two reasons for this. The first is that a focus on the process of stereotyping reveals that the "Indian" stereotype has only one set of characteristics that can be put to different uses. This helps explain why Leland and many others since can combine good and bad "Indians" in virtually the same breath or paragraph. The same "Indian" stereotype meets different, but sometimes coincident, needs. The second is that it is too easy to confuse the "image of the good Indian" with a "good image of the Indian." As I have argued above, the "Indian" stereotype is ultimately destructive, even when used approvingly. Its persistence means that most of us who identify with the hegemonic North American culture use the stereotype of the "Indian." We all can admit with Sam Gill—painful though it may be—

that we're all in the boat with Columbus.[72]

The question that arises from this admission is why has the dual use of the "Indian" stereotype persisted for so long? Responding to this question will require us to return to the touchstone of our investigation, Charles Godfrey Leland. If we can learn about Leland's approving use of the "Indian" stereotype, we may have a perspective on more contemporary approving uses, and thus on the persistence of the "Indian."

Chapter 6

Weaving Himself into the Landscape
Charles Leland's Use of the "Indian" Stereotype

T he stereotype of the "Indian" no doubt serves many uses. In the last chapter I noted that the disparaging use of the stereotype, which Roy Harvey Pearce coined "savagism," has been used from the time of contact between Native American and European cultures to justify the attempt to conquer the indigenous peoples of North America. Olive Dickason puts it this way:

> By classifying Amerindians as savages, Europeans were able to create the ideology that helped make it possible to launch one of the great movements in the history of western civilization: the colonization of overseas empires.[1]

In the last chapter I also noted that the approving use of the "Indian" stereotype—which scholars typically discuss under the rubric of primitivism—was most often used as a way of criticizing the society of the stereotype-user. As Alice Kehoe caustically notes,

> Cultural primitivism, constructed as the opposition to civilization with its discontents, has been part of Western culture for close to three thousand years. This fiction is picked up by credulous scholars and by common charlatans, by neo-romantic writers and by earnest counterculture pilgrims. Borrowing from and serving one another, poets and plastic medicine men earn a living from the hoary tradition of ascribing virtue to nature.[2]

There is evidence that some of the earliest Europeans to come to North America borrowed from both savagism and primitivism. In other words they found it useful to make both disparaging and approving use of the "Indian" stereotype. Berkhofer calls attention to an English missionary, Alexander Whitaker, who in 1613 had to convince his "funding agencies" that the "Indian" was "savage" enough to need saving, yet human enough to warrant saving. He had to establish both the need for and capability of conversion. Thus in the same brief pamphlet he portrayed "Indians" as liars, deceivers, cannibals, in cahoots with the devil on one hand; and, on the other hand, as crafty, of good government, industrious, and with laws.[3] Despite the pronouncements of hopeful scholars, there is little evidence to suggest that this practice of double borrowing has waned in the intervening four hundred years.

Most simply put, the persistence of the "Indian" stereotype can be attributed to its usefulness to not-Natives. The obverse character of its dual use gives it the versatility both to justify conquest and to criticize not-Native society, both to rationalize cruel intrusion and brutal invasion as well as to engage in critical self-reflection. Both disparaging and approving uses of the "Indian" stereotype have histories far more complex and subtle than appear here. It is not my intention to exhaust by analysis either way of using the "Indian" stereotype. Rather I want to point out that the "Indian" stereotype with its prominent characteristics and its dual use is a motif in a story cherished by hegemonic popular culture. It is first and still foremost a story that speaks to not-Native values and needs. The questions currently arising from our inquiry (and thus the ones now driving it) might be put something like this: *What needs does the "Indian" stereotype meet for contemporary hegemonic North American popular society? How does the "Indian" fit into the stories not-Natives tell about themselves?*

Questions like these—questions of meaning-making and story—point to the larger religious issues lurking just beneath the surface of our inquiry. We began with the story of Kluskap and Malsum, a story of powerful twin brothers, betrayal, and fratricide. The story we are trying now to understand seems amorphous and hazy because it belongs to many of us. Rather than try straightaway to grapple with this story and its underlying religious issues, I suggest we double back on Leland and his story to ask, from the vantage point of history, similar questions. If his story resonates with the story of hegemonic popular culture, we shall have a different perspective on the study of Native North American religions.

When Leland used the "Indian" in an approving manner, he had a clear if peculiar agenda. He was determined, over a hundred years ago, that his audience attend to and come to respect the stories he collected and rewrote. He felt comfortable altering drawings and stories because he trusted that "Injun" part of himself to know what the "Indians" would do or say if they only had his aesthetic skills. He felt the need to alter drawings and stories because he perceived what he saw as a significant oversight on the part of his compatriots:

> There is no subject in the world which is of so little interest to the American people as the early legends attached to their country. . . .
>
> One might by seeking find, almost any day, in some print the admission that America is wanting in romantic legends, and all the sweet, wild charm of Elfin land. The Hudson is not for us as the storied Rhine. Yet, if we did but know it, every hill and vale and rock and rivulet around us was once consecrated by all these "sweet humanities of old religion." . . . Had our scholars taken but a little pains they might have shown the Old World that all that is sweet and strange is spirit and dream-love haunts our forests; that Puck as the *Mik-amwes* frolics by moonlight in the *d'jeh-ka-mee-gus*, or forest-openings.[4]

Leland's agenda begins from this perceived oversight and moves to rectify it by means of his well-told stories gleaned from the "Indians."

When Leland makes approving use of the "Indian" stereotype in relating his story, it is not unlike the cultural primitivism we have been following. There is implicit in his story a criticism of his society—it is a society with a secondhand sense of nature—but this is not foregrounded. Indeed, his critique of society is subsumed under a larger concern, a concern for a sense of belonging to the land, for Place. I will argue that Leland meant to instruct his countrywomen and men on how to learn the secrets of the land in order to bring a sense of Place into being.

For Leland, access to those secrets was through "Indian" stories, especially those that reveal most clearly humankind's "first religion," "Shamanism." As we have seen, one of the indicators of Shamanism for Leland was magic. Thus in the stereotype-charged passage I quoted in the last chapter Leland begins by extolling the "Indian's" feeling for the poetry of nature:

But the greatest cause for a faith in magic is one which the white man talks about without feeling, and which the Indian feels without talking about it. I mean the poetry of nature, with all its quaint and beautiful superstitions.

Then, in a few sentences—ones I omitted in the last chapter—he turns the discussion to magic:

Meeko, the squirrel, has the power of becoming a giant monster; flowers, beasts, trees, have all loved and talked and sung, and can even now do so, should the magician only come to speak the spell. And there are such magicians. Why should he doubt it? If the squirrel once yielded to such a power in man, it follows that some man may still have the power, or that he himself may acquire it. And how much of this feeling of the real poetry of nature does the white man or woman possess, who pities the poor ignorant Indian? A few second-hand scraps of Byron and Tupper, Tennyson and Longfellow, the jingle of a few rhymes and a few similes, and a little second-hand supernaturalism, more 'accepted' than felt, and that derived from far foreign sources, does not give the white man what the Indian *feels*. Joe, or Noel, or Sabattis may seem to the American Philistine to be a ragged, miserable, ignorant Indian; but to the *scholar* he is by far the Philistine's superior in that which life is *best* worth living for.[5]

For Leland "Indian" stories, especially ones featuring "magic,"[6] are the key to understanding these secrets. When Leland writes, just after comparing Kluskap to Nanabozho, "It is absurd to laugh at or pity the Indian for believing in his magic," he is chastising Schoolcraft and his followers. Similarly, he concludes his tirade against Henry David Thoreau with, "Such a writer can, indeed, peep and botanize on the grave of Mother Nature, but never evoke *her* spirit."[7] This is, in fact, the ultimate criticism Leland can make: Thoreau (unlike Leland himself) has a false relationship with nature. Thoreau assumed he *had* this feeling of the real poetry of nature when in fact he did not. Remember, from Leland's point of view he *could* not; after all he did not respect or appreciate the "Indian's" stories. Worse, Thoreau's "peeping and botanizing" thwarted the nation's need to understand the land, the secrets of which were known only to "the Indian."

It is not immediately clear to a contemporary reader why feeling the poetry of nature is what makes life *"best* worth living for." It is not even clear why this *might* be so. Consequently we are apt to dismiss Leland's concluding claim in the above passage as a bad punch line. This would be unfortunate. It is on this "punch line" that much of Leland's story is based. If it is to make any sense, however, the feeling of real poetry of nature as synonymous with that which is *"best* worth living for" needs to be set in context if it is to make any sense.

There is little question that Leland valued the "poetry of nature" in part because his experience was primarily urban. He was, all his life, a city dweller who enjoyed periodic forays into the countryside. In his formative youth that countryside was in New England. It is helpful to read passages like the following in that light:

> I venture to express the hope that all who love nature in New England will turn to the study of its folk-lore and thereby secure the final flash of gold on the mountain tops, . . . I wish with all my heart, and truly from no selfish point of view, that every lover of rock and river and greenwood tree would master these old Indian tales or poems, and see in all Nature new charms.[8]

Leland's specific concern for New England may have stemmed in part from its serious economic decline in his time. By the end of the 1880s more than one thousand farms had been abandoned in Vermont, more than thirteen hundred in New Hampshire, nearly fifteen hundred in Massachusetts, and in Maine, the state in which Leland met with Tomah Joseph and other Passamaquoddies, the total of abandoned farms was over thirty-three hundred. What accounted for this remarkable (and as it turned out temporary) misfortune? The rural New Englanders were moving on, and a primary destination was the city.[9]

The cities most attractive to the former New Englanders and to the immigrants arriving in large numbers were some of the same cities Leland knew well—Philadelphia, New York, Boston. These cities, and others, were growing in the nineteenth century, and their growth was so rapid as to be breathtaking. Here are some numbers. From 1820 to 1860 the total population of the United States increased by about 226 percent, but the urban population rose by 797 percent. In the two decades between 1840 and 1859, while the total population of the

United States increased slightly less than 36 percent in each decade, the registered urban population rose by 92.1 percent and 75.4 percent, respectively. The population of Philadelphia in 1800, twenty-four years before Leland's birth, was 69,403. By 1860 it had topped half a million. In the same period New York grew from 60,489 human beings to over a million.[10] Percentage increases of population in the urban United States were unprecedented before and have remained unmatched since. One scholar of the United States concludes that by 1880, four years before Leland published *Algonquin Legends,* "urbanization for the first time became a controlling factor in national life."[11]

Leland would not have been able to ignore the fact of cities even if he had not been living in them. He was, however, a citydweller, and, due to his father's business acumen, an upper-middle-class citydweller. It is worth reflecting on Leland's day-to-day urban experience, and on that of his less-privileged neighbors. What is now described as "quality of life" was then, for the majority of people, not good. Even the most commonplace features of contemporary cities, for example the paved street, could not be taken for granted. Not until the last years of the nineteenth century were streets paved, and then only infrequently with asphalt. This meant that most people had to contend with choking dust and dangerous ruts much of the time, and serious mud whenever it was wet.[12] There were, however, more profound problems. There was no organized rubbish removal, thus garbage was thrown in street gutters or piled up in backyards and alleys. Sewage systems, when they existed, were inadequate, so water supplies were usually contaminated. The presence of so much decaying organic matter required that there be a symbiotic relationship between citydwellers and a number of different animals:

> Hogs, geese, and dogs scavenged in the streets, and in Charleston even vultures were protected by law because of the public role they performed in removing the remains of dead animals. Bands of rats lived under sidewalks and infested the larger buildings in the downtown sections of cities.[13]

Housing was in this period often poor, with crowded conditions and—especially in cellar rooms—poor ventilation, thus contributing to people's susceptibility to diseases like cholera and tuberculosis.[14] Fire was a constant danger, with organized professional fire-fighting departments not established in most cities until the latter half of the century.[15] Similarly, policing was haphazard if not corrupt at a time when crime was a growth industry.[16] Many people hadn't enough to eat, nor an adequate place to stay—they were poor. Most urban families were able to make ends meet because their children worked.[17] While historians have tended to stress the determination and ingenuity of the people of the United States to find technological solutions to these problems, it is clear that the urban life Leland knew, even protected as he was by his relative wealth and his position among the literati, was risky and dangerous.[18]

This sounds familiar. Leland experienced Philadelphia, New York, and Boston as overwhelming, frightening, disorderly; in the same way that many of us experience large cities. The quality of chaos in late-nineteenth-century city life—the animals, disease, stench, noise, mud, poverty— would have given Leland and his urban readers a sense of being disrupted, cut off, upset, and unsafe.[19] Similarly, many of us experience urban life as more dangerous and alienating than we would like. There is a difference, though. Leland's experience of city is unlike a contemporary experience of city in one important way. We feel cut off from nature by the concrete and pavement. In contrast, nineteenth-century urbanites were not shielded from natural processes—nature was not yet physically or metaphorically paved over. Rather the natural processes of nineteenth-century urban North America—the decay of garbage in the streets, the stench of outhouses servicing even tenement buildings, the foraging birds and animals, the daily confrontation with the elements while moving about on city streets—all suggest a natural cacophony, not the poetry of nature.[20] In Leland's urban environment nature was, in the vernacular, "in his face, all the time." In his day-to-day experience, the idyllic nature of his New England childhood vacations was constantly elbowed aside by the rude, vulgar, chaotic nature of his nineteenth-century urban existence.[21]

While Leland's reflections on idyllic nature depend on his mostly urban experience, and that experience was no doubt shaped by the turbulent changes in the cityscape of the United States, this is not sufficient for our inquiry. Leland's experience of cities only begins to explain his determination that his readers attend to the "Indian" secrets of the poetry of nature, or that feeling this poetry is what makes life worth living.

Leland's determination makes best sense in the context of his intellectual roots in German Romanticism. His "official biographer" tells us that he was influenced by Fichte and Schelling, a fact Leland confirms in his *Memoirs*. He read the two philosophers while at Princeton, noting in his diary that of all the considerable material he read during his senior year, two works, one by Schelling, the other by Fichte, drew his greatest interest.[22] Leland's deep interest in Fichte, Schelling, and the other German Romantics was not only intellectual. After graduating from Princeton, Leland, a retiring youth in poor health, decided to travel in Europe. He left in the spring of 1846 and of the next three years abroad, spent just over one year in Germany, much of it as a student, first in Heidelberg and then in Munich. His health improved immeasurably, and his love of the German Romantics deepened with lectures in philosophy, largely on Schelling. In April of 1847 he wrote to his brother, Henry, telling him to read everything of Jean Paul Richter, a Fichtean author. While at Heidelberg Leland did more than just attend lectures. He developed an outgoing persona and an affection for lager beer. He visited villages and there attended dances, which he admitted might be considered "shockingly vulgar" by the standards of home. He also hiked with companions in the countryside, and by his own account grew strong and vigorous. By the time he moved to Munich he was completely enamoured of Germany. He attributed his good health to his German activities. He was, he thought, speaking, smoking, eating, drinking and waltzing like a German. In the remaining time that he was in Europe, he compared all the places he visited with Germany, and nothing, in his estimation, ever equalled it.[23] Leland's love for Germany and things German give his appropriation of the romanticism of that country an authenticity it would otherwise lack.[24]

The aspect of German Romanticism central to Leland's story is the one to which we now turn: its understanding of the relationship between nation, community, and land. George L. Mosse states that according to the Romanticism of Johann-Gottlieb Fichte:

> unity of thought and action could be achieved only within that nation which was a valid historic community, . . . Within the unity of this community, the highest individual freedom could be found, not the individualized freedom of sentiment and emotion but the freedom found through group integration. This group was defined in the terms of the *Volk*. People had to be integrated with the national memories and the poetry of the *Volk*.[25]

The "poetry of the *Volk*" could best be accessed by reading their folk tales where the "innate correspondence between the individual and nature"[26] common to virtually all romanticism could be perceived. In German Romanticism, through the vehicle of the *Volk* with what were seen as their unchanging customs, "the romantic worship of nature became a romantic worship of those who lived closest to it."[27] Drawing on these intellectual roots, Leland perceived connections between nation ("a valid historical community"), nature, landscape, and the folklore of the people closest to nature.[28]

All this provides a context for the words of Leland's preface to *Kulóskap, the Master*, an attempt by Charles Leland and John Dyneley Prince to rework the Kluskap stories into an epic in poetic verse.[29] Writing in 1902 near the end of his life, Leland reflected on all the beautiful natural places he had seen. He recalls Florence, the Alps, and the Rhine, then admits,

> I never found in it all that strange and sweet charm like a song without words which haunts the hills and valleys of rural New England.

He admits there have been some passable New England poets, then goes on,

> Yet with all this, there was still one thing wanting; that which nature itself would not give fully, even to a Wordsworth; the subtle final charm of human tradition, poetry or romance. . . . the most inspired poet can never feel that he is really "heart-intimate" with scenery, if it has for him no ties of tradition or folk-lore. When I was young, I felt this lack, and bore in patience the very common reproach of Europeans that we had a land without ancient legends or song, but now that I am older grown, I have learned that this want is all in our own ignorance and neglect of what we had only to put forth our hand to reach.

It is obvious to whom Leland is going to direct his audience to reach their hands for the folklore and tradition necessary to become "heart-intimate" with nature. He continues,

> We bewailed our wretched poverty when we had in our lap a casket full of treasure which we would not take the pains to open.

Few indeed and far between are those who ever suspected till of late years that every hill and dale in New England had its romantic legend, its beautiful poem, or its marvelous myth—the latter equal in conception and form to those of the Edda—or that a vast collection of these traditions still survives in perfect preservation among the few remaining Indians of New England and the Northeast Coast.[30]

The connections so important to the German Romantics—land, nation, poetry, *Volk* stories— are clear in Leland.

What is also clear is his concern for Place. Mircea Eliade calls this "the religious experience of autochthony; the feeling . . . of *belonging to a place.*"[31] Yi-Fu Tuan calls this religious response to the land "geopiety," and includes the earth, the soil, homeland, country, and family in its purview. Tuan turns to the contemporary ecological movement to show "the roots of certain modern concepts, such as that of reciprocation in nature, lie in profound human experiences that were given other (largely religious) expressions in the past."[32] From the persistance of the idea of Place, he turns to the example of the ancient Greeks and Romans to demonstrate the rootedness of Place—their family hearth/altar was, once established, all but unmovable. The geopiety of these people, he says,

rested on the sense of country as one's native home, on the sense that one had sprung out of its soil and was nurtured by it, on the belief that one's ancestors since time immemorial were born in it. The autochthony of the Athenians was a common boast of Athenian poets and orators.[33]

Finally, and not surprisingly, Tuan turns to the Germans for evidence of a deep emotional attachment to place mediated by stories. He quotes from a translation of a popular almanac, *Reimmichls Volkskalender* to the show the power of *Heimat,* a word of multileveled meanings beginning with "birthplace":

Heimat is first of all the mother earth who has given birth to our folk and race, who is the holy soil, and who gulps down God's clouds, sun, and storms so that together with their own mysterious strength they prepare the bread and wine which rest on our table and give us strength to lead a good life.[34]

This cosmological dimension of Place is linked with a people's story about themselves. Thus, says, Tuan, "A people's present attachment to the land is secure because it has numerous ties with the deep strata of the past. Rootedness stems from geneology—yes, but also from significant events shared by, or woven into, the myths of a people."[35]

The process by which human beings construct their Place by weaving themselves into their landscapes is part of a larger human endeavor to make Place for ourselves. This essentially religious endeavor is an immense and endless undertaking. It involves a simultaneous and ongoing constructing and being-constructed-by a worldview, a cosmology. We "make Place" all the time, often by telling stories that locate us in our families, in our communities, in our nation, in our world. This inquiry cannot help but be concerned with authochthony, with geopiety, with Place, the religious feeling of belonging to a place.[36] It is what Leland was engaged in, what Native American religions often center on—making sense of the relationship of human beings to their landscape, to the physical world.[37] We shall return to this later.

If Leland's intellectual roots in German Romanticism and the idea of Place help us understand something of the logic of his story, we need to look to the historical situation of the United States in the second half of the nineteenth century to understand the urgency of that story. German Romanticism appealed (and may still appeal) to people in times in which they feel they are living in a world at risk.[38]

The Civil War had certainly contributed to that feeling. Leland's own experience as a soldier in the Civil War was apparently profound. In an 1877 article written for an English magazine, he recounts that after the war had ended he had seen a group of starving Confederate soldiers stumbling out of their mountain hiding place:

> We saw many such sights in those days. One single case of utter misery—of gasping starvations elbowing Death in the black border-land of despair—is *horrible,* but a multitude of such is hell. I never understood Dante until our war.[39]

Closer to home, that war also claimed Leland's brother, Henry, who died in middle age from injuries sustained while on duty with the Union Army.

The so-called Gilded Age of the United States, the period immediately following the Civil War, was also a time during which people felt their world threatened. According to historian, Curtis Hinsley,

Between the Civil War and the First World War the United States underwent fundamental social reorganization. Patterns of daily work and community life before 1860 had been predominantly local and personal. If small communities restricted acceptable behavior, within those horizons they also provided a sense of comfort, coherence, and control. With faith, the world was manageable; men and women could cope. The rapid appearance in the second half of the nineteenth century of giant corporate structures, masses of laboring poor, urban filth, and rural poverty—the negative social and economic indices of modern growth—permanently destroyed antebellum America. Personal rootlessness, impotence, and retreat to the thin securities offered by industrial and farm unions, professional groups, and embattled family circles became the signs of a maturing industrial society. The organizational revolution of the second half of the century was a response to the dislocation and group leverage against impersonal, unpredictable economic forces.[40]

When his father died shortly after his brother, Leland inherited the family wealth. Some years later, mulling over his personal situation during this historical period, Leland wrote:

The death of my father and brother within a year, the sudden change in my fortunes, . . . and above all, the working hard seven days a week, had been too much for me. . . . I began to apprehend that a break-down in my health was impending. I needed a change of scene, and so resolved, finding, after due consideration, that I had enough to live on, to go abroad for a long rest. It proved to be a very wise resolve. So I rented my house, packed my trunks, and departed, to be gone "for a year or two."[41]

This also marked the end of Leland's career as an editor and a political writer.

The unsettledness of Leland's personal life resonated with the unsettledness of the Gilded Age in the country as a whole. Leland puts shudder quotes around "for a year or two" because it would be almost eleven years before he returned to the United States. Four years after that return, stabilized by his years in Europe and worried for the country of his birth, Leland prepared *The Algonquin Legends of New England,* his first response to the uncertainty of the times, and to the European criticism that the United States "had a land without ancient legends or song." It is no wonder he tried so hard and with such urgency to impress on his audience the importance of the stories he collected, even to committing scholarly misdemeanors to attain his end.[42]

Later, near the end of his life, Leland seems to feel more despair than urgency about the state of the nation. He writes his niece-biographer about some humorous stories she has sent him.

> There was something Indian-like, aboriginal and wild in the American fun of 40 years ago . . . which has no parallel now . . . we were wilder in those days, and more eccentric. All of these [stories] which you send are very good, but they might all have been made in England. They are *mild.* Ere long, there will be no *America.*[43]

In other words, the wild and strong are connected with the "Indian" and the "Indian" with the heart and soul of the United States.[44] Leland, taking that characteristic of the stereotype that vouchsafed the "Indian" was close to nature, employed it in an approving manner in order to meld the tenets of German Romanticism into the unsettled milieu of the Gilded Age of the United States. His aim: to protect the country's heart and soul, to see it "repeopled with the fairies of yore,"[45] to call Place into being. His efforts to shape, edit, and finally improvise Abenaki and Micmac stories are about making meaning; and not Abenaki or Micmac meaning. They shore up the last part of his story. Leland's anticipation that the nation would come to forge a connection to the natural landscape it had come to inhabit through the vehicle of "Indian" stories is essentially a concern for Place.[46]

Nowhere in Leland's work on Native Americans is there an indication that he is aware that he is telling a story about "Indians" and nature, nation and land that stems from his needs and those of his readers. Nowhere, for example, does he speak directly about "Place." Nonetheless we know that according to Leland's story, his compatriots in the United States must attend to "Indian Legends" so they might learn the secrets of feeling the poetry of nature. We know Leland believed, after the German Romantics, that this feeling was essential to developing a sense of belonging to the land, what I am calling a sense of Place. But where is Leland himself in this story? What role does he play?

In his own story Leland gave himself the role of intermediary between "White" and "Indian," between "his own people" and the Others.[47] This part of Leland's story draws on that characteristic of the "Indian" stereotype that claims obversity—an almost unbridgeable gulf between *Them* and *Us*. In one sense this characteristic relies on and sums up all the others. *Them* means the generic "Indian" who is traditionally timeless as if fixed in amber, doomed to extinction, and linked inexorably to nature. *Us* means just the opposite—a people innovative, progressive, who are conquerors able to transcend the bounds of nature. Between these two, according to the stereotype, is a gulf so great as to be virtually unbridgeable. The one can never know the other, at least not without help. In Leland's words, "It must be borne in mind that in this [tale] . . . here are associations and chords which make as gold to an Indian that which is only copper, or at best silver, to the civilized reader of my translations."[48] Leland is clear that his "civilized readers" needed help understanding his "Indian" stories. It was just this help that Leland understood himself to be providing.

As we have seen, Leland identified a special "Injun" quality in himself, a quality, he said that was recognized by real "Indians." This allowed him to understand the "chords and associations" of "Indian" stories as fully as "Indians" did, as gold rather than merely copper or silver. This quality also allowed him to alter Abenaki and Micmac stories and create "Passamaquoddy" birchbark drawings since he knew what the "Indians" would do if they possessed his literary and artistic abilities.[49] Finally, this quality allowed him to gain the trust of the Passamaquoddies, to "go to their tents . . . and sit over the fire in the real loafer attitude by the hour," to learn of the existence of Abenaki and Micmac stories:

> They have rarely met with white men who understand their legends as they themselves do. The result is that they are very reticent as to communicating them. I had at first great difficulty in getting even the most trifling tales from them. They have been accustomed to being told by the religious that *m'teolin* [Power] is only another name for the devilish; at best, they have never talked with white people who believed in any way in their myths. But he who lives in and loves nature sincerely has *faith* in the deepest and sweetest magic, and feels with the Indians, as Heine felt, that there is a wonderful truth in this artless sorcery.[50]

Leland's role in his own story is, not surprisingly, that of a hero. He is the one who brings the secret knowledge of the "Indian" to our attention. He is the one who, by his "translations," grants access to the secret knowledge. In addition, he provides an analysis of the stories' hidden meaning that will effect a response in his readers so profound that they will have the feeling of the poetry of nature so critical for answering the crisis of the Gilded Age.[51]

Leland's "official biographer" thought he was remystifying the United States, putting that country back in touch with its wild, powerful, magical roots by extracting those "Indian" stories that would give the land back its native mystery. This would serve to rescue it from the morass of classical names that threatened to stultify and strangle it. Her observations:

> One reason of his love for the Children of Light of his own country was that they, with their myths, had given "a fairy, an elf, a naiad, or a hero, to every rock and river and ancient hill in New England," and that he, by collecting these myths, could repeople his native land with the fairies of yore, and walk in spirit-trodden paths, and find goblins in the woods, and transform every foolish "Diana's Bath" into the "Home of the Elves" it really was.

She reiterates this throughout the biography. For example, "To him the true value of the Indian's myths and legends was in the new beauty they gave to the country he knew best and cared for most, though so long away from it."[52]

Leland's story is striking enough, but more arresting is the evidence that his story is not unique. Leland, although he may have been one of the first, is not alone. As the frontier closed in the United States, according to Curtis Hinsley, anthropologists took the role of intermediary. The role was not a new one. Hinsley, basing his argument on the work of Richard Slotkin, says:

> American literature and national mythology have been populated from the beginning by a series of intermediaries between savagery and civilization: captives, hunters, frontiersmen, Indian fighters, mountain men. In each case the mediating figure, through immersion in the wilderness and savage ways, returns to civilization with a gift, or boon, to his troubled people. From the forest and savagery he learns the secret of regeneration and prosperity.

Ethnologists and anthropologists, says Hinsley, stepped into this role of intermediary, "offer[ing] a gift of romantic aboriginal cosmology to a callow, disenchanted people."[53] Charles Leland was moved by the same currents that swirled around his scholarly colleagues, although the fit between Leland as the hero of his own story and this pattern of cultural intermediary between the "savage" *Them* and the "civilized" *Us* is not exact.

The points at which the fit is inexact are as important for our inquiry as those where the fit is tight. Leland collected and offered his stories just as ethnology and anthropology were becoming professions in the United States. The conventions of those professions were still being negotiated. Like many who would become identified with anthropology, Leland saw himself as a folklorist, and a unique one. He wrote Mary Owen, then a relative newcomer to the study of Black folklore: "Real folk-lorists like us live in a separate occult, hidden, wonderful fairy-land,—we see elves and listen to music in dropping waterfalls, and hear voices in the wind."[54] A participant-observer in and of folklore, Leland understood himself as distinct from the ordinary scholar:

> There is a great difference between collecting folk-lore as a curiosity and *living* in it in truth. I do not believe that in all the Folk-Lore Societies there is one person who lives in it in reality as I do. I cannot describe it—what it *once* was is lost to the world. You cannot understand it at second hand.[55]

Professional folklorists (and later, ethnologists and anthropologists) were not supposed to write like this. Leland commonly did.[56]

There is, however, a more important way that the fit between Hinsley's cultural intermediary and Leland as the hero of his own story is not exact. Following Slotkin, Hinsley's cultural intermediaries go into the wilderness and emerge with gifts that will bring regeneration and prosperity.[57] Leland's gifts—his stories, their "translation," his analysis—are not about regeneration and prosperity; they are about establishing Place. From Leland's postbellum point of view the problem in the barely united United States was not simply that people were disenchanted and in need of regeneration. For him disenchantment and the need for renewal were symptoms of a larger, deeper deficiency. This deficiency, clearly visible from the vantage point of German Romanticism, was that the United States was not a viable historical community connected to the landscape by its attention to nature. That attention was directed and shaped by the oral expressions, the songs,[58] and stories, of the *Volk*, the people who lived closest to the land. In the case of the United States the *Volk* were the Aryan-like "Indians" of the Northeast, as his story collection amply demonstrated.

One other aspect of Leland's story demands our attention—its failure to catch his readers' imagination. It was his hope that his story about learning from the "Indians" the secrets of the land would transform the United States from a gawky adolescent country with disruptive growing pains into a mature nation—a "valid historic community"—which could hold its head up in the family of European nations. Instead, his work is remembered and used for its ethnographic richness, but his story has been lost to the extent that a reconstruction like this inquiry is necessary to see its internal logic. Leland's second effort to tell his story in poetic epic in 1902 failed as unambiguously as his first in *Algonquin Legends* in 1884.

This failure no doubt rests on a number of causes, but foremost has to be that Leland was twenty-five years too late. According to Robert Berkhofer, by 1860 the heyday of what he calls "the romantic savage" was over, especially in the Northeast United States where Leland's colleagues and readers clustered.[59] Says Berkhofer,

> Although Longfellow's *Hiawatha* achieved great success during this decade, it was quickly ridiculed in one satirical imitation after another. Other satires mimicked the standard Indian subjects of earlier plays and poems. . . . The use of the Indian as a subject for an *American* literature in the quest for cultural identity and nationalism had run its course.[60]

The waning of the "Indian" as prime subject matter for literature and the existence of satires that punctured the "Indian"-used-approvingly give a new perspective on Leland's attempt to get his audience to take the Algonkian stories seriously. It is no wonder he was not willing to let the stories stand as he received them; they might well be laughed at. Considering what he felt was in the balance, he could not just pass them on untouched. He must show that they were worthy of attention, even if that meant adding a little here and there, changing a lot here and there. There was also the matter of his ego. The stories had to be worthy of his name, too. Leland never missed a chance for self-aggrandizement. His efforts, finally, were in vain. Leland, it would appear, was hopping a train that had left the tracks twenty-five years earlier.

Berkhofer characterizes the period of the popularity of the "romantic savage" as having the "tendency to romanticize the safely dead Indian." It was replaced, he says, by a story on which the "ideological geography of the American West" rests.[61] This story is the one Pearce has investigated so thoroughly—the story of civilization over savagery. There is little room in that story of conquest for the approving use of the "Indian" stereotype.

That story of civilization versus savagery received its foremost academic retelling from Frederick Jackson Turner. Turner delivered his seminal paper setting forth his "Frontier Thesis" before the American Historical Association in 1893, between Leland's two attempts to promote *his* story. The essence of Turner's thesis, according to Berkhofer, was that the

> American character had been shaped primarily by the frontier experience of westward migration and settlement. As initially presented, the thesis rested upon premises of social progress and evolution fashionable in the later nineteenth century, and so, naturally, the Indian was pictured as an obstacle to White settlement and the coming of civilization.

Berkhofer notes that although as he developed his thesis, Turner "dropped the social Darwinian trappings," "the Indian remained the stage of society before the evolution of White American civilization from frontier settlement to agricultural development to full-fledged urban society." This theory persisted for at least the first half of the twentieth century, dominating the conversation in academic parlors and school books on U.S. history.[62] It came to be on Turner's story, and not on Leland's, that the people of the United States based their truths about who they were. As Turner's famous essay has it,

> The frontier is the line of most rapid and effective Americanization. The wilderness masters the colonist. It finds him a European in dress, industries, tools, modes of travel, and thought. It takes him from the railroad car and puts him in the birch canoe. It strips off the garments of civilization and arrays him in the hunting shirt and the moccasin. It puts him in the log cabin of the

Cherokee and Iroquois and runs an Indian palisade around him. Before long he has gone to planting Indian corn and plowing with a sharp stick; he shouts the war cry and takes the scalp in orthodox Indian fashion. . . . At the frontier the environment is at first too strong for the man. . . . Little by little he transforms the wilderness, but the outcome is not the old Europe. . . . The fact is, that here is a new product that is American.[63]

What is noteworthy about Turner's story for our inquiry is how it meets the need of a people in the last years of the nineteenth century to understand themselves in relationship to the landscape they inhabited, and to the "Indians," the people closest to the land. To see that landscape as "frontier," the "Indians" as conquered by necessity, and themselves as a conquering people is to call Place into being in a particular kind of way. Central to Turner's frontier story, based on the repeated triumphs of civilization over savagery, is the disparaging use of the "Indian" stereotype.

It is on this point that the failure of Leland's story turns. Leland's perception that there was in his time a need for Place in the postbellum hegemonic culture of the United States was accurate.[64] His perception that meeting this need for Place would require the ingredients of landscape, "Indians," and nation was similarly correct. But his approving use of the "Indian" stereotype was out of fashion. The experience of the people of the United States resonated more with a story that featured conquest with its attendant disparaging use of the "Indian." In Leland's story, the physical conquest of the land and its inhabitants was a past event. Furthermore, the physical conquest, his story presumed, was not enough. Leland's Place story required his countrywomen and countrymen to rely on the "Indians" among them and to attend to their secrets. No amount of editing and recasting, adding and improvizing could make such a story attractive to the people of the United States in the late 1800s between Custer's defeat at the Little Big Horn and the massacre at Wounded Knee.[65]

If this were simply a story of a dead man's scholarly skulduggery made merely curious by the intervening one hundred years, I would not be retelling it. Rather, aspects of Leland's story—the agenda that shaped his treatment of his Passamaquoddy, Micmac, and Maliseet consultants and their cultures—are unfortunately contemporary. The contemporary scene is dotted with "Indian" imitators with the latest take on the role of cultural intermediary. The present-day study of Native American religions—both "popular" and more academic—is often skewed by the same Place-based concerns that undergird Leland's work. And just as the approving use of the "Indian" stereotype was a distinctive feature in Leland's story, so it is today. Not only was Leland's story thirty years too late, it was also a hundred years too early.

Chapter 7

In the Absence of the Wisdom of the Elders
The Contemporary Use of the "Indian" Stereotype

The central characteristics of Leland's story emerge from what at first seem like idiosyncratic academic twitches: his identification of Kluskap with the heroes of the Norse epics, his description of "Algonquin" stories as Aryan-like, his insistence that his readers attend to his stories so as to develop a feeling for nature, and of course his scholarly chicanery. He engages the "Indian" stereotype in an approving manner, making use especially of the generic "Indians," their affinity for nature, and the almost unbridgeable gulf between *Them* and *Us*. If the central vehicle of Leland's story is the "Indian," the *Volk* of North America, the story's theme derives from his concern for Place, a sense of belonging to the land. These central characteristics, I will argue, are shared by the stories of contemporary popularizers and scholars writing about Native American religions.

I am not talking about Leland's direct influence. It is true that his Kluskap-Malsum story has influenced virtually all contemporary manifestations of the Kluskap twin tale. It is also true that Leland's work, including his improvisation and peculiar theories directly influenced Joseph Campbell, who recycles them in his *Historical Atlas of World Mythology*. They have also influenced less reputable scholarship.[1] Still, that is not what I want to dwell on here. Rather my argument is that the needs of his readership, the ones Leland was trying to address, are similar to the needs felt today by popularizers and scholars of the "Indians," as well as by their audiences.

That contemporary inhabitants of North America might identify some of the same Place-related needs as the nineteenth-century inhabitants of this same space may well reflect some of the same existential situations. As I noted in the last chapter, many of us find large North American cities to be threatening, risky centers of disorder.[2] Rather than experiencing natural processes as overwhelming, as did their nineteenth-century fore-dwellers, many urbanites feel disconnected from nature, cut off from both the nurturing and the ferocity that typifies life connected to the land. Similarly, like our foreparents of the U.S. Gilded Age, we experience our world as at risk. While the nearness of war arches over both centuries, much has changed. Our sense of crisis has different triggers—fear of impending atomic annihilation, deep anxieties about the ecological state of the physical world, an uneasiness or exhilaration with shifting gender roles.

There is another important difference—a change of venue. For Leland and his audience the trouble was with the nation; for many in contemporary hegemonic North American culture the trouble is with the entire globe, the whole earth. There is a corresponding change in the stereotype's labels. I notice an increasing proclivity to use descriptive labels for "Indians" that globalize the stereotype. Two labels that appear to be coming into prominence are "indigenous peoples" and "aboriginal peoples" (or even "the aboriginals"). So, for example, in the 1992 *Wisdom of the Elders* the authors use "Native" to mean any "indigenous person" or "aboriginal person" in the world.[3] The United Nations designated 1993 the International Year of Indigenous People. This change in labels reflects the fact that hegemonic culture's contemporary need for Place is a global rather than national or continental matter.

This move from nation-centered Placing activities to those that are globe-centered speaks to the primacy and endurance of the human need for Place. Those of us who identify with hegemonic popular culture express that need in a variety of ways. Here is my version of our Place-driven story:

> We feel environmentally estranged. Improbably, we are global exiles. There is nowhere we belong because there is nowhere we have not polluted. By our mindless obeisance to progress we have "fouled our nests" like no other people on earth. We feel dis-Placed by our own culpability. Many of us have land (which we call "property") that belongs to us, but we have no feeling that we belong to that or any other land. We have a sense that we have had this feeling, but we lost it. We feel, I am arguing, that we do not belong here on the planet. We feel like we are NoPlace. We need to be SomePlace. We need, in other words, to call Place into being.

Responding to these Place-driven needs, some of us turn to the timeless, tradition-respecting "Indian" who has a deep abiding relationship to Mother Earth. Perhaps, this part of our story goes, the "Indians" can help us to feel a sense of belonging, just as they helped our nation's foreparents when they arrived in North America (or better, this part of "Turtle Island"). Perhaps we too can feel we have a home on the lap of our Mother. If the "Indian" would only teach us some of her or his timeless secrets, we too would have access to this sacred sense of Place.[4]

The geopious response of the array of "Indian" imitators—Boy Scouts or Bear Tribe, "Indian" hobbyists or Lynn Andrews's workshoppers—to the Place-needs expressed in this story is embarrassing, but obvious.[5] Less graphic responses become clear on some reflection.

Just as Leland recognized and responded to the Place-related needs of his readers, so contemporary writers recognize and respond to similar needs in hegemonic culture. A deft and versatile author, Leland wrote for two readerships at once—one more general, one more scholarly. Contemporary writers on Native American religions more often than not direct their work more specifically to one group or another. In this chapter, then, our inquiry will first consider examples of those works directed at more general audiences, and next examples of those authors whose readership is more scholarly.

Among the former group, *In the Absence of the Sacred* stands out.[6] The book's subtitle, *The Failure of Technology and the Survival of the Indian Nations* points to the agenda of its author, Jerry Mander. Really two books in one, *In the Absence of the Sacred* first details the dangers of the "megatechnology" that holds the "West" in its grip—Mander singles out computers, television, corporations, and genetic engineering—and then catalogs the ongoing attempts of "technological peoples" all over the world to steal the land of and otherwise wage war on "native peoples." Juxtaposing the two "books" allows Mander to suggest that the needs of technological peoples require the suppression and conquest of native peoples. *In the Absence of the Sacred* is not without problems,[7] but I am sympathetic to the book's central thesis. I am also struck by Mander's efforts to sift through the stereotypes affecting Native Americans in the media, in racist perspectives, and in New Age movements. Mander has engaged himself in the political struggles of Native Americans, and cautions against "skim[ming] the 'cream'—art, culture, spiritual wisdom—off the Indian experience," ignoring the day-to-day existences of "living Indians."⁸ And yet the "Indian" stereotype runs throughout *In the Absence of the Sacred*, bursting off the surface of the pages at different points in the book.

One such point is in chapter 12, "Indians Are Different from Americans." Here, in a four-page subsection (214–19), Mander presents a "Table of Inherent Differences" between "Technological Peoples" and "Native Peoples." The generic "Indian" with timeless religious teachings, close to nature with some added generalities about economics, social organization, architecture, and political structure combine to provide an overwhelming sense that *They* are completely different from *Us*. "It is clear from this big picture of both cultures," says Mander, "that they are incompatible. They do not and probably cannot mix." According to Mander, not only "Indian" but "aboriginal peoples" the world over

> all share very similar attitudes toward nature. To the degree that they have not been overtaken by Westerners, they still engage in collective production, share commodities, and live in extended families. They have similar ideas about art, architecture, time, and dozens of other dimensions of life. Their religions are nature based; they believe in a living planet.

Mander also characterizes the "incompatible Westerners." In a remarkable passage he notes,

> we wear ties and wristwatches, drive cars, live in nuclear families in permanent structures alongside pavement walkways. We work for fixed hours of the day for years at a time for a person we call "boss." We use money to purchase commodities. (215)

All but a couple of these "Western" characteristics apply to a majority of Micmacs, Maliseets, Passamaquoddy, and Penobscot that I know.⁹ The attempt to create this incompatibility would seem even more silly if it were not so offensive. The question it raises is why the well-intentioned Mander needs this wholly other generic "Indian"? The answer would frankly be beyond me if it were not for the example of Charles G. Leland.

We are again confronting the Place-needs of the author and his reading audience. The contrasts in Mander's "Table of Inherent

Differences," which seem at first very persuasive, dissolve under careful scrutiny. Examining even a few Native American nations and their histories overturns the "Table." Unfortunately this kind of stereotypic comparison only serves to exclude some Native Americans who self-define as Micmac or Penobscot or some other nationality because they do not fit the model. Apparently they have, despite their own self-understanding (and despite Mander's contention that the differences are "inherent"), "been overtaken by Westerners." Perhaps in a twisted way they have. They have been overtaken by "Westerners" who need them to be "authentically Indian" and Other in order to invoke their nature-centered teachings to grant the "Westerners" Place on the planet.

For Mander this is not a romantic, backward looking enterprise. He counters that "What is romantic is to believe . . . that technology itself can liberate us from the problems it has created." Instead, his project is "going *forward* to a renewed relationship with timeless values and principles that have been kept alive for Western society by the very people we have tried to destroy." He concludes, "It is native societies, not our own, that hold the key to future survival."[10]

As I indicated earlier, I find much in Mander's project attractive. I remain wary, however, of any attempt, regardless of how good-hearted, that relies on the "Indian" stereotype. That Mander is not content to learn from Navajo people, Hopi people, Cree people, and/or Dene people, but needs to conflate them into "Indians" indicates he is snagged by "technological peoples'" need for Place.

Although more careful than Jerry Mander, Peter Knudtson and David Suzuki are, in the Canadian best-seller *Wisdom of the Elders,* just as drawn to respond to the Place-needs of their readers by resorting to the "Indian" stereotype. Again the overall project is commendable; again the "Indian" stereotype sabotages the authors' best attempts. The central idea that drives the book is, I think, a good one. It is worth turning to the Chewong, the Hopi, the Dunne-za, the Kayapó, and the Waswanipi Cree to try to understand something of the way each culture understands its relationship with what we call "nature." It may be that those of us who identify with the hegemonic popular culture might learn from these different peoples and from our "elders" in the scientific community.

Perhaps even more significantly, Knudtson and Suzuki call our attention to an important feature of Native American religions—their concern for Place.[11] As Sam Gill has shown, this placed-ness or way of configuring reality so central to Native American religions, is difficult if not impossible to generalize about. In the few examples Gill uses, the Zuni have a concern for the "middle place" that signifies their niche in cosmic harmony; the Seneca fold the negative aspects of their lived reality into their worldview; the Navajo concern is most often with righting the imbalance caused by the sheer fact of living in the world.[12] Each Native American worldview is complex and dynamic, so that careful study of a single worldview as it has changed over time yields a deep matrix of meaning that belies the standard "the world is like a sacred circle and all nature is worshipped" cant of users of the "Indian" stereotype.

The geopious expressions we have been trailing for the past few chapters—the sense of belonging to the land—is one part of this larger cosmological place or worldview. Given the diversity of Native American worldviews, only if the "Indian" stereotype is invoked can Place be distilled down to "closeness with nature." For all their care with sources and their awareness of the pitfalls, it is precisely here that Knudtson and Suzuki cross themselves up. Phrases like "the Native Mind," "Native nature lore," "Native wisdom," and "indigenous knowledge"—all singular—pervade the book. Also front and center are the almost unbridgeable gulf, closed only by a few scholar-elders (and of course the authors), the timeless teachings of peoples on the brink of extinction, and so on.[13]

Again it is adherence to the stereotype that causes harm. In his "Personal Foreword," Suzuki writes that "the destruction of indigenous people is now occurring with frightening speed." He likens this phenomenon to "the current spasm of species extinction" and states that "Once these people have disappeared, their body of priceless thought and knowledge, painstakingly acquired over thousands of years, will disappear forever." And then the clincher:

> And like a species that has lost its habitat and survives only in zoos, indigenous people who have lost their land and eke out a living in tiny reserves or urban slums lose their uniqueness and identity.[14]

Where in Suzuki's vision, I wonder, are the Passamaquoddy and Penobscot, the Micmac and Maliseet people I know, most of whom are "living in tiny reserves or urban" communities? Would they agree that they had lost "their uniqueness and identity"? Many, I think, would admit to struggling every day with alcoholism, family violence, substance abuse, and petty political wranglings in their communities, and with racism outside their communities, but most still identify themselves as Passamaquoddies and Penobscots, Micmacs and Maliseets and celebrate that fact. Suzuki, bewitched by the "Native" stereotype—extended to cover the global context of our own needs as exiles—has by his well-meaning words, discounted and disenfranchised most Passamaquoddy, Penobscot, Micmac, and Maliseet people. These are real people who, largely due to their own particular histories of conquest, cannot meet Suzuki's or his readers' needs for timeless secrets for understanding their relationship to the Earth.

Just as in Leland, Place in Knudtson and Suzuki takes the fore, overshadowing the persistent primitivist critique of society. Here is just one of many passages in *Wisdom of the Elders* that depends on the global "Indian" stereotype, "the Native," to tell the authors' version of our story:

> But if Western science does not need the Native Mind, the *human* mind and, in particular, the Western mind and society *do*. We will always need the Native Mind's vibrant images of a living natural world that can penetrate to the deepest and most heartfelt . . . realms of human understanding. We need the Native Mind's bold assurance that while much of the universe is accessible to human sensibilities, it possesses dimensions that may remain forever beyond human logic and reason, and that the cosmic forces of mystery, chaos, and uncertainty are eternal. Perhaps more than anything else, we need the glimmer of hope for the kind of future that indigenous nature-wisdom foreshadows—by its historic precedent of sustaining a long-term ecological equilibrium with the natural world, despite occasional lapses.[15]

It is all here. The generic "Indian" (here, "Native"), in danger of extinction, has timeless wisdom. Although the "Native Mind" is completely different from "Western minds," the authors have traveled among these people (and read the books of respected scholars) and have managed to bring back the secrets of living in this world (if we are not too blind to see). Although we polluters don't deserve it, we can have the gift of Place if we accept the teachings about long-term ecological equilibrium.[16]

It is as easy to criticize these biologists' approving use of a stereo-type in order to tell the hegemonic culture's story of Place as it is to appreciate that culture's deep-seated need for just such a story. It is not as easy to identify the same approving use of the stereotype in scholars who do not claim to be telling us a story about Place, but to be describ-ing "Indian religion." Nonetheless, as Robert Berkhofer points out:

> Like other intellectuals [in the 1960s], many anthropologists [and religionists] came to see Indian societies as embracing a unified way of life often with values superior to those found in the frag-mented culture of modern industrial life. Insofar as they por-trayed Indian cultures as manifesting the wholeness of man, the humanity of interpersonal relationships, and the integrity of organic unity, these [scholars], like writers, artists, and social philosophers of modern times, had abandoned the liberalism of the mid-nineteenth century for the liberalism of the mid-twenti-eth as their way of judging the presumably splintered culture of their own industrial society.[17] (68)

Berkhofer goes on to affirm what we have learned from our study of Leland—that scholars tell their own stories when doing scholarship. In Berkhofer's words, scholars, "like other members of their society stud-ied other cultures according to the premises of their own."[18] Thus, as we turn from that generality to the more specific study of religions, we should not be surprised to find scholars tangled in the web of the "Indian" stereotype.

It is not immediately obvious that Joseph Epes Brown is snared by the "Indian" stereotype. He appears, for example, to avoid the largest bugaboo, the generic "Indian." He says in the first essay in *The Spiritual Legacy of the American Indian*,

> there has developed, through time and in accord with the great geographical diversity of the Americans, a rich plurality of highly differentiated types of religious traditions, making it impossible to define or describe American Indian religions in generalities.[19]

On the essay's next page, however, Brown delineates what he calls the "primal elements" out of which Native American religions grew. Not surprisingly Brown identifies one of these elements as "a special quality and intensity of interrelationship with the forms and forces of their natural environment. . . . a metaphysic of nature." By resorting to his "primal elements" Brown uses generalities to describe Native American religions—a project that he himself says is impossible. Even assuming he can accurately discern the earliest religious "foundations" of the people who were the ancestors of Native Americans, Brown's effort is akin to trying to generalize about Christianity from its Jewish and Hellenistic roots, ignoring its historical and contemporary manifestations. Brown falls back on the generic "Indian" in part at least because he feels it necessary to claim that "American Indian living religions have the right to a legitimate place alongside the great religious traditions of the world."[20]

One might suspect that Brown was championing "Indian" religion in part to claim respectability and significance for his own work. This would be unfair. Brown's agenda is more well-intentioned, though hardly more well-advised. The following passage from *The Sacred Pipe* reveals the heart of Brown's intent. He has just given a quick sketch of Black Elk, detailing his first meeting with the famous *heyoka*. In that meeting, according to Brown, the old holy man had been expecting him.[21] He portrays Black Elk as a special sagely elder concerned that the "flowering tree" of Lakota religiousness was withering. Not only was Black Elk concerned in Brown's description, he felt powerless. In Brown's biblically derived phrase, "Black Elk knew not what to do." To demonstrate his point Brown quotes a poignant prayer of Black Elk from Neihardt's *Black Elk Speaks*, and then he writes,

> Because of this mission to keep alive his religious heritage, Black Elk wished to pass on to his people and the world those aspects of his religion that were recorded in *Black Elk Speaks*, and in the book I recorded for him in 1953, *The Sacred Pipe*. It is in keeping with his wish, and for the sake of the values themselves, that I present the following material.[22]

He goes on to describe what he sees as the central features—sacred circle, closeness to nature, vision quest, sweat lodge, sacred pipe—of Plains religiousness.[23] From this passage it is clear that Brown understands himself as a mediator between the *Them* of the Plains "Indians" and the *Us* of his reading audience. Like Leland, he is bridging the gulf between the *Them* and *Us*, not for his own glory, but for a higher purpose. In Brown's case that higher purpose is twofold: (1) it was the old man's last wish and (2) because he cherishes the values inherent in Black Elk's teachings.

Much has been written about those teachings and the men who gave them to the world, especially since Raymond DeMaillie's edited version of the Black Elk interviews.[24] Black Elk was interviewed by John G. Neihardt first in 1931 and again in 1944. It was on the basis of the first interviews, translated by the elder's son Ben, and transcribed by Neihardt's daughter in shorthand and then typed by her, that the poet laureate of Nebraska wrote *Black Elk Speaks*. Neihardt considered the book primarily "a work of art with two collaborators," and admitted as early as 1971 that he was responsible for the beginning and the ending. "They are," he said in a phrase that Leland would have sanctioned, "what [Black Elk] would have said if he had been able."[25] There is still considerable debate as to just how much of *Black Elk Speaks* is Neihardt and how much Black Elk. What is not in dispute is that for at least forty years of his life Nicholas Black Elk was a Roman Catholic, active in teaching and missionizing for the church. Flowing from this fact is a heated conversation about how to understand the apparent puzzle of the Roman Catholic Oglala *heyoka* telling his great vision for the first time to a not-Native poet. We are not likely to add much light to that conversation with this inquiry.[26] What is more important is that Joseph Epes Brown, who lived with Black Elk in the winter of 1947–1948 and visited in the summers of 1948 and 1949, must have known of his devotion to Roman Catholicism.[27] Brown was not, ostensibly at least, a poet. He was a student of religions. That he didn't tell his audience that Black Elk, the old holy man he studied with, was a devout Christian, or that the seven rituals of *The Sacred Pipe* were organized to correspond to the seven sacraments of Catholic Christianity,[28] is hard to understand. It is reminiscent of Edward Jack's (and by extension Charles Leland's) portrayal of Gabe Acquin from whose lips came a version of the Kluskap twin story "as he sat in front of the fire in my room this evening smoking his tobacco mixed with willow bark." Like Black Elk, Acquin was a Roman Catholic who had traveled in Europe, as well as a man well versed in the other traditions of his people.[29]

It would appear that Brown's understanding of his role as a mediator of Oglala religious values overrode his academic standards. Those values, which he calls the "transcendent metaphysical principles central to the spiritual ways of the Plains Indians," are vital to the search of both Native Americans and not-Natives for answers to the "detraditionalization or despiritualization" that plagues the lives of both. In this search, Brown avers, the Native Americans have "a certain advantage" because "their indigenous traditions are deeply and intricately rooted in this very land, unlike the more recently transplanted Europeans."[30]

I want to admit, my first reaction on coming to this understanding of Brown's scholarship was anger. My anger was rooted first in feelings of embarrassment—I felt a fool; I taught from Brown's work—and second in feelings of injustice that rise up when stereotypes are applied in any manner, disparaging or approving. No doubt my anger leaks into this discussion.[31] I am retaining those leakages for reasons that will become apparent.

While Brown says that the search of "Indians" and not-"Indians" will ideally result not in imitation, but in both groups "ultimate[ly] regain[ing] and reaffirm[ing] the sacred dimension of *their own* respective traditions," it is evident that he sees the Plains "Indian" values he is transmitting as vital to both. Identifying "the tipi, the hogan, or the longhouse" with sacred centers "of antiquity" like the temple or the cathedral, Brown notes that "such primordial types of formulations found within our American land may serve as reminders to those who have lost or forgotten the sense of a center."[32] This, of course, is the language of Place. Brown sounds like an updated Leland when, in *The Spiritual Legacy of the American Indian*, he says,

> each being of nature, every particular form of land, is experienced as the locus of qualitatively differentiated spirit beings, whose individual and collective presence sanctifies and gives meaning to the land in all its details and contours. Thus it also gives meaning to the lives of people who cannot conceive of themselves apart from the land.

"People who cannot conceive of themselves apart from the land"? I find it easier to excuse Leland writing in 1884 than Brown who, in 1976, might have known better than to disenfranchise the thousands of Native Americans living in North American cities. But, like Leland, Brown needs to meet the need of his readers for Place. He labels the "Indian's" close relationship to nature, "a polysynthetic metaphysic of nature," and, armed with that expensive label, this is what he says:

Such a polysynthetic metaphysic of nature, immediately experienced rather than dangerously abstracted, speaks with particular
force to the root causes of many of today's problems, especially to
our present so-called ecological crisis. It is perhaps this message
of the sacred nature of the land, of place, that today has been most
responsible for forcing the Native American vision upon the
mind and conscience of the non-Native American.[33]

Mustering all of the characteristics of the "Indian" stereotype except
the "Indian doomed to extinction,"[34] Brown manages a scholarly
sounding response to the global Place-needs of his readers. As for the
responsibility "for forcing the Native American vision upon the mind
and conscience of the non-Native American," Joseph Epes Brown has
to accept some of that. He not only managed some of the "forcing," but
had a large role in forging "the vision" itself.

I mentioned that my first reaction to seeing Brown's scholarship in
this way was anger. Rather than remove the evidence of the anger, I
want to use it as an occasion for reflecting on the power of my need for
Place. It is clear to me now that the times I read Brown's work before
this inquiry, I needed to hear what he was saying. I felt some religious
lack and needed to hope that this might be filled by "Indian" wisdom.
Hinduism scholar David Kinsley still chuckles about the cheeky first-
year graduate student who in 1971 exclaimed to him with obvious
incredulity, "You *haven't* read *Black Elk Speaks?!*" That graduate student
was me and, like many of my contemporaries, I found in Neihardt's
Black Elk hope that even our troubled world might be resacralized.[35] If
my memory serves me, as a student I never wrote an academic paper
on Neihardt's Black Elk. The teachings were too important. Over twenty
years later, I find Nicholas Black Elk a far richer, more complicated,
riveting teacher than Neihardt's Black Elk. Had I the choice between
the two Black Elks, would I have preferred Nick Black Elk back then? I
would like to think as much, but I am frankly not so sure. The old
bireligious *heyoka*/catechist could not have met my need for Place as
elegantly as Neihardt's tragic figure who I might help redeem if I
attended to his vision. In my 1971 "sixties" war-resisting context,
Neihardt's telling of the Black Elk story resonated deeply with my own
sense of alienation, with my own sense that the hoop of my birth-
nation was broken. Over twenty years later, the more complicated,
nuanced story of Nicholas Black Elk fits much more my current context
of undeconstructed uncertainty.

Joseph Epes Brown's approving use of the "Indian" stereotype has been singled out before. His exhortatory style attracts attention among his less exuberant colleagues. While taking him to task for his "cultural primitivism," for example, Alice Kehoe points out that his central notion that fundamental elements thirty to sixty thousand years old survive in contemporary Native American religions is nonsense. "Brown's enterprise," she concludes, "is built upon an unverified and probably unverifiable premise."[36] Kehoe also singles out Brown's teacher for criticism.[37] This is initially surprising since, unlike Brown, Åke Hultkrantz is widely known for his solid scholarship. In fact, there is little doubt that he is one of the preeminent scholars of native American religions in our time. A Swedish scholar, Hultkrantz is a prolific, multilingual professor whose thirteen books and approximately three hundred papers signal a lifetime of research in an area of religious studies where, until relatively recently, few have worked. Reviewing the sheer bulk of Hultkrantz's work, it is possible to excuse Christopher Vecsey's ebullience when he writes,

> he has established in his own writings a cross-referencing to his other publications, a mighty fortress of interconnected observation, a veritable intellectual world-view with coherence and continuity over his productive lifetime, a unified corpus of data and theory.[38]

Clearly Åke Hultkrantz is a major figure in the academic study of Native American religions. Yet here too we find the "Indian."[39]

Hultkrantz seems prone to the approving use of the "Indian" stereotype when he is discussing the "Indian attitude toward nature."[40] Like Brown, he begins a major article on this topic by warning against generalizing about "Indian" relations with nature, pointing out very clearly that there is "no universal American Indian" and thus no "common Indian attitude toward nature." He then proceeds to show why such generalization is impossible. It seems Hultkrantz has stepped clear of the "generic Indian" and, perhaps, the "Indian" stereotype. Two pages later, however, he is drawing a generalization about "the Indian veneration of nature,"[41] a sure sign the stereotype is taking hold.

Hultkrantz claims he wants to show that the relationship of "Indian" and environment is complex, that "the Indian veneration of nature is specific, not general." He admits that there are "many complications in the Indian attitude to nature," although he never seems to work out that his adherence to the generic "Indian" characteristic is one of the complications. In spite of his best efforts not to generalize, Hultkrantz effectively postulates a pristine "Indian" past in which natural ecologists roamed precontact North America engaged in "nature conservationism and nature veneration."[42] Alas, this paradise could not last. First, there were Native farmers, and then "the white man's value patterns." Hultkrantz reflects on the way the "common idea" of Mother Earth is weakened by agriculture and then destroyed by the "secularization which started in the wake of white colonialism." Christianity, too, works to "disenchant" the "Indian" worldview. He bemoans this loss: "Where the old beliefs are gone, red man's particular relationship to nature is there no more."[43]

This version of events is certainly central to the hegemonic culture's need for an "Indian" worldview that might enrich and revitalize one that is ecologically bankrupt. But it violates the histories and present situations of Native Americans. The notion that the (singular) "Indian" worldview was "shattered" by European contact is incongruous with what we know of many Native American nations' active efforts to respond to the religious ideas of European newcomers. Kenneth M. Morrison has, in a number of studies, shown the complexity of the religious coevolution between Native Americans and not-Natives.[44] For example, in the case of the Montagnais (Innu) the process of becoming Christian involved, among other things, understanding Jesus as a Guardian of Animals. Says Morrison, "[Father] Le Jeune relates one instance when two Montagnais reported that Jesus offered to aid them: 'I have seen thy Manitou, and I thy Jesus . . . .' 'Oh what a good year he promised us! What Beavers, what Elks!' The Jesuits were undoubtedly dismayed when the two men stipulated that Jesus expected tobacco in return for his assistance."[45] While some Native American nations were shattered, indeed destroyed, by European conquest, many were not. Those that remain have of necessity developed creative responses to the "dominant society." Their continued existence is a tribute to their ability to resourceful innovation, to change. The adherence to the timeless "Indian" stereotype leads to a denial that Native Americans who change are "really" Native Americans. So when Hultkrantz says, "Where the old beliefs are gone, red man's particular relationship to nature is there no more," it is clear the "Indian" is at play.[46]

I interrupted Hultkrantz's essay just as he was about to begin his conclusion. Here is how he begins; listen for the story about Place:

No wonder that many thoughtful Indians long for the days when nature was virgin and unspoiled, when the Great Spirit offered his children a rich flora and fauna, and revealed his own essence in the beauty and dramatic force of the landscape.[47]

It is not only "thoughtful Indians" who long for those days. Many of us who identify with the hegemonic culture do too.[48] Here Hultkrantz is making approving use of the "Indian" stereotype to call Place into being for that part of his audience that identifies with the hegemonic culture.

It is important to emphasize that Hultkrantz's use of the "Indian" stereotype is approving. While it is true that his tone can be patronizing, Hultkrantz's scholarship is free of the disparaging use of that stereotype. Instead, Hultkrantz uses the stereotype of the "Indian" relatively sparingly and approvingly. I stress that Hultkrantz does not use the stereotype of the "Indian" in a disparaging fashion, because it plays a role, I will argue, in the often volatile conversation that swirls around Sam Gill's discussion of the way scholars have used the Mother Earth story. That volatile conversation both warranted mention in and informed the electronic discussion about teaching Native American religions I described in the first chapter. I recall the Mother Earth story here, for Hultkrantz's version of it dovetails with Charles Leland's story, and the neat fit shows us something of the dangers that can befall even the most experienced of students of Native American religions. The most famous evidence of Mother Earth as a Native American goddess is the quotation from Smohalla,

My young men shall never work. Men who work can not dream, and wisdom comes to us in dreams . . . . You ask me to plow the ground. Shall I take a knife and tear my mother's bosom? You ask me to dig for stone. Shall I dig under her skin for bones? You ask me to cut grass and make hay and sell it, and be rich like white men. But how dare I cut off my mother's hair?[49]

The runner-up piece of evidence is the statement attributed to Tecumseh: "The earth is my mother—and on her bosom I will repose."[50] Gill contextualizes these and other bits of evidence to show that they are not sufficient for the scholarly pronouncements about the ubiquitousness of Mother Earth.[51] These pronouncements constitute the scholars' story of Mother Earth. One representative example is this one from Hartley Burr Alexander's 1953 *The World's Rim:*

> It is difficult to realize the deep veneration with which the Indian looks upon his Mother the Earth. She is omniscient; she knows the places and acts of all men; hence, she is the universal guide in all the walks of life. But she is also, and before all, the universal mother—she who brings forth all life, and into whose body all life is returned after its appointed time, to abide the day of its rebirth and rejuvenation. The conception was not limited to one part of the continent, but was general.[52]

Another example of such pronouncements is Hultkrantz:

> Mother Earth is a common idea among Indians over large parts of North America, it occurs among hunters as well as among agriculturists. Whereas in myth she may be portrayed as an individual, anthropomorphic goddess, she appears to be identical with earth in ritual and everyday beliefs.[53]

He follows this, of course, with the requisite quotation from Smohalla.[54] This is precisely the sort of scholarly storytelling that Gill identifies in his inquiry.[55]

There is little question that the role Gill sees Hultkrantz playing in the European-American story of Mother Earth has generated some heated debate.[56] There is, however, another take on Hultkrantz's role in the Mother Earth story, one hinted at by the story of Charles Leland. I suspect Gill has missed an aspect of the Mother Earth story and has thus made himself vulnerable to even more vehement attacks than he might otherwise have had to endure for what he labels with grim irony, his "heresy."[57]

According to Gill, when Hultkrantz relies on Smohalla's famous Mother Earth quotation, then writes passages like "Many hunting tribes in North America manifest the same primitive belief in `our mother,' 'Mother Earth'"[58] he is one of the chief players in the European-American story of Mother Earth. That story, says Gill,

> is a story of the development of human religiosity and culture. It is a story of the evolution of religious structures and forms, a

story enriched by the patterns and categories derived from Western antiquity. It is a story of society's growth from the simple to the complex, from the primitive to the civilized, from a nonliterate to a literate culture. It is a story in which native Americans, by virtue of the statement made by Smohalla in 1885, could be placed at a very early stage of cultural and religious development.

Gill maintains that to tell the European-American version of the Mother Earth story is to participate in a logic of dominance.

In the European-American story of Mother Earth the logic of dominance appears under the rubric of the dichotomy between primitive and civilized. Here the theme of dominance may be more subtle, but it is also more sinister.[59]

In Gill's analysis, then, Hultkrantz, as one of the primary tellers of the European-American story of Mother Earth, comes off as a purveyor of an old story of the ladder of humankind's cultural evolution in which the "simple primitive" from the "many hunting tribes in North America" is on a bottom rung.

As Gill points out, the central theme of this story is civilization battling and winning out over savagism. As we have seen, the civilization versus savagism theme depends on the disparaging use of the "Indian" stereotype for its rationalization of conquest. Gill foregrounds this essential dominance when he retells the scholars' Mother Earth story. So, for example, this explanation from the scholars' story of the apparently simple concepts of some of the original inhabitants of North America: "Because of the simplicity of their minds they could not yet comprehend the complex idea of the heaven as a father, they could only conceive of the simpler idea of the earth as a mother." To stress the dominance he sees as central in the European-American story of Mother Earth, Gill has its proponents like Hultkrantz using the stereotype of the "Indian" in disparaging ways. This reading of the Mother Earth story may well fit some of the early Mother Earthologists like Tylor, Gatschet, and even Mooney. In Hultkrantz's case this reading is incongruous with his use of the "Indian."

While she can be found in much of Hultkrantz's work, Mother Earth as an "Indian" goddess is a focus of only one major article.[60] There is something unusual about this essay. Normally a staid and distant scholar, Hultkrantz bookends the article with his own personal experiences of Mother Earth. Of the first experience he says, "I made the acquaintance of this goddess during my fieldwork among the Shoshoni Indians of Wyoming in the 1940s and 1950s." The second personal experience is even more revealing. He is discussing Peyote Woman who he says is "a divinity probably created after the pattern of Mother Earth." Hultkrantz goes on, "Those who take peyote during a peyote ritual may hear her sing, as I did once when I attended a peyote ceremony. Certainly Indian goddesses also appear to white people."[61] Gill notes that the rhetorical device of framing his evidence for the existence of Mother Earth in Native American religions with his own personal testimony has "much persuasive power." He goes on acerbically, "What can be stronger evidence than the personal testimony of one who has met and heard the goddess whose story he is telling?"[62] Like Gill, I think there is more to Hultkrantz's strategy than mere description. I contend that by citing his own personal experience, Hultkrantz is tacitly acknowledging his participation in the Mother Earth story. By that I mean he is recognizing that the story of Mother Earth has power for him and for his largely not-Native readers. In a rare intimate account of the man, Christopher Vecsey catches Åke Hultkrantz musing about the possibility of not-Natives appropriating "Indian" values:

"Their values and their ways," he says, "developed from their conditions. We can learn from them, surely, but we cannot expect to become them. I am moved by the Indian concern for harmony and balance with nature in its more general sense, but we Europeans cannot adopt all Indian nature-ways in detail."[63]

But in general the appropriation of the "Indian" seems possible. Hultkrantz, Vecsey tells us, is a member of a Swedish "Indian Club," like those described in chapter one. Vecsey quotes Hultkrantz himself on this matter: "'We Swedes are crazy for Indians,' he remarks, 'we always have been.'" Vecsey continues,

Swedish youths and even grown-ups continue to set up teepees in the wood around Stockholm, playing at being Indians. Advertisements in Swedish newspapers picture Indians in headdresses and face paint, gazing at canoes on the waters.
In Hultkrantz's own office we find a Shoshoni headdress, a

buffalo skull complete with sagebrush and sweetgrass offerings, a bust of a Dakota Indian.[64]

Clearly the appeal of the "Indians" and Mother Earth is global. Borne by the scholar's approving use of the "Indian" stereotype, "Our Mother Earth" is a story whose powerful themes meet Hultkrantz's needs. A central component of those needs is the need to feel a belonging to the physical world, to "nature"—the need for Place.

It is my hypothesis that when contemporary scholars describe Mother Earth as an essential part of "Indian religion" or ("religions") they are usually telling that part of the hegemonic culture's story, which is about Place. That story, as we have seen, tells about healing the relationship between exiled human beings and the physical world. For Leland the issue was national; for us it is global. Leland found a solution to a world at risk in the vigorous "Northern" stories of the "Algonquin" hero, Kluskap. Hultkrantz and other well-intentioned Mother Earthologists have found a solution to match the seriousness of our sense of global exile. We are ecologically guilty enough to question our right to a Place with the rest of creation. Calling Place into being entails for us, as for Leland, turning to the nature-sensitive "Indians," now with their goddess Mother Earth, made accessible through the approving use of the "Indian" stereotype.

What Gill misses is that whether in 1967 when Hultkrantz writes that "many hunting tribes in North America manifest the same primitive belief in 'our mother,' 'Mother Earth,'" or 1983 when he authored "The Religion of the Goddess in North America" for a volume entitled *The Book of the Goddess*, he intends his "Indians" to be seen in a positive light.[65] He invariably uses the stereotype in an approving fashion. When Gill lumps Hultkrantz in with the earlier Mother Earthologists, he adds the insult of the disparaging use of the "Indian" to the injury of exposing our scholarly role in the Mother Earth story.

I would like to be able to show that this use of the "Indian" in an approving manner to gain access to a relationship to "our Mother Earth" frees the user from the "logic of dominance." I cannot. I have argued that any use of the stereotype, "Indian," harms real human beings. Discussing those not-Native misunderstandings of Native Americans sometimes thought of as "positive," Michael Dorris writes,

It makes a great story, a real international crowd-pleaser that spans historical ages and generations, but there is a difficulty: Indians were, and are, *Homo sapiens*. Unless the presence of a shovel-shaped incisor, an epicanthic fold or an extra molar cusp (or the absence of Type B blood) affords one an extra foot in the metaphysical door, native people have had to cope, for the last 40,000 or so years, just like everyone else. Their cultures have had to work consistently and practically, their philosophical explanations have had to be reasonably satisfying and dependable, or else the ancestors of those we call Indians really would have vanished long ago. . . . In the paradigm of European confusion, Indians have been objects of mystery and speculation, not people.[66]

Further, I take seriously Rayna Green's assessment of the approving use of the "Indian." "It doesn't," she says, "help real Indian people survive and thrive . . . don't think the positive images help us."[67]

I would take Dorris's and Green's assessments one step further. The "positive images" are in fact the one "Indian" stereotype used approvingly. As we have seen, that stereotype is characterized by a number of features—the generic "Indian" who is everywhere the same, who is unchanging through time, who has an innate harmonious relationship to nature, who is doomed to extinction (or more recently, assimilation), who is so different from hegemonic culture as to create an almost unbridgeable gulf between *Them* and *Us*. Used approvingly, the "Indian" stereotype clouds the vision of all who would study Native American religions. Although he speaks of historians, Michael Dorris's words describe most accurately scholars of Native American religions bewitched by their own approving use of the "Indian":

> They may have come to first "like" Indians because they believed them to be more honest, stoic, and brave than other people, and forever after have to strive against this bias in presenting their subjects as real, complicated people. Or they may discover to their disillusionment that all Indians are not pure of heart and have to suppress, consciously or unconsciously, their abiding resentment and disenchantment.[68]

The "Indian" stereotype has been used in North America since the time of contact with European peoples in disparaging and approving ways. This obverse or dual usage, coupled with one other characteristic—the stereotype's persistence—leads me to hypothesize one further danger of the approving use of the "Indian." Hegemonic popular culture has known periods in which its approving use of the "Indian" stereotype has equalled or surpassed its disparaging use.[69] Since all the features of the stereotype are susceptible to approving or disparaging use depending on the needs of the hegemonic culture, and since approving use has always been followed by its obverse, I see no reason to suppose the approving use of the "Indian" that seems to be waxing in the early 1990s will not falter and flip to a disparaging use in the future. In other words, public attitudes toward the "Indian" have always flipped from disparaging use to approving and then flopped back, often quite rapidly. So long as the "Indian" stereotype informs hegemonic public attitudes (and government policy), relations between real Native Americans and those of us who identify with the hegemonic culture will be fraught with unmet and unmeetable expectations at best, and charges of deceit and fraud at worst. If that were not enough, there is a further problem with the approving use of the "Indian" stereotype.

I admit the approving use of the stereotype may well be grounded in genuine affection. If Yi-Fu Tuan is right, however, we must beware of affection, for affection—as opposed to love—is premised on a hierarchical relationship, on a power discrepancy. We show affection to those to whom we feel superior. Implicit in affection, warns Tuan, is dominance.

> Affection is not the opposite of dominance; rather it is dominance's anodyne—it is dominance with a human face. Dominance may be cruel and exploitative, with no hint of affection in it. What it produces is the victim. On the other hand, dominance may be combined with affection, and what it produces is the pet.[70]

Gabe Acquin, the linchpin of Leland's story of Kluskap and Malsum, Maliseet leader, hunting guide, and world traveler, is often referred to by Edward Jack as "my Indian."[71] I do not doubt Jack's affection for Acquin,[72] but I also do not doubt Jack felt superior to Acquin. The phrase "for an Indian" lurked always between the lines of his letters to Leland. Lieutenant-Governor Gordon twenty years earlier described Acquin as "the pet guide and huntsman of the [British] garrison" in Fredericton. It is easy today to scoff at the phrase, "pet guide," but I suggest that it is precisely this relationship of master and pet that is implied by the approving use of the stereotype of the "Indian."[73]

Good intentions do not automatically free us from the use, even the approving use, of the "Indian."[74] We can know, like Brown and Hultkrantz, that generalities drawn from the myriad different Native American religions are impossible, and yet succumb to the generic "Indian" if our need for it is strong enough. We can know, like Hultkrantz, that respectful, good scholarship requires that we attempt to understand a Native American religious tradition "on its own terms" and yet still be played by the "Indian" stereotype.

Retelling the story of Placelessness earlier, I felt an ache. This is my story, too. The Place-driven need to weave ourselves—often by means of stories—into the landscape we find ourselves in is real. The alienation of the exile—political, ecological—is real. I too feel the need to make sense of this not-belonging. The needs are real. We of the hegemonic popular culture, especially its scholars, need to find ways to get these needs met, however, that do not include the use—disparaging or approving—of the stereotype of the "Indian."

Chapter 8

Reworking the "Indian" for Place

Scholars and Native Americans

T hroughout our inquiry, the story of Kluskap and Malsum has remained our narrative touchstone. Whatever its origins, I suggested near the beginning of chapter 4, that story belongs in some sense to the hegemonic popular culture. My reasoning was simple. It is that culture, not any Native American culture, that has recollected and passed on the story.[1] Remember, it appears in a number of story collections and in a cinematic retelling, all derived directly or indirectly from the Kluskap-Malsum version of Charles Godfrey Leland. The question to which I want to turn now is why has this story remained popular? For Leland it was important as a critical link in his Place-driven story of "Indians," nation, and land. A more global version of that story, I have argued, still moves students of Native American religions, thus shaping their findings. Why, though, does this particular story of Kluskap and Malsum begin to turn up in the hegemonic popular culture? And why does it still persist? And what are we to make of the story's tentative existence among Micmac and Maliseet people? Does geopiety—the persistent religious bond between people and land—play a role here? Finally, what does all this have to do with the academic study of Native American religions?

To explain why the story is well-liked in hegemonic popular culture, we can begin with the central themes of the story. There is Good, there is Evil; both are personified as brothers. This is most obvious in the version of Cyrus Macmillan, but it occurs in all the versions based on Leland's. They do cosmic battle and the Good brother wins, destroying the Evil brother. These are themes with which any culture apprehending the world dualistically would be comfortable.

In this case, the story is not just any story. It is an *"Indian"* story. As such, it meets the Place-needs—for conquest, for belonging—of the hegemonic culture. This it shares with the more influential stories of Carlos Castaneda and Lynn Andrews.[2] But unlike those stories that attempt to present an alternate (although still hegemonic and still "popular") way of being in the world, the Kluskap-Malsum story is for hegemonic popular culture authentically "Indian" *and* it upholds truths with which that culture is already comfortable. This combination helps explain why this story remains popular enough, but without the enthusiasm that has greeted Castaneda's and Andrews's stories. Kluskap-Malsum is a sort of middle-of-the-road story offering little new to hegemonic popular culture, but demanding little of it too. Perhaps this is why it has taken its most enduring form as a "children's story."

When the story is remembered and retold not in the context of hegemonic popular culture, but in Native American cultures, its significance shifts along with its context. I mentioned in passing in chapter 2 that Michael William Francis painted a scene from the story and that it was told by Viola Solomon from the Tobique community in 1962. I also noted that as far as I knew only two Micmac elders currently told versions of the Kluskap-Malsum story. Returning to this matter now, I feel a mixture of eagerness and anxiety. Eagerness, because I find challenging the effort to understand the process by which Micmacs have appropriated a story that has such a mixed pedigree. Anxiety, because at this point our inquiry moves from considering the story of hegemonic popular culture to the story of Micmac and Abenaki people. At this point, in other words, this inquiry and I as its guide become much more vulnerable to the power of the "Indian" stereotype, and more open to the "consequences" Vine Deloria, Jr., warned about. This admission does not obviate the need for care as we move from *the study of the study* of Native American religions to *the study* of one or two of those religions.

Michael William Francis, the Micmac artist now in his late sixties who first painted the scene of Malsum turned to rock, his face eternally slapped by waves, also tells a version of the story. His is a brief story of two brothers, one who turns against the other "for political reasons" while the other is away. On his return the brother who was away, Kluskap, confronts his brother, Malsum, kills him, and "turns him into some mountains."[3] Francis's story seems to be a caution against political wrangling within families. In the 1911 version Mrs. Catpat tells Michelson,[4] the younger brother, Amkotpigtu, perpetrates violence against family members whom Kluskap—because he was the older brother—had the responsibility to protect. Thus, it is by battering weaker members of the family that Amkotpigtu turns against Kluskap. Otherwise the two versions have more in common with each other than either do with Leland's version.

The late Mrs. Viola Solomon told her version of the Kluskap-Malsum story to a student from a folklore class while visiting her daughter who no longer lived in the Tobique community. Fifty-one at the time, she told the story in Maliseet, trying to ignore the tape recorder running beside her. Her daughter, a neighbor of the folklore student, later translated, sitting between two tape recorders.[5] Mrs. Solomon's version begins with the twins conversing in their mother's womb, then moves to the birth during which the mother dies, although Malsumsa's (her "Malsum's") fault in her death is only suggested. Mrs. Solomon identified Malsumsa with "the Indian Devil," the wolverine. She continues,

> So anyway they brought themselves up. And they was always together, 'til one day they tried their strength against each other which one would have more power than the other, although they were twins. Well he [Malsumsa] said, "how would a person kill you anyway? How could a person kill you?"

Kluskap, she says, lied and said a white owl's feather would kill him. They continued to test their strength while on a hunting trip. "Anything they tried Kluskap was always the strongest of the two. Malsumsa didn't like it; he envied his brother all the time." One night while Kluskap was sleeping, Malsumsa found a white owl, plucked a feather, and tried to kill Kluskap. Kluskap woke up.[6]

Here Mrs. Solomon's story takes a turn from all the other versions we have seen. Kluskap turns Malsumsa into a beaver and, when the beaver threatens to "always eat up your woods," he drives the rodent away by throwing huge rocks at him. Those piles of rocks, Mrs. Solomon says, speaking directly to her daughter, could all still be seen before they built the dam, hiding one of them. Two sites—the Pokiok Falls and Grand Falls—can still be seen and mark the places where Malsumsa/beaver tried to escape the barrage of Kluskap's rocks. Unlike the Kluskap-Malsum story, this latter description of Kluskap tossing huge rocks at a giant beaver and thereby forming the (now-hidden) Tobique Rocks, and various other falls along the river, occurs frequently in Maliseet story collections.[7] Mrs. Solomon uses it to validate the point of her story—that when a person feels envious of a family member's accomplishment, there is danger, perhaps even violence. The rocks are still there; the point of the story is therefore true.

We do not know where Mrs. Solomon learned of the Kluskap-Malsum story. It is hard to help noticing that all of the story elements that might appeal to hegemonic popular culture—the dualism, the battle of Good and Evil, and so on—are missing from Mrs. Solomon's story. I suppose more intrepid investigators would exult that they had finally found the *ur*-story of Kluskap and Malsum, the original, the real thing, the authentic version.[8] I suggest our inquiry ought to be more tentative. Mrs. Solomon's story, it seems to me, is an authentic version, if by that we mean a story appropriated to make sense of and provide support for a lived truth. This, however, is not unusual, nor particularly "aboriginal." It does demonstrate the creativity and power of this Maliseet storyteller to appropriate and shape stories to make meaning in her community. These characteristics, I will argue, also typify the two elders currently telling their versions of the Kluskap-Malsum story.

George Paul, one of the elders who tells the Kluskap-Malsum story, is in his forties, the other, Noel Knockwood, is in his sixties. The former remembers learning the story from a book, perhaps in school; the latter is more circumspect about where he learned the story. He remembers that he read the story in a book, but was not sure where. It was important to Knockwood that he had verified the accuracy of the story with two elders from his home community before he started telling it. This would have been at the beginning of the 1970s at the earliest. The point is that there was a time when neither had the story as part of a story corpus passed on to them. I am all but certain that the Leland Kluskap-Malsum story, in either Leland's or Kay Hill's version, was a source story for both these elders.

The two elders who share the telling of the Kluskap-Malsum story also share some life experiences. Both now live off-reserve; both attended the residential school in Shubenacadie, Nova Scotia; both identify themselves as traditionalists. Traditionalism is in Maine and the Maritime Provinces a relatively new phenomenon, dating from the mid- to late 1970s. Abenaki and Micmac people who identify themselves as "traditionalists" understand themselves to be reclaiming the spiritual ways of their ancestors. Central to their teaching is abstention from alcohol and recreational drugs. More apt to describe their spiritual path as "Indian" than as "Micmac" or "Maliseet" or "Passamaquoddy" or "Penobscot," traditionalists most often conduct the rituals central to their practice in English, although prayers and songs in Micmac or Passamaquoddy/Maliseet are not uncommon.[9] Mindful that this process of reclaiming traditional ways began in the late 1970s among Abenaki and Micmac people, and that devout Micmac Catholics refer to *their* religion as "traditional," I am here using the label "neotraditionalism" for this religious movement. In this way I hope to avoid confusion with the older "traditional" Micmac and Abenaki Catholicism.

When describing their reasons for telling the Kluskap-Malsum story, it is clear that both Micmac elders have made the story their own. George Paul, who has also painted a scene from the story (see Figure 8.1), is only beginning in the early 1990s to tell the story. He is a respected neotraditionalist teacher and artist. He shares on cassette tapes songs and chants some of which he has received during ceremonies. They are becoming popular among Micmac neotraditionalists. Paul tells that Kluskap and Malsum were born in the Spirit World. Because Malsum killed his mother he was banished to earth as a way of "doing time." The message of the story, according to Paul, is that when we get overwhelmed by negative energy, we risk ending up turned to stone, the waves slapping our face. When I talked with Paul, I had a sense that he was early in the process of becoming comfortable with the story.[10] In contrast, the story fits Noel Knockwood like a favorite wellworn sweater.

Noel Knockwood has been telling the Kluskap-Malsum story for at least fifteen years. He is a pipe carrier who has done extensive work for "his people" in the areas of prison reform and education. For him the story is a "creation story" because his version tells of how things came to be. In Knockwood's story Kluskap and Malsumsis[11] create in tandem. For everything Kluskap creates that is positive and good, Malsumsis creates something negative. Diseases, misfortune, murder, poisonous plants are all part of Malsumsis's creation. When Malsumsis was defeated by Kluskap in battle, it was to Malsumsis's kingdom that he was banished. Knockwood explained that,

According to tradition, [Kluskap] had turned to the heavens to seek advice from his father, and his father said not to kill Malsumsis for Malsumsis will have to keep this creation of evil,

Figure 8.1. George Paul's "Glooscap Turns His Evil Brother to Stone" from *Micmac Legends of Prince Edward Island* (Lennox Island Band Council and Ragweed Press, 1988)

his kingdom of disease, misfortunes, murders, fights, poisonous plants and all these things that are of his kingdom. He created them and he has maintained them. So those individuals who are called back to the Creator and have spent some amount of negative time on earth and are very cruel and rugged individuals—to their own group, to their own village people, to their own parents, things like that—had to go after death through the kingdom of Malsumsis. And you cannot define it as hell because it is not as such; it is the Kingdom of Darkness where they will go there for a while but eventually will be forgiven and will be called into the Kingdom of God.

Knockwood went on to say,

> That's the reason . . . our world is still full of disease, is still full of
> anger and bitterness and all these characteristics that we humans
> develop and sometimes we walk that path; sometimes uncon-
> sciously . . . sometimes deliberately we make people envious of us
> or jealous of us or things like that because it's the human charac-
> teristic. But then we have to pull ourselves out of that. And this is
> Malsumsis's kingdom too, because it's all negativity—it's anger,
> it's bitterness, it's jealousy, it's hatred, it's all these things.[12]

For Knockwood the story's importance is twofold. First, it describes
the duality of creation; second, it encourages the individual's acceptance of his or her duality, especially negative aspects. By affording the
individual's acceptance of the negative part of his or her own nature
(and here Knockwood includes substance abuse), the story encourages
Native people to get back on the right road. The "traditionalist" solution, said Knockwood, is to do ceremonies to put the person back on
the right road. This he equated with being in balance:

> You have to balance heart, mind and soul; and when these are in
> harmony you're in balance; you're on the right road. You
> acknowledge and accept all these other [negative] things around
> you, yet you walk a path between the two extremes of right and
> wrong.[13]

When I suggested that Malsumsis's kingdom seemed a lot like pur-
gatory, Knockwood agreed. Then he reminded me that he had taken
courses in religious studies toward completion of his degree at St.
Mary's University in Halifax. There he had learned, he said, that there
were similar ideas in many different religious traditions. That did not
mean these ideas were the same. He returned to a theme he had woven
throughout our talk— not-Native and "Indian" ways were different. In
this case, one important difference was "the definition of angels and
saints and all this structure within heaven." The difference is between a
hierarchical not-Native afterlife and a nonhierarchical "Indian" afterlife. For Knockwood this hierarchical-nonhierarchical difference permeates all aspects of not-Native and "Indian" cultures.

The versions of the Kluskap-Malsum story Knockwood and Paul

tell, like the one of Viola Solomon earlier, show little evidence of Leland's interference. Gone are his equation of Little Wolf with the evil brother and his description of the past as a time of widespread human evil. Yet the story has not caught on. It still is an insignificant story even among those Abenaki and Micmac for whom it would seem most likely to be meaningful—neotraditionalists. Knockwood says he has not heard anyone else tell the story in any detail. It is hard to say why his teaching that this story is central to Abenaki and Micmac neotradition-alism has not been received with more enthusiasm. It may be because some neotraditionalists, needing to put more distance between them-selves and the religious traditions of hegemonic culture, are uncomfort-able with the Christian echoes in the story. It may be that this Kluskap story still suffers from its curious origins and does not resonate with the experience of most Abenaki and Micmac people. And of course it may also be that this story will soon catch on and be told and retold at neotraditional gatherings and ceremonies across the northeastern part of Turtle Island. Perhaps George Paul's recent interest in the story is a sign of this coming popularity. This story is tenacious; it's too early to count it out.

More important, it seems to me, is that the story has provided a way for Knockwood and others who listen to him to simultaneously (1) set themselves apart from the traditions of hegemonic culture and (2) maintain connection with some of the values and story-realities of their parents' and grandparents' Micmac Catholic religious traditions. By appropriating this story Noel Knockwood can on the one hand set him-self apart from the hierarchical, repressive structures of the "dominant society," for which the residential school stands as a potent example in his memory.[14] This story is not part of that culture: it is a *Micmac* cre-ation story. It is *not* a "White" story. While he remembered reading it somewhere while "researching the past," it has been validated by his mother and another elder from Knockwood's community.[15] On the other hand, by removing the fratricidal elements and understanding Malsumsis as the cause of "negativity" and the ruler of a purgatory-like kingdom that wrongdoers must pass through before they can go to heaven, he is consistent with three centuries or more of Micmac Catholicism. Whether the vision of a hell-less cosmos in which one's own negative or dark side must at some level be accepted as part of creation is the influence of Micmac tradition or the popular culture of the late 1960s and early 1970s, or both, is conjecture. It does, however, represent another example of Knockwood's talent for appropriating this story into his own religious context.

However laudatory, this process whereby these two elders are teaching using a story that they take to be authentically "Indian," but which has a much more complicated history, gives me pause. In fact, initially I was quite uneasy. Indeed, one possible response to this kind of assembly of culture out of apparently "corrupt" elements is outrage. William K. Powers, commenting on the appropriation of Neihardt's Black Elk and his eclectic rendering of Lakota religion as normative by not-Natives and neotraditionalists, says,

> some Lakota today . . . look to spiritual guidance from books. The new generation of Indians has moved to the cities away from their direct source of inspiration. . . . For these young Indians, *Black Elk Speaks* and other fabrications of the white man become not only increasingly acceptable but desireable. . . .
>
> It is undeniable that the myth of Black Elk has captured the minds and emotions of white Americans and Europeans. . . . But even from this Euroamerican background is it not immoral to witness the creations of an Indian religion by a romantic white man? The religious zeal of even more romanticists is overshadowed by their total ignorance of a Lakota religion learned first hand from those ritual specialists who are not the subjects of books, and who are therefore more nearly akin to the ideal type of Lakota medicine man accepted by Lakota culture.[16]

"Is it not immoral?" The question, coming from an established scholar of Lakota religions, is not easily dismissed.

I respect Powers's scholarship and think I understand his response, but I cannot join him. I worry that those of us from the hegemonic culture have little ground from which to gain a perspective on this phenomenon—except perhaps our history of colonialism and dominance. That worry informs my reluctance to form negative judgments about this process of meaning-making.

Nonetheless Powers's observation about the way Neihardt's Black Elk is used widens the scope of our inquiry. It would appear that the phenomenon of the two Micmac elders telling the Kluskap-Malsum story is not an anomaly but rather part of a broader pattern of appropriation. Within that broader pattern, some contemporary Native

Americans incorporate into the expression of their religiousness "Indian" elements that derive most directly from not-Native cultures. At the heart of this pattern, then, is the stereotype of the "Indian." Indeed, I contend that neotraditionalism is appropriating the stereotype of the "Indian" used in an approving fashion, as one basis for self-identification.[17] I have been clear in my censure of both approving and disparaging uses of the "Indian" stereotype by those of us who identify with the hegemonic culture. When Native Americans themselves appropriate the images from the approving use of the "Indians" to define themselves, however, the matter is far from clear cut. It is precisely here that I am most wary of coming to conclusions prematurely.

My understanding of this appropriation rests on the current use of the "Indian" stereotype. By way of "editing and recasting" that usage I would ask you to stretch a bit and imagine a game show set. There's the stage, and on it is a revolving platform divided in two by a partition. The audience can only see one side of the partitioned platform at one time. There are two realistic-looking Disney-style, "life-like" humanoid robots on the stage, one on each side of the revolving platform. We know that there are two robots because the platform has just spun around revealing what appears to be a good "Indian." She appears in fringed deerskin traditional dress, tall and strong. Her face commands respect, but simultaneously shows the audience they have nothing to fear. This message is underscored by the fruits of a bounteous harvest—squash, beans, corn—which she holds cradled in her arms. This robot stands in marked contrast to the one that was just whirled out of sight. He is scruffy in appearance, his scant clothing of animal skins torn and soiled. This appears to be a bad "Indian." He is slouching, scowling, and his shifty eyes never meet those of the audience. In one hand a small dead animal dangles, its head crushed; in the other he holds a club, blood dripping from its stone head. The atmosphere around this robot is as dangerous and threatening as the one around the other one is friendly and inviting.

Fifteen years ago Robert Berkhofer identified the two aspects of the "Indian" stereotype that I have personified as robots on a rotating platform. What has become clearer in the intervening years is that the two images of the "Indian" have many features in common. These I have catalogued in the previous three chapters. Perhaps most significantly, the button that controls the movement of the platform is in the hands of not-Natives. Michael Dorris puts it this way:

In a certain sense, for five hundred years Indian people have com-
peted against a fantasy over which they have had no control.
They are compared with beings who never really *were*, yet the
stereotype is taken for truth.[18]

In other words, the needs that determine which of the whirling images
appears on stage at any given moment are those of the hegemonic popular culture, not those of Native Americans whose realities are by and
large misunderstood or ignored. As Berkhofer noted, "the debate over
'realism' will always be framed in terms of White values and needs,
White ideologies and creative uses."[19] Perhaps this last fact helps
explain why some Native Americans have begun to appropriate the
images from the approving use of the "Indian" stereotype as descriptive of themselves. It is, at its most basic, a way to wrest control of the
image-spinning by fixing one montage of images as normative, as the
way "Indians" really are.[20]

This phenomenon takes many forms among Micmac and Abenaki
people. There are references to images that stem from the stereotype in
the poetry of Micmac poet Rita Joe.[21] Urban Maliseet neotraditionalists
claim an innate close relationship with nature. In an eloquent plea to
heal the earth, Abenaki writer and storyteller, Joseph Bruchac, uses a
story featuring Kluskap that demonstrates that same relationship.[22]
Religious rituals recently initiated are described as "belonging to our
ancestors for a thousand years." Teachings like the Medicine Wheel,
new to the area, are described as ancient "Indian" wisdom belonging
therefore to the Micmac, Maliseet, Passamaquoddy, and Penobscot.[23]
Finally, there are the more extreme neotraditionalists who identify
completely with the timeless generic "Indian." From the latter's point
of view they are so completely different from representatives of
"Western" cultures that there is barely room for dialogue. Proponents
of this position, who their detractors call "born-again Indians," claim
that "traditionalism" is the cure for all the ills of "Indian people."[24]
Traditionalism will end spousal battering, drug and alcohol problems,
child sexual abuse, political wrangling—all the problems of contemporary Native American communities.

This effort to gain control of the whirling "Indian" stereotype has its
parallel in academe where, as we have seen, Native American scholars
are concerned about the not-Native imitation of the "Indian," and are
often truculent about fencing off "Indian" religion from not-Native

academics. It may well be that these efforts are about trying to get some control over the language and images that shape the discourse about themselves. I am reminded of Vine Deloria, Jr.'s reference in the electronic discussion to "basically insulting categories of analysis," and to his criticism of "non-Indian frameworks of analysis" that are used "to control the definitions of what is being said and thought about regarding Native religions."[25] I have shown that even the not-Native approving use of the "Indian" stereotype is motivated by geopiety. Given that these Place-needs are in fact about conquest, albeit a less violent conquest, this response makes sense from one point of view. It seems clear that besides making an effort to take control of the use of the "Indian" stereotype, neotraditionalists—extreme and not-so-extreme, academic and not-academic—are engaged in the religious process of making sense of their lives.

Ellen Badone confronted a similar religious phenomenon in Brittany in the mid-eighties when she tried to understand *radiesthésie,* "both a method of diagnosing illness and a divinatory technique for discovering things hidden beneath the earth."[26] She discovered that *radiesthésistes* "are not merely following tradition. Nor are they inventing traditions that are entirely new. More accurately, they are reworking older indigenous ideas and combining them with diverse elements from multiple external sources." Part of this process depended on having access to paperback books about Breton traditions written by folklorists and ethnographers. This, says Badone, "has encouraged people to adopt a reflexive stance toward their own culture."[27] I take neotraditionalism among Micmac, Maliseet, Passamaquoddy, and Penobscot people to be a parallel phenomenon.

The availability of books by Kay Hill, John Neihardt, Joseph Epes Brown,[28] Knudtson and Suzuki, Storm, Andrews, and many others has afforded Native Americans the adoption of a reflexive stance toward their own cultures. This, in turn, has led to Micmacs and Maliseets, Passamaquoddies and Penobscots reworking "older indigenous elements from multiple external sources." One element in the resulting constellation of religious meaning is images from the approving use of the "Indian" stereotype.

In a way, for scholars in the hegemonic culture to dismiss this process of meaning-making is to slip into the grip of that stereotype. The *Them* and *Us* and timeless components of the "Indian" require an impossible cultural purity.[29] As Badone points out:

In the postmodern world, the notion that cultures represent bounded, impermeable units is no longer tenable: "Human ways of life increasingly influence, dominate, parody, translate and subvert one another. . . . Since cultural forms are always socially constituted and reinterpreted in light of historical and contingent concerns, all traditions are, at some level, "invented."[30]

Badone recommends we take those traditions seriously. I concur.

Neotraditionalism is, of course, not the first instance of creative adaptation in the history of Native American religions. The Northeastern North American ancestors of contemporary neotradition-alists forged a complex religious alliance with French Catholics.[31] More generally, Joel Martin has found that Native American prophetic or transformative movements were creative in responding religiously to oppressive circumstances:

Cognizant that tribal tradition alone could not provide adequate orientation, participants in these movements considered multiple options and energetically borrowed ideas and forms of non-native neighbors (including Christians) and other Native American groups (often from a great distance). The Delawares of 1760, the Shawnees of 1805, the Creeks of 1813, and the Sioux of 1890 used a wide range of cultural resources. From Europeans, they appropriated Christian ideas about the sacred book and the savior. From other Native American groups, they borrowed purification practices. Of course, as they innovated, they took pains to insure that the new religious forms meshed well with tra-ditional indigenous forms. Among the Delawares and Shawnees, the Christian ascent to heaven was correlated with the shaman's sky journey. The Sioux Ghost Dance clearly resembled the old Sun Dance.[32]

Many of the features of the these transformative movements parallel those of neotraditionalism.[33]

Neotraditionalism among Micmac, Maliseet, Passamaquoddy, and Penobscot peoples is at the very least a religious response to the experi-ence of social injustice rooted in colonialism. The appropriation of a montage of images from the approving use of the "Indian" stereotype is at the very least an attempt to take some measure of control over one of the most oppressive tools the hegemonic culture has—the power to image Native Americans in ways that will meet that culture's needs of the moment. More often than not those needs have been overwhelmed by the singular need to justify the conquest of the lands and bodies of Native Americans. Neotraditionalism among Micmacs, Maliseets, Passamaquoddies, and Penobscots is only the most recent religious evidence that the minds and spirits of these Native Americans remain active, creative, and free.

With a shove in the right direction, this discussion of the social construction of cultural forms directs us back to the central character in the story I have been telling—Charles Godfrey Leland. It also leads back to the cultural form that has arrested our attention here—the academic study of Native American religions.

When Charles G. Leland penned "Of Glooskap's Birth . . . "—his version of the Kluskap-Malsum story that opens *The Algonquin Legends of New England*—he could not have any awareness that he was telling a story of Place in a conversational milieu dominated by the "Indian" stereotype, let alone that he was engaged in "the social construction of cultural forms." Yet we have seen that his carelessness about his sources and his deliberate additions to and alterations of the Kluskap-Malsum story lead to that interpretation. He attempted with his *Algonquin Legends* to meet the needs of a country still damaged by the Civil War. Drawing on his intellectual roots he identified the nation's primary need—to become spiritually connected with the physical landscape its inhabitants occupied. He knew from the German Romantics that this sense of Place had to be established by tapping the mystical secrets of the people closest to the land. For the German Romantics this meant attending to the songs and fairy tales of the *Volk;* for Leland this meant attending to what he saw as the epic stories of the "Indians." Some of those stories, Leland was sure, showed the influence of Norse mythology and contributed greatly to the Aryan-like quality of the "epic." "Of Glooskap's Birth . . . " was one such story. It was Leland's fervent hope that his presentation of Algonkian stories would capture the imagination of the adolescent nation, giving it the impetus to claim these stories as its own and thereby call Place into being. This would have the effect (although of course not by itself) of transforming the United States into a "valid historic community" like the mature nations of Europe Leland so admired.

It was not to be. Leland's larger story (although not "Kluskap and

Malsum") has been forgotten. Instead, a competing idea of self-definition—one that looked West rather than East, one that was conflictory rather than mystical, one that made disparaging rather than approving use of the "Indian" stereotype—the Frontier Thesis of Frederick Jackson Turner caught the collective imagination of the United States. For over fifty years the people of the United States defined themselves in ways consistent with Turner's story. As the twentieth century wanes, there is continuing evidence that this perennially pubescent nation is still casting about for an enemy in a world devoid of frontiers to conquer and defend.

Such reflections on larger cultural constructions are really a distraction from the matter at hand. Charles G. Leland's treatment of Native American religions is not anomalous in the history of the study of those religions. Rather it resonates with studies done in the intervening one hundred years. True, the story itself has changed in work done for both general and scholarly audiences. But the stories of the hegemonic culture still call Place into being. For those of us who identify with that culture, the stories we tell are still geopious, still about creating a Place for ourselves in the landscape.

It is hard to imagine how it could be otherwise. Scholars of religion, like people everywhere, need to experience their Place. We all need to feel "the religious experience of autochthony; the feeling . . . of belonging to a place."[34] Geopiety is not new. It resounds in this passage from Isocrates from over two millennia ago:

> We did not become dwellers in this land by driving others out of it, nor by finding uninhabited, nor by coming together here a motley horde composed of many races; but we are of a lineage so noble and so pure that throughout our history we have continued in possession of the very land which gave us birth, since we are sprung from its very soil and are able to address our city by the very names which we apply to our nearest kin; for we alone of all the Hellenes have the right to call our city at once nurse and fatherland and mother.[35]

We students of religions, like people everywhere, will tell stories that meet our religious needs, including the need to be connected to the physical landscape in which we find ourselves. We are drawn, naturally enough, to the stories that intersect our own. We hope, clandestinely, that at the intersection of these stories, if they are stories of the land, we will find our Place.

Vine Deloria, Jr., in *God Is Red,* tells us not to get our hopes up. He points to a "profound difference" between the people I have here called Native Americans and those who are not-Native. According to Deloria, a Native American is "indigenous" and thus has a "deep emotional sense of knowing that he or she belongs" to the land, while a not-Native has "a deep psychological burden of establishing his or her right to the land." While he admits that "it is significant that many non-Indians have discerned this need to become indigenous and have taken an active role in protecting the environment," he is pessimistic about not-Natives ever assuaging that "strange feeling of alienation which the intruder experiences."[36]

Not surprisingly North Americans have not let neotraditional voices like Deloria, Jr.'s—here sounding very much like Leland's a hundred years earlier—deter them from their quest for Place. The idea is powerful. This is why the hegemonic popular culture engages so wholeheartedly in the imitation of the "Indians," "characteristically" so close to nature as to be indistinguishable from it. This is how Daniel Francis in *The Imaginary Indian* puts it:

> There has also been a strong impulse among Whites . . . to transform themselves into Indians. Grey Owl simply acted out the fantasy. Each time they respond to a sales pitch which features an Indian image, each time they chant an Indian slogan from their box seats, each time they dress up in feathers for a costume party or take pride in the unveiling of yet another totem pole as a symbol of the country, non-Native Canadians are trying in a way to become indigenous people themselves and to resolve their lingering sense of not belonging where they need to belong. By appropriating elements of Native culture, non-Natives have tried to establish a relationship with the country that pre-dates their arrival and validates their occupation of the land.[37]

Notice that Francis understands that what I call not-Native Place-needs function in a national (Canadian) context. He also contends that not-Natives want to "become indigenous people." On these two points I disagree with his otherwise fine analysis. I am arguing that the context for the "Indian," while once national, is now global. Furthermore, I am convinced that not-Natives are trying to become, not Native Americans, but "Indians." It is not a matter of "appropriating elements of Native culture." The disparaging and approving uses of the "Indian" stereotype have existed virtually since European immigrants made contact with Native Americans. The central characteristics of that stereotype have been constant for five hundred years. The "Indian" contemporary imitators want to become has no more to do with the real lives of Native Americans than it did five hundred, three hundred, or thirty years ago.

Nonetheless, many of us who identify with hegemonic culture hanker to incarnate the image we have created, not to do harm or to offend, but out of geopiety. We, like people everywhere, have a religious need to forge a connection between ourselves and the land on which we find ourselves. This "land" has become the whole earth. The well-meaning imitators in our midst—Boy Scouts, "Indian" hobbyists, Bear Tribe members—serve both as extreme cases of geopious place-obsession, and as a signal that the almost unbridgeable gulf between *Them* and *Us* can be mediated. I am embarrassed by these Wannabees because they broadcast too garishly, too graphically, too clearly the Place-needs I feel too.

Our task as students of Native American religions, it seems to me, is not to excise our person and our needs from our work, but rather to come to know, acknowledge, and honor those needs. Most important, we must determine if, by meeting our needs through our scholarship, we are harming others. In the case of the use of the "Indian" stereotype I have argued that this is precisely what we have done.

The solution to the harmfulness of our scholarship on Native American religions is not to cease feeling the need for Place or even to squelch our appreciation of stories of Place. It is rather to try to identify our use of the stereotype of the "Indian" wherever is occurs, to assess how the stereotype is useful to us, then return to the study of Native American religions without it. It follows from what I have said that I am wary of studies that generalize about Native American religions. We are too inexperienced in our work to get along without the crutch of the generic "Indian," unless, of course, the focus of our inquiry is neotraditionalism or some other "pan-Indian" religious phenomenon. In my judgment, the academic study of Native American religions will, for the next while, have to content itself with careful and tentative studies of the religious traditions of specific Native American peoples. When careful inquiries into the histories of specific Native American religions are well under way—inquiries suspicious of textual evidence and attentive to oral traditions and performative evidence—only then will we have the luxury of more general studies. Only when, for example, more of the religious histories of the Micmac, Maliseet, Passamaquoddy, and Penobscot peoples are fully engaged with care and suspicion, can we begin to speak with authority of the religious traditions of the Algonkian-speaking people of the Northeast.

I have stressed in this part of this concluding chapter the points of similarity between what contemporary neotraditionalists and scholars have done by way of "reworking older indigenous ideas and combining them with diverse elements from multiple external sources." The process of meaning-making in both is doubtless similar. There is an important difference. Neotraditionalists are most often clear that their ends are spiritual or religious and that their sources are appropriate to those ends. Thus, besides what Abenaki and Micmac neotraditionalists read, they rely on prayer and other ceremonial contact with their ancestors and with spirit helpers to inform their meaning-making. We scholars usually present ourselves as being about something quite different. Whatever else scholars admit to be doing, they do not normally include constructing a sense of belonging to the land for their audience and themselves.

It is tempting to argue that we scholars simply need to clean up our act, that we need to expunge those vile religious needs from our scholarly work. Excise all tinges of geopiety, and solve our problems of autochthony on our own time. Get back to the good old days when the academic study of religion was one thing and theology the rest. Perhaps; but I doubt it. Rereading the seminal texts from those good old days, I am struck not by their clean lines and crisp interior, but by how like Charles Godfrey Leland our scholarly foreparents were. I am led to another conclusion: if our cloak of objectivity in the study of Native American religions has caused such harm, perhaps it is time to admit our sidelong glances at these religious traditions have always been rooted in religious needs. Perhaps it is time to explore—overtly and honestly—*those* needs while we deepen our stereotypeless understanding of the religious traditions of Native American peoples.

Appendix

Three Versions of the Kluskap-Malsum Story

T hese three versions of the Kluskap-Malsum story are arranged to illustrate how Charles Leland worked with the stories his consultants passed on to him. The story running in the left-most column is the one Edward Jack claims to have taken down as Gabe Acquin was speaking. Jack's handwriting in the letter recounting the story seems unusually messy—his letters are ill-formed and hurried, making it difficult to make out some words; he uses almost no punctuation. This gives credence to his claim that he recorded it as Acquin spoke it, as does his ingenuous character, a quality which comes through in his writing and that written about him.[1] Certainly he wants to give Leland the impression he is taking the story down as it was told to him.

In the middle column is the version of the story that Leland places late in his first chapter of *Algonquin Legends*. Although sharing the main points with the story that Jack reports Acquin told him, Leland's version shows both the deftness and heaviness of his editorial hand. The final version in the third column is the one featured in *Algonquin Legends* and in first part of this book. As I noted in the third chapter, Leland had four sources for this story; only one—the Gabe Acquin story—appears here.

1. Gabe Acquin's version, as it appears in Edward Jack's letter to Charles G. Leland, dated March 18, 1884:

Jack's letters to Leland can be found among the manuscripts of the *Charles Godfrey Leland Papers*, Pennell-Whistler Collection of the Papers of Joseph and Elizabeth Robins Pennell and James A. Whistler. Washington, D.C.: Library of Congress, container 373.

Glooscap & his brother were twins they talked to one and other before they were born, the youngest said to the oldest they must be born right away, they must get out into the world, the oldest said we must wait he could not stop him the other however he must get into the world. So he went out of his mothers side, this killed the mother, they agreed to go then after this;

2. Charles G. Leland's treatment of Jack's rendering of Acquin's story:

The Tale of Glooskap as told by another Indian. Showing how the Toad and Porcupine lost their Noses. from *Algonquin Legends.*

(Micmac)

In the old time. Far before men knew themselves, in the light before the sun, Glooskap and his brother were as yet unborn; they waited for the day to appear. Then they talked together, and the youngest said, "Why should I wait? I will go into the world and begin my life at once." Then the elder said, "not so, for this were a great evil." But the younger gave no heed to any wisdom: in his wickedness he broke through his mother's side, he rent the wall; his beginning of life was his mother's death.

3. Charles G. Leland's treatment of *Of Glooskap's Birth, and of his Brother Malsum the Wolf.* From *Algonquin Legends,* quoted in chapter 3:

Now the great lord Glooskap, who was worshiped in after-days by all the Wabanaki, or children of the light, was a twin with a brother. As he was good, this brother, whose name was Malsumsis, or Wolf the younger, was bad. Before they were born, the babes consulted how they had best enter the world. And Glooskap said, "I will be born as others are." But the evil Malsumsis thought himself too great to be brought forth in such a manner, and declared that he would burst through his mother's side. And as they planned it so it came to pass. Glooskap as first came quietly to light, while Malsumsis kept his word, killing his mother.

The two grew up together, and one day the younger, who knew that both had charmed lives, asked the elder what would kill him, Glooskap. Now each had his own secret as to this, and Glooskap, remembering how wantonly Malsumsis had slain their mother, thought it would be misplaced confidence to trust his life to one so fond of death, while it might prove to be well to know the bane of the other. So they agreed to exchange secrets, and Glooskap, to test his brother, told him that the only way in which he himself could be slain was by the stroke of an owl's feather, though this was not true. And Malsumsis said, "I can only die by a blow from a fern-root."

It came to pass in after-days that Kwah-beet-a-sis, the son of the Great Beaver, or, as others say, Miko the Squirrel, or else the evil which was in himself, tempted Malsumsis to kill

Now in after years, the younger brother would learn in what lay the secret of the elder's death. And Glooskap, being crafty, told the truth and yet lied; for his name was Liar, yet did he never lie for evil or aught to harm. So he told his brother that the blow of a ball or handful of the down of feathers, would take away his life; and this was true, for it would stun him, but it would not prevent his returning to life. Then Glooskap asked the younger for his own secret. And he, being determined to give the elder no time, answered truly and fearlessly, "I can only be slain by the stroke of a cat-tail or bulrush."

And then the younger, having gathered the down of bird's feathers, struck the elder, so that he fell dead, and therein he told the truth. But he soon recov-

after a few years the younger brother asked the older how to kill him (the older) he thought a long time, he did not tell him what would kill him dead but only what would stun him, he then told him that down (feathers) would kill him.

The older then asked the younger the same question, the younger told the truth as to what would kill him (the younger) that was cattails (bull rushes),

after that the very first oppor-

Glooskap; for in those days all men were wicked. So taking his bow he shot Ko-ko-khas the Owl, and with one of his feathers he struck Glooskap while sleeping. Then he awoke in anger, yet craftily said that it was not by an owl's feather, but by a blow from a pine-root, that his life would end.

Then the false man led his brother another day far into the forest to hunt, and, while he again slept, smote him on the head with a pine-root. But Glooskap arose unharmed, drove Malsumsis away into the woods, sat down by the brookside, and thinking over all that had happened, said, "Nothing but a flowering rush can kill me." But the Beaver, who was hidden among the reeds, heard this, and hastening to Malsumsis told him the secret of his brother's life. For this Malsumsis promised to bestow on Beaver whatever he should ask; but when the latter wished for wings like a pigeon, the warrior laughed, and scornfully said, "Get thee hence; thou with a

ered, and in that was his deceit. Howbeit it was well for the world and well for him that he then gathered bulrushes and smote his younger brother, so that he died. But the plant never grew that could harm the Master, wherefore he is alive to this day.

tunity the younger brother had he got some down, and struck his older brother with it knocking him down. After a little while the elder brother came to, he then looked about him for some cattails and the first opportunity he had he struck his younger brother with a cattail killing him dead the younger brother was dangerous and that was why he killed him.

tail like a file, what need hast thou of wings?"

Then the Beaver was angry, and went forth to the camp of Glooskap, to whom he told what he had done. Therefore Glooskap arose in sorrow and in anger, took a fern-root, sought Malsumsis in the deep, dark forest, and smote him so that he fell down dead. And Glooskap sang a song over him and lamented.

The Beaver and the Owl and the Squirrel, for what they did and as they did it, all come again into these stories; but Malsumsis, being dead, was turned into the Shick-shoe mountains in the Gaspé penisula.

Who was his mother? The female Turtle was his mother.

The Master was the Lord of Men and Beasts. Beasts and Men, one as the other, he ruled them all. Great was his army, his tribe was All. In it the Great Golden Eagle was a chief; he married a female Caribou. The Turtle was Glooskap's uncle; he married a daughter of the Golden Eagle and Caribou. Of all these things there are many and long tradi-

The older brother is living yet their mother was a female turtle Glooscap got up an army of animals of which the great golden Eagle was a chief, the golden Eagle married a caribou, Glooscaps uncle the turtle was commander in Chief.

tions. Our people tell them in the winter by the fire: the old people know them; the young forget them and the wisdom which is in them.

When the Turtle married the Master bade him make a feast, and wished that the banquet should be a mighty one. To do this he gave him great power. He bade him go down to a point of rocks by the sea, where many whales were always to be found. He bade him bring one; he gave him power to do so, but he set a mark, or an appointed space, and bade him not go an inch beyond it. So the Turtle went down to the sea; he caught a great whale, he bore it to camp; it seemed to him easy to do this. But like all men there was in him vain curiosity; the falsehood of disobedience was in him, and to try the Master he went beyond the mark; and as he did this he lost his magic strength; he became as a man; even as a common mortal his nerves weakened, and he fell, crushed flat beneath the weight of the great fish.

The Turtle married one of the daughters of the Golden Eagle and the Caribou,

after the wedding Glooscap told his uncle that he must make a feast Glooscap had given the turtle power to do anything he chose he asked him what to do so Glooscap told his uncle the turtle to go down to a long point running out into the sea about which there were always plenty of whales and for him to get one and shoulder it, when the turtle brought back the whale Glooscap told him he must not go one inch beyond a place which he pointed out to him, When the turtle brought the whale up he thought that he would go a foot or so beyond the mark.

When he did the whale crushed him down, the rest of the animals rushed to Glooscap and told him what had happened, he said never mind cut up the whale and the turtle will be all right in the end, they then cut up the whale, When the turtle made his appearance stretching out his leg and saying how tired I am I have overslept my self, the animals were all afraid of Glooscap, he was a spirit.

At last the Turtle got so big in his own opinion that he thought that he would make away with Glooscap, he got up a council of the animals, and tried to find out how he could destroy him

Glooscap knowing what they were about turned himself into an old squaw, he got into the council house, just inside of this there were two old squaws one of them was a toad the other has a porcupine in the shape of squaws. When

Then men ran to Glooskap, saying that Turtle was dead. But the Master answered, "Cut up the Whale; he who is now dead will revive." So they cut it up; (and when the feast was ready) Turtle came in yawning, and stretching out his leg he cried, "How tired I am! Truly, I must have overslept myself." Now from this time all men greatly feared Glooskap, for they saw he was a spirit.

It came to pass that the Turtle waxed mighty in his own conceit, and thought that he could take Glooskap's place and reign in his stead. So he held a council of all the animals to find out how he could be slain. The Lord of Men and Beasts laughed at this. Little did he care for them!

And knowing all that was in their hearts, he put on the shape of an old squaw and went into the council-house. And he sat down by two witches: one was the Porcupine, the other the Toad; as women they sat there. Of them the Master asked humbly how they expected to kill him. And the Toad answered

Glooscap got in he seated himself beside them and begin asking questions he wanted to find out how they intended to destroy him.

The old toad being questioned first answered him very savagely and said Why do you want to know? Glooscap said he did not mean any harm, so just touched her nose and went over to the other one and asked her the same question she said the same thing and he did the same as he had did to the other, then he went out, after he had gone out the two old squaws looked at each other; each asking the other where is your nose gone to for their noses were both gone that is the way the toad and the porcupine lost their noses, and have none to this day—

Glooscap had two dogs one was the Loon (po-queem) and the Wolf (mol-som), Glooscap sent all the animals away from him in their natural shapes as they are now, formerly they were when they were Glooscap's army in the shape of men.

savagely, "What is that to thee, and what hast thou to do with this thing?" "Truly," he replied, "I meant no harm," and saying this he softly touched the tips of their noses, and rising went his way. But the two witches, looking one at the other, saw presently that their noses were both gone, and they screamed aloud in terror, but their faces were none the less flat. And so it came that the Toad and the Porcupine both lost their noses and have none to this day.

Glooskap had two dogs. One was the Loon (Kwemoo), the other the Wolf (Malsum). Of old all animals were as men; the Master gave them the shapes which they now bear. But the Wolf and the Loon loved Glooskap so greatly that since he left them they howl and wail. He who hears their cries over the still sound and lonely lake, by the streams where no dwellers are, or afar at night in the forests and hollows, hears them sorrowing for the Master.

The Loon and the Wolf were so fond of Glooscap that they are still lamenting for him.

I give it to you just as it came from his own lips as he sat in front of the fire in my room this evening smoking his tobacco mixed with willow bark, he has any quantity of Indian lore. (container 373)

I am indebted for this legend to Mr. Edward Jack, of Fredericton, N.B. "I give it to you," he writes, "just as it came from an Indian's lips, as he sat before the fire in my room this evening, smoking his tobacco mixed with willow bark. He has an endless store of Indian lore." (*Legends*, 106–09)

For this chapter and parts of others I am indebted to the narrative of a Micmac Indian, taken down by Mr. Edward Jock; also to another version in the Rand MS. (*Legends*, 15–17)

Notes

Chapter 1

1. A record of this electronic discussion, "On Teaching Native American Religions," has been compiled by Ron Grimes (rgrimes@mach1.wlu.ca). Grimes's compilation is from three electronic discussion groups: Religion, a discussion group on religious studies (religion@harvarda.harvard.edu); Anthro-L, whose focus is anthropology (listserv@ubvm.cc.buffalo.edu); and Natchat, a discussion group on native issues (natchat@tamvm1.bitnet).

In my discussion of the conversation, the numbering in brackets refers to Grimes's numbering scheme in "On Teaching Native American Religions."

Ron Grimes has himself reflected on this conversation in "Teaching Native American Religions" in *Spotlight on Teaching*.

2. Russ Hunt, personal communication, June 25, 1993.

3. Paul Simon, "Train in the Distance," *Hearts and Bones*, 1983.

4. In this criticism of Gill, Deloria follows Ward Churchill, ("A Little Matter of Genocide: Sam Gill's Mother Earth, Colonialism and the Expropriation of Indigenous Spiritual Tradition in Academia," in Fantasies, 202–03). I find Deloria's criticism of Gill's work on this point curious. My reading of *Mother Earth: An American Story* has it that it is precisely the scholarly insistence on a generic *deity*, Mother Earth, that was one of the tip-offs that the scholar's story—the one Gill is exposing—is being told. Thus, it is after citing two pages of significant "female figures" from the story and ritual of a number of Native American religious traditions, that Gill says, "My knowledge of many tribal traditions was and remains superficial, but for all the tribes I knew, I could think of none that considered the earth as a major goddess" (*Mother Earth*, 5). Reading this statement in context, then, I take it that Gill means what he says: there are a great number of important female Powers in a large number of Native American nations; but there is no *goddess* who is the Mother Earth scholars have "recorded." It is not, therefore, a surprise to find Gill bemoaning the fact that scholars have spent much more time and energy arguing about

whether or not Mother Earth precedes the development of agriculture: "This has been a hotly contested issue, gaining much more attention, sadly, than the careful examination of the multitude of female figures in North America" (*Mother Earth,* 113). That some Native Americans use goddess language neither invalidates their experience of Mother Earth nor reflects on the variety of other experiences of female Power in various Native American religions.

As to whether or not the concept "gods" is useful in understanding Native American religions, I would hazard it is not in Micmac, Maliseet, Passamaquoddy, or Penobscot religions prior to and immediately following contact with Europeans in the sixteenth century. Following that time, it becomes useful enough to keep, with caution.

5. Grimes's posting of the collected responses to his initial query generated a discussion on the Religion List about the distinction between public and private e-mailings and how they should be treated.

6. "So here I am blowing a whistle of some sort" (*On Teaching* . . . , 1.1). I also knew of the volatility of this discussion from Ward Churchill's reviews of Gill's *Mother Earth* ("A Little Matter of Genocide"; "Sam Gill's *Mother Earth"*; *Fantasies*), and from Gill's response ("The Power of Story"). I knew from James A. Clifton's defensive stance: "Whether I or the contributors to this book may be fairly characterized as 'anti-Indian' or 'racist,' our readers may see for themselves. Such smears, I think, are no more than part of the sanctions protecting an othodox politicoacademic position. Lively, provocative, well-informed, thoroughly disciplined scholars willing to serve as intellectual dissidents would be a more accurate assessment of my colleagues, I believe." ("Introduction: Memoir, Exegesis," in *The Invented Indian,* 23); and from Churchill's review of it ("The New Racism: A Critique of James A. Clifton's *The Invented Indian"* in *Fantasies,* 163–84]. Ward Churchill's assessment of Clifton and his colleagues is different: "If there is any utility at all to the release of *The Invented Indian,* it lies in the open self-identification of a whole cast of North American neo-Nazis. Now we know beyond any reasonable doubt where they stand. All those involved should be accorded the degree of disgust they have so richly earned" (181).

I knew, as well, from corridor gossip and conference discussions. Since this online discussion, I have experienced the nature and intensity of the conversation more fully with the publication of Jordan Paper's rejoinder to my review of his Offering Smoke: The Sacred Pipe and Native American Religion in Studies in Religion.

7. Daniel Francis, *The Imaginary Indian,* 9.

8. Berkhofer, xvii; Francis, in *The Imaginary Indian* updates Berhofer, setting his ideas in a Canadian context.

9. See Marianna Torgovnick (*Gone Primitive*, 20) and Robert Gordon (*The Bushman Myth*, 4–8) for other points of view on naming.

10. Dippie noticed this oscillating quality as well, 6.

11. It should be obvious that the appellation, "North American culture," is a convenient but imprecise generalization. One only need consider that when I use it here, it rarely includes the cultures of that North American country, Mexico.

12. Wilcomb E. Washburn, "Introduction," 2–4.

13. Linda P. Rouse and Jeffery R. Hanson refer to stereotypes as "overgeneralized beliefs that attribute certain characteristics to a particular group" (1). Their conclusions, while not startling, are telling:

> While most [university] students agreed that American Indians are culturally diverse, their average scores were low on specific knowledge of American Indian history and culture. Also, they tended to share some traditional cultural stereotypes that reflect a pervasive generic "folk ethnography" promulgated by the media and recreation and leisure industry. Correspondingly, for all three samples, the highest ranked source of information about American Indians was TV/movies. (15)

14. The disparate "European" comes to mind, as do the Indians of India where fourteen different major languages means that for a large part of the country the common language is most people's second language. Moreover that second language is everywhere in the South and many places in the North, English, a language of conquest.

15. The names recorded by the Europeans in the region include Etchemin, Amalecites, Souriquois, Tarrantine, and Almouchiquois. The latter, according to Whitehead, is a derogatory Micmac word meaning "dog-people" (*The Old Man Told Us*, 23). Similarly "Maliseet" derives most probably from the Micmac meaning "lazy speaker" (Erickson, 135). For further information on synonymy see the *Handbook of North American Indians*, v.15, 135, 146.

16. Walker, Conkling and Buesing, "A Chronological Account of the Wabanaki Confederacy," use "Wabanaki" to refer to the Micmac, Maliseet, Passamaquoddy, and Penobscot despite this citation of Penobscot historian, Joseph Nicolar, and anthropologists, Frank Speck, and Wilson and Ruth Wallis: "Nicolar [1893:238] also states that the Micmacs were separate and distinct from the Wabanaki, by which he meant the Penobscots, Passamaquoddies, and Maliseets. This assertion is confirmed by Micmac statements reported by both Speck ("Eastern Algonkian Wabanaki Confederacy") and the Wallises (51). See also Snow, 137.

17. The appellation—"Algonkian-speaking people of Northeastern North America"—also includes Innu (Montagnais, Naskapi) and Cree people. In Maine, where most Passamaquoddies and Penobscots currently live, I have heard the term "The Four Tribes" used, but I have not heard it frequently in New Brunswick and would be surprised to hear it in Nova Scotia, where "Mi'kmaq" is replacing Micmac in common usage.

18. In his *The Embattled Northeast* Kenneth Morrison writes,

> Abenaki refers to the various tribes that inhabited the river basins of New Hampshire, Maine, and New Brunswick. From west to east these peoples were the Pennacook, Saco, Androscoggin, Kennebec, Wawenock, Penobscot, Passamaquoddy, and Maliseet. When appropriate, . . . I have drawn on the experience of the other Algonkian (especially the Micmac . . .) to illustrate the forces that affected the Abenaki as a whole. (5)

Morrison could have added "Vermont" to his list of current states and province.

19. I have compiled the reserves from the Canadian government's 1990 *Schedule of Indian Bands, Reserves and Settlements Including—Membership and Population Location and Area in Hectares.* I have added to the total of Maliseet reserves the community in St. Basile, N.B. That it is missing from the *Schedule* gives weight to my sense that these figures should be taken as approximate at best. Census figures are even more suspect.

20. I later found that Gordon Day's curiosity was also picqued by this story: "There is reason to question whether this episode really belongs in Wabanaki mythology, and the student who eventually attempts to settle the question should consider the following points" (Gordon M. Day, "The Western Abenaki Transformer," 78). I am grateful to Andrea Bear Nicholas for this reference.

21. Ralph Smith, *Charles Godfrey Leland: The American Years, 1824–1869*, 1961; Varesano, *Charles Godfrey Leland: The Eclectic Folklorist*, 1979.

22. Ralph Smith, 38–39, 78–87.

23. Leland, *Memoirs*, 86, cited in Ralph Smith, 81.

24. Pennell, I, 46. Smith contradicts this, saying that "the study of theology remained his goal in June, 1847, because he inquired about completing his studies in Germany and entering his duties immediately in America" (121–22). His source is a letter from Leland to his brother, quoted at length in Pennell's biography. I think Smith misreads Leland here. The letter, dated June 3, 1847, is from Munich and begins, "Today is a *festa,* a regular lump of laziness." He goes on to describe how "Roman Catholic Munich had a real good holiday after its

own way." His description is brief, beginning a long chatty conversation of beer drinking, the Volkstheater, a manuscript whose publication Leland wants his brother to orchestrate, how cheaply he can live, and, again, beer drinking. Without transition, he moves to his increasing prowess at waltzing, some Dürer engravings he wants his brother to sell, and then back to beer drinking. This last narrative of his encounter with German beer sets the context for his remarks on studying theology, so I'll quote it at length:

> Talking of drinking, the only time I ever had beer get into my head, since I have been in Munich, was one evening when I held with five *professors* a grand beer celebration in the Hildebrand in honour of the arrival of an old *professor of theology* from Tübingen, and, upon my honour, my very good friend the *professor of mathematics* was pretty considerable drunk! This was an extraordinary occasion, understand now. I hope I can make you feel the truth. When a man drinks in America he's a rowdy—he belongs to the caste of the dissipated; in quiet, slow, solemn Deutschland, everybody drinks beer, nobody gets drunk. . . . The prof. of theology drank like a Christian. Ah, you can't understand how *very* different Germany is from our *Amerique!* (Pennell, 123–24)

It is at this point in his letter home that Leland, without a word of transition, writes of theology:

> I must say a word about studying. I propose theology, and I want to know if a man can study in Germany and then enter upon his duties immediately in America? My money-spending days I hope are over, and if you were only here I'd show you a few things. I don't believe a man can lead a happier life than I can here.

I have found no other references to his "theological studies." Immediately following this discussion of "studying theology" Leland tells a humorous tale of his time before the police commissionaire for neglecting to pay his residence fees. That Smith misses the humorous intent of Leland's line about studying theology is not surprising. Leland is writing to his brother who knows him well, thus he has the luxury of tempering his usually broad humor. Only the context of his words provides the incongruous gap at the heart of his joke.

He has been describing what in Philadelphia of the mid-1800s must have seemed a wild and bohemian life. His confidante is his brother with whom he had for a while toured Europe. He proposes the most outlandish course of study he can. This question about "taking up his duties" as a minister immediately on returning to America is meant to sound incongruous and thus preposterous.

From his letters, it *is* clear he is reading German philosophers; his favorites are Fichte and Schelling (Pennell, 33–35; Leland, *Memoirs*, 16–17, 77–78, also cited in Smith, 41; while Leland was at Princeton: Smith, 73).

25. Ralph Smith, 159–65.

26. Ralph Smith, 296–97, citing Leland in *Knickerbocker*, LVIII (Sept. 1861), 265–67 and (Nov. 1861), 377–83.

27. Leland, *The Union Pacific Railway*, 68–69.

28. Leland, *The Algonquin Legends of New England; or, Myths and Folk Lore of the Micmac, Passamaquoddy, and Penobscot Tribes*, Boston: Houghton, Mifflin and Co., 1884. The book was republished in 1968 (Detroit: Singing Tree Press) and in 1992 (NY: Dover Publications). This latter was titled simply *Algonquin Legends*, but was "an unabridged republication of the work originally published as *The Algonquin Legends of New England; or, Myths and Folk Lore of the Micmac, Passamaquoddy, and Penobscot Tribes*."

29. Leland, *Memoirs*, 147–55; Pennell, I, 233.

30. The Canadian Broadcasting Corporation announced on March 30, 1993 that the number of people in Canada who claimed Native ancestry had risen from 2.8% in 1986 to 3.7% in 1991. The Statistics Canada figures on which this report was certainly based are, in 1991, 1,002,675 people (of 27,296,859) "reported Aboriginal origins," while, in 1986, 711,725 people (of 25,309,331) made a similar claim. The government document suggests: "Public attention on Aboriginal issues may have increased reporting of Aboriginal origins" (Statistics Canada, i).

31. Powers, "The Indian Hobbyist Movement," 557.

32. Daniel Francis, 145–58. The quoted phrase is from 157.

33. Powers, "The Indian Hobbyist Movement," 557–61; Conrad, 455–71 (especially 455–56, 464); Taylor, 562–69. An exception to this generalization about the lack of political awareness are the Indianklubben of Sweden (Taylor, 567).

34. Brand, 570–72.

35. *The Bear Tribe Directory*, 8–10. I do not know why some names have shudder quotes around them and others do not.

36. Kehoe, 199–201; Albanese, 156–63.

37. *Bear Tribe Directory*, 4–5.

38. *Bear Tribe Directory*, 5.

39. *Bear Tribe Directory*, 1, 8.

40. Kehoe, 196; Daniel Francis, 110.

41. Daniel Francis, 123–31.

42. Daniel Francis, 136, 131–41, the quotation is on 133.

43. Doxtator, 31.

44. Rose, nt 26, p. 420; the "Cults and Culture Vultures" section is 414–15; the information on Sun Bear's participation is on 414. Rose is, of course, not alone in her condemnation of Sun Bear. See, for example, Vine Deloria, Jr., *God Is Red*, 40–41.
Ron Grimes has written thoughtfully about what he calls "parashamanism" in *Ritual Criticism*, 109–44.

45. Rose, 405. See also Deloria, Jr., *God Is Red*, 281.

46. I find unintentional irony in Rose's last words in this article:

> Perhaps we can treaty now. Perhaps we can regain a balance that once was here, but now seems lost. If poets and artists are the prophets and expressers of history—as thinkers of both the American Indian and Euro-derived traditions have suggested in different ways—then it may well be that our task is simply to take back our heritage from the whiteshamans, shake it clean and bring it home. . . . Perhaps then we can at last clasp hands, not as people on this land, but of this land, and go forward together. As Seattle, leader of the Suquamish people, once put it, "Perhaps we will be brothers after all. . . . We shall see." (418)

We don't know exactly what Seattle said in 1854, but he didn't say this. English professor Ted Perry wrote it as part of a screenplay in the early 1970s. The two earlier probably less fictional versions of the speech Perry embellished for his own work (which he did not intend to pass off as Seattle's) do not include this line (Kaiser). Perry's Seattle speech is a fine example of the approving use of the "Indian" stereotype. Rose's use of it is indicative of how powerful and pervasive that stereotype is.

47. Jonathan Z. Smith, *Map*, 309.

Chapter 2

1. Arthur Hamilton Gordon, 56–58. Rand, *Legends*, 239–40. Leland, *The Algonquin Legends*, 15–17. Leland and Prince, 43–49. Ives, 16–18.

2. The Big Cove and Red Bank communities are in New Brunswick. Michael William Francis's mural of Malsum's stone face appears briefly in a video entitled *Jipuktewik Sipu, River of Fire: Nuji-atukwet Mi'kmaqa'j, Micmac Storyteller* (Michael William Francis, Site 10, Box 6, Big Cove, NB. E0A 2L0). A color photograph of George Paul's painting, "Glooscap turns his evil brother to

stone," graces the cover of John Joe Sark's *Micmac Legends of Prince Edward Island*, Illustrations by Michael Francis and George Paul (Lennox Island, PEI: Lennox Island Band Council, 1988). It appears again on p. 13. The Indian Island School video, called Indian Island School 1992 Animations, is available from Indian Island School c/o Michael E. Vermette, 15 Rolling Thunder Drive, Old Town, ME, USA 04468.

3. "Malsum" is the Passamaquoddy/Maliseet word for "wolf." The "sis" in Malsumsis is a diminutive, thus "Little Wolf," or as we shall see, "Wolf, the Younger."

4. Sweetser, iii. For a more contemporary use of Micmac stories about Kluskap see "Glooscap Country," a 1962 Canadian National Film Board film showing the scenic delights of the Cape Blomidon area of Nova Scotia. Much of what it says about Kluskap is inaccurate. For example, the film notes that Kluskap's voice was the wind; that his anger the thunder; that "his pleasure was the sunlight that warmed the sea and land;" and that "When Kluskap slept, each flower and leaf stood still." All of this comes from the minds of the film's makers.

5. Spence, 141–44.

6. While he does not claim personal experience of Native Americans, Spence enthuses about those "men who possess first-hand knowledge of Indian life and languages, many of whom have faced great privations and hardships in order to collect the material they have published." He goes on to assert that "the direct, unembellished verbiage of these volumes conceals many a life-story which for quiet, unassuming bravery and contempt for danger will match anything in the records of research and human endurance" (Preface, vi–vii).

7. Spence, 362–74.

8. "Publisher's Note," *Wonder Tales*, iv, London: The Bodley Head Ltd., 1974.

9. Macmillan, *Wonder Tales*, 62–64.

10. Peterson in Macmillan, vii.

11. Macmillan, *Wonder Tales*, xii.

12. Macmillan, *Wonder Tales*, xi.

13. Macmillan, *Micmacs*, 9.

14. Sapir to R.W. Brock, September 9, 1914, *Edward Sapir's Correspondence*. Barbeau's work, cited by Sapir, is also in manuscript form in the archives of the Canadian Museum of Civilization.

15. The original 1918 edition was printed in London and New York by John Lane, then reprinted in 1920, 1928, and 1938. In 1955 Oxford University Press issued two of Macmillan's collections, *Canadian Wonder Tales* and *Canadian Fairy Tales*, as one book, *Glooskap's Country and Other Indian Tales*. This volume was reprinted in 1956 and 1962. The 1974 edition of *Canadian Wonder Tales* cited earlier is this two-collection compilation: "being the two collections . . . collected from oral sources by Cyrus Macmillan."

Macmillan apparently did not lack gall. He nagged Sapir for the last $180 and then, in April 1915, wrote to ask about the possibility of further work "in any of the fields" (Macmillan to E. Sapir, April 3, 1915, *Edward Sapir's Correspondence*).

16. Hill, *Glooscap*, 7, 190.

17. Hill, *More Glooscap*. The illustration, by John Hamberger, is on p. 6; the story is pages 1–9. In Hill's *Glooscap and His Magic* the story is told on pp. 11–25.

18. Kay Hill, "Glooscap and His People," in *Childcraft, The How and Why Library; Vol. 3: Stories and Power*. Chicago: World Book, Inc. 1985, 143–51. The illustration is on pp. 148–49. Ms. Hill showed me seven other anthologies which contained her stories, most often "The Rabbit Makes a Match." At least one was in hard- and softbound editions.

19. Kay Hill, *Glooscap and His Magic: Legends of the Wabanaki Indians*, London: Victor Gollancz Ltd. 1964. The Japanese edition is in kanji script. The English publication information read, "Glooscap and His Magic—Legends of the Wabanaki Indians by Kay Hill @1963 . . . Japanese translation rights arranged through Kaigai Hyoron Sha, Tokyo. Japanese edition published by Akane Shobo Co., Ltd. Tokyo. Translated by Yasuka Kakegawa."

20. Kay Hill, interview, November 14, 1992.

21. Hill, *Glooscap*, 7–9. The introduction has "romantic dreams," but Ms. Hill was emphatic that this was a typographical error. "Romantic dramas" is what she had written (Kay Hill, interview, November 14, 1992).

22. Hill, *Glooscap*, 8, 9.

23. After he provides the People with the means to hunt and the ways to make use of the products of the hunt (as he does in Abenaki and Micmac stories), Hill has Kluskap say, "'Now you have power over even the largest wild creatures,' . . . 'Yet I charge you to use this power gently. If you take more game than you need for food and clothing, or kill for the pleasure of killing, then you will be visited by a pitiless giant named Famine, and when he comes among men, they suffer hunger and die.'" As far as I can tell, Hill's sources do not include this idea.

24. This from Ms. Hill's working notes (dating from about 1960) is a reminder to herself: "Remember, to make stories lusty, gay, robust, full of sly humour; not sentimental, solemn or virtuous. Glooscap [is] full of tricks and laughter, as well as morality" (Kay Hill, interview, November 14, 1992).

25. Michael E. Vermette, Art Director, Old Town School, interview, July 9, 1992. Vermette was enthusiastic about the animation-making process. In his opinion, it helped the students remember the stories much better. The new technology facilitates the easier retelling in animation. They could shoot a sequence and then play it back seconds later, viewing it on a small monitor. This allowed them to decide very quickly whether to keep something or not. Vermette said the children became very engaged with the project, an assessment borne out by the quality of the video itself.

26. Michael E. Vermette, interview, July 9, 1992. *The Wabanakis of Maine and the Maritimes*, C-2–C-6. The blurb for the book says, "This Resource Book was planned by a Native Curriculum Committee which included Native People from Maine and the Maritime Provinces of Canada." The committee members are listed on p. v and include 12 people, 11 of whom self-identify as Micmac, Maliseet, Passamaquoddy, or Penobscot.

27. *The Wabanakis of Maine and the Maritimes*, p. C-2.

28. The note (*The Wabanakis of Maine and the Maritimes*, C-2, nt. 2.) identifying the source adds, "A few sentences were omitted and a few words changed from Kay Hill's original." The word changes from Hill's version include spellings of names (Koluskap, Malsom, Mus), and the phrase for the way the story ends. And these: "chose someone" for "chose a servant"; "small creatures" for "small hairy creatures"; "made the people" for "made men"; "any elderly woman" for "any elderly female." These I take to be small changes in editing. The first paragraph of Hill's story is omitted, probably because it is setting up the whole "Kluskap cycle," most of which is not included in the resource book. I found no other sentences omitted. The rest of the story is virtually as Hill wrote it in the early 1960s.

29. John Martin, "Gloosgap the Great Chief, n.d." In his report Martin writes:

> So it was that the Great Spirit sent these two supernatural beings on earth to do his work. The Great Spirit had his reason for sending two supernatural beings, one of which was good and the other was bad. In doing so he made sure that we would have a will. We would have the power to choose right from wrong. (2)

Photocopies of this report and a second, more wide-reaching document, "General Outline of the Series," were generously provided by Diane Bertolino of Via le monde.

30. John Martin, interview, January 6, 1994; Silas Rand's *Legends of the Micmacs* is most familiar as a blue, cloth-bound book to me, too.

31. The *Indian Legends: Glooscap* video is available in Canada from Via le monde, 326, rue St-Paul ouest, Montréal, Québec, Canada. H2Y 2A3, (514) 285-1658; and in the United States from Films for the Humanities and Sciences, PO Box 2053, Princeton, NJ, 08543-2053, (800) 257–5126. The latter distributor lists its title as simply "Glooscap."

32. Campbell, *Historical Atlas,* illustration number 272, p. 187. The story, pp. 186–87. The illustration is almost certainly by Leland.

Chapter 3

1. Campbell, *Historical Atlas,* Endnotes, ix.

2. Campbell, *Historical Atlas,* Endnotes, ix. Of the fourteen Abenaki and Micmac stories Campbell retells, two-thirds are taken from Leland's collection. Hill, *Glooscap*, 7–8. Marion Robertson relies on Leland for her version of the Kluskap-Malsum story in *Red Earth: Tales of the Micmacs*, 62–63, 92.

3. That he valued his folklore studies above his more profitable endeavors is clear from his correspondence with his niece-biographer and others (Pennell, II, 246, 420). He wrote the humorous ditties as Hans Breitmann and became famous for them both in Europe and the United States. According to Ralph Carlisle Smith, "Though almost completely forgotten now, they were known to nearly every American in the late nineteenth century. To Leland's distress, he became Hans Breitmann" (257). Here's an example:

> Hans Breitmann gafe a Barty,
>   Dey had biano-blaying;
> I felled in lofe mit a Merican frau,
>   Her name vas Madilda Yane.
> She hat haar as prown ash a pretzel,
>   Her eys vas himmel-plue,
> Und ven dey looket indo mine,
>   Dey shplit mine heart in two.

Hans Breitmann's Ballads, 29–30, cited in Smith, 247.

4. Ralph Smith indicates that prior to going to England in 1869 Leland was an economic failure, often looking for work (164–65, 193, 263–65, 308, 365). When he returned to the United States in 1879 it was primarily to promote industrial arts training as part of general education. His summer respite from this work brought him in touch with the Passamaquoddy people.

5. Leland, *Algonquin Legends,* 15–17, 106–110; Leland and Prince, 43–49.

6. Parkhill, "'Of Glooscap's Birth,'" 4–8.

7. Leland, *Algonquin Legends,* iii; Pennell, II, 233–35.

8. Leland's correspondence is archived with the rest of his papers in containers 365–73, the Pennell-Whistler Collection of the Papers of Joseph and Elizabeth Robins Pennell and James A. Whistler, Library of Congress; hereafter referred to by container number. While I have examined only one side of Leland's correspondence—the letters he kept—the pattern of correspondence is not difficult to piece together. For one thing Leland wrote very frequently during the latter part of 1883 and the first half of 1884. For another his correspondents either responded promptly acknowledging his letters or were apologetic when they didn't, always acknowledging the date of their last correspondence.

9. Leland, "Passamaquoddy," 668.

10. Lester, *History on Birchbark,* figure 14, 10.

11. Leland, "Passamaquoddy," 677.

12. A letter from a Hartford correspondent says, "In yours of last August [1883], you asked a question that I couldn't then—or now—answer,—as to a book from which stories about 'Glooscap' were copied into the Guide Book for Canada." The letter is dated January 5, 1884, and is from J. F. Trumbully or Frumbully; container 373.

13. January 13, 1884; container 373.

14. Sweetser. The first edition of *The Maritime Provinces* was published in 1875; the newest edition Leland could have seen was published in 1883. All the editions to that date featured the Kluskap twin story on p. 41.

15. Container 373.

16. Rand made the offer in a December 21, 1883 letter: "I will also send you the volume of Legends if you desire it. My object in gathering them was to make them known, and thus contribute to the course of *Science, Ethnology etc.* I might not find it possible to attend to it myself." Rand's precarious financial situation informed the details of this offer: "If you would like to borrow it to make any use of it you choose, say so and I will send it on. It weighs five pounds. You must give me a receipt when you get it and promise to return it. And perhaps I must require the *postage* to be *prepaid*—or would this be to make myself too little? (I am already small enough.)" (Emphases are Rand's.) In the version of the manuscript published after Rand's death there are eighty-seven stories. A brief discussion of Rand's collection and its value is found in Ruth Holmes Whitehead, *Stories From the Six Worlds: Micmac Legends,* Halifax:

Nimbus Publishing, 1988, 218–19. The most recent biography of Rand is Dorothy Lovesey's *To Be a Pilgrim.*

17. Just how big was the manuscript which Rand sent Leland is a bit uncertain. In "The Edda among the Algonquin Indians" Leland says there were "eighty-five Micmac tales, forming a folio volume of one thousand pages" (223). In *Algonquin Legends* he says there were "eighty-four Micmac tales, making in all nine hundred folio pages" (7). In Rand's published volume, *Legends of the Micmac,* there are eighty-seven stories.

18. Rand, *Legends,* 339.

19. Both letters are in container 373. After he received the longer works that Lewy Mitchell collected and translated for him, Leland bound a number of them together into a series of booklets. This makes it difficult to date the stories in these booklets. In one there is a long story called, "The Origin of Gloscop By Lewy Sock Toma" (container 373). I mention this here because this story is not about Kluskap's origin, but it does feature Kluskap fighting his brothers, much like the Solis fragment. It is not wild speculation, I think, to propose that in response to Leland's increasing pressure, Mitchell gave one of his consultants the title and outline of a story along with pressure of his own to fill in the rest. Perhaps he did the job himself. The result was "The Origin of Gloscop By Lewy Sock Toma." However it came to be, I find "The Origin of Gloscop . . ." unusual in the Leland's unpublished story collection. I get the same feeling reading this story as I used to get occasionally reading the essay answer on students' exams. It is clear the students knew what they were talking about, but they were answering another question, not the one asked. Often only the first and last sentences made any reference to the exam question. So it is with this story—the title is right as is the theme of Kluskap's difficulty with his brothers. The rest is very interesting, but not related to the first part of the title, which I speculate was supplied by Leland in a letter to Mitchell prior to the latter's story-collecting forays, 19.

20. The "Edward Jock" of Leland's acknowledgment is clearly Edward Jack of Fredericton. While the typesetter read "Jock" for "Jack," and the editor missed it, the error is clear from the original manuscript in container 372, as well as from Leland's "The Edda Among the Algonquin Indians," 223. See also *Algonquin Legends,* vii, ix, and 109.

21. Container 373.

22. In his paraphrase Leland retains only two of Thomas's (or Rand's) phrases—"how they had best enter the world" and "burst through this mother's side" (Rand, *Legends,* 339; Leland, *Algonquin Legends,* 16). The rest is Leland's wording.

23. Leland retains more of the original Sweetser paraphrasing than he does the Thomas/Rand phrasing; he seems to favor this sort of rococo language (Sweetser, 41; *Algonquin Legends* 17).

24. See Sam D. Gill's brief discussion of explanatory elements as a symbolic way of validating a story's power to define the world in *Native American Religions*, 48.

25. Michelson, "Micmac Tales." Michelson's first footnote indicates that the stories were published with the permission of the Bureau of American Ethnology. *The Twenty-eighth Annual Report of the Bureau of American Ethnology, 1906–07* (Washington, D.C.: Government Printing Office, 1912) includes Michelson's "Preliminary Report on the Linguistic Classification of Algonquian Tribes" in which he indicates he visited the Micmacs of Restigouche "in the season of 1910" (225). Ruth Whitehead suggests (personal communication, December 1992) that the etymology of Amkotpigtu's name might well be *mkobit-pigtu*. The first is archaic form of *kopit*, "beaver"; the second a rendering of *piktu*, "fart." That a Micmac or Maliseet storyteller might name its story's villain "Beaver Fart" or "The-one-who-farts-like-a beaver" strikes me as delightful and possible.

26. Nicholas, 3–4.

27. Rand, *Diary*, 1–18. Although Rand includes the story in his collection, *Legends of the Micmacs*, his diary indicates that "friend Gabriel" (18) was from the St. Mary's community in Fredericton. In late August 1870 Rand recorded five stories from Gabriel Thomas, four having to do with Maliseet/Mohawk hostilities and the Kluskap twin story. I am grateful to Thomas S. Abler for this reference.

Curiously, on the one hand, the New Brunswick censuses for the years 1871, 1881, and 1891 do not know of Gabriel Thomas anywhere in the province, let alone at St. Mary's. Gabriel Acquin, on the other hand, is recorded in all the censuses. While it is possible that Rand confused Gabriel Acquin and Gabriel Thomas, it is more likely that Rand's "friend Gabriel" was a literate Passamaquoddy, Gabriel Tomah, from the Peter Dana Point community of Maine. He would have been twenty-eight years old in 1870. See Willard Walker, "Gabriel Tomah's Journal."

28. While it does not have the same detail, the Thomas version recorded in Rand's diary has "Tortoise" as Kluskap's uncle (*Diary*, 6). Rand leaves this detail out of his published version.

29. In his diary Rand says, "I have finished reading Leland's 'Legends of the Algonkins,' and he has certainly made an interesting book of it. But when he expotates on Indian Philology, or Etymology, he slips. He has made

sad havoc of my Micmac, Hood is Flood, and words are separated, and put together, and letters are confused and confounded in all manners of ways," (*Diary*, October 16, 1884, 48). I am grateful to Thomas S. Abler for this reference.

30. I am indebted to Andrea Bear Nicholas for this information.

31. April 16, 1884, container 373: "My indian's name is 'Gabe' he is a Melicite." Jack is not entirely clear on this. In an earlier letter (December 17, 1883) he says, "There is a very intelligent Wabanaki residing opposite Fredericton he is generally known as 'Gabe.'" Jack may mean "Abenaki" which would be accurate. Or he may mean what he says. While the Wabanaki Confederacy included Micmac and Maliseet nations among others, Leland's mistake in this text remains. Nowhere in *Algonquin Legends* does Leland refer to the Maliseet people, yet in his "The Edda Among the Algonquin Indians," apparently published a few months earlier, he refers to "legends and folk-lore, Malisete and Micmac," (223).

32. Gordon, 56–57. Clote Scarp is an (admittedly unusual) variation on the spelling of Kluskap.

33. Gordon, p. 56.

34. Container 372, *Algonquin Legends* handwritten Ms., 49–50. I speculate that Leland made these changes after studying Jack's March 18 recording of Gabe Acquin's twin story at the end of which Kluskap's "dogs," loon and wolf are spelled out in Maliseet, "po-queem" and "molsom" (container 373).

35. Gordon, 53.

36. Gordon, 56. The example of Campbell Hardy might well make us suspicious of this fireside setting in which Gordon tells his story. In a lecture delivered around 1910, Hardy's text indicates he said the following:

> The Night in question was our last night in the woods, and the blaze of our campfire attracted the Owls . . . who came into the neighbouring trees and hooted, answering one another for a considerable time.
> We glance at the Indians enquiringly—
> "Why are the Owls so noisy tonight, Glode"?
> "Owls say `I'm sorry. Oh, I'm sorry.'"
> "Why Glode?"
> "Glooscap gone" was the answer.
> "And weren't you saying something about Glooskcap and the Beaver, the other day, Glode?"
> "Ah mooch," yes, sure, and then he begins a story, which, if you were a good listener and appear interested, will tell you much about Glooskcap and his twin-brother, Malsumsis, the Wolf, who was bent on

his destruction from his birth, and how Kohbeet, the Beaver, from his place of concealment in the lakeside sedges overheard the secret of the charmed life of Glooskcap, and how it could be destroyed. ("In Evangeline's Land," 9)

I am grateful to Ruth Holmes Whitehead for this reference. The story is straight out of Leland—"Reward? You with a tail like a file? Get thee hence!" Reminders to be tentative with the results of our inquiry are everywhere.

37. Gordon, 9.

38. Susan Squires, 14. Susan Squires's father, Samuel Dayton, ran a general story less than a half mile from the St. Mary's Maliseet community from 1853 to 1893. Mrs. Squires sometimes helped out in the store and in her late teens kept the books for a number of years. Her daily journey from home to school took her past the Maliseet "Camp" twice a day.

39. Nicholas, 4.

40. Susan Squires, 15.

41. In an introduction to her story, "Gabe Acquin and the Prince of Wales," Carole Spray notes that the late Dr. Peter Paul from the Woodstock Maliseet community once showed her "a collection of calling cards and invitations received by Gabe from the British nobility" (*Will O' The Wisp*, 27).

42. Austin Squires, 51.

43. Susan Squires, 16.

44. See Chapman, 18–19, for evidence of Gordon's aristocratic disdain for provincial colonials. Gordon, in 1883 between assignments as governor of New Zealand and governor of Ceylon, (Chapman, 264–65) was in London during most of the time Acquin was there. They almost certainly became reacquainted.

45. Douglas Hyde, who was a professor at the University of New Brunswick before he was the first president of Ireland, noted that Acquin "had learned his European manners from the English officers who used to be quartered in Fredericton, and he used to put his hands behind his coat tail and stand with his back to the fire just like one of them!"

It is also worth noting that Acquin called himself a Roman Catholic, as would, almost certainly, his ancestors of the previous two hundred years.

46. The Peter Solis fragment calls Kluskap's brother "wicked" in Jack's translation, but that brother is almost certainly Amkotpigtu who abuses the vulnerable members of his family while Kluskap is absent.

Chapter 4

1. Leland, *The Union Pacific Railway*, 27. Many examples of Leland's disparaging use of the "Indian" stereotype can be found here and in "Indian Impudence."

2. See for example his reference to his publisher, John Forney, as being prodded "to the very highest pitch of his fighting `Injun'" (*Memoirs*, 139).

3. *Memoirs*, 183–84, 200.

4. Varesano notes Leland's fascination with the frontiersman, James P. Beckwourth, and suggests it stems from his understanding of him as an "Indian white man," that is one who had a "gift" to "go among the wildest tribes safely," and in whom the "Indian" would confide (Beckwourth, 17, quoted in Varesano, 155).

5. *Memoirs*, 153–54. Leland's self-understanding in this matter of the "Indian" within him was well known. His belief that he had "Indian blood in his veins" appears in one of the notices of his death ("A Wandering Scholar," *The Outlook*, March 28, 1903, 708–10).

6. Leland, *Algonquin Legends*, 119–20.

7. Pennell, II, 234–35.

8. In the preface to *Kulóskap the Master* Leland gives an assessment of his skill in Passamaquoddy: "I regret that, though I had certainly acquired some knowledge of 'Indian,' it was, as a Passamaquoddy friend one day amiably observed, 'onl baby Injun now, grow bigger some day like Mi'kumwess s'posin' you want to,'" (Leland and Prince, 12).

9. Quoted in Pennell, II, 248–49.

10. Letters of Oct. 16, 1882, and April 30, 1883; container 373.

11. August 6, 1883; container 373.

12. March 30, 1883.

13. December 31, 1883, container 373.

14. February 29, 1884, container 372.

15. May 3, 1884, container 373. Mitchell consistently spells Passamaquoddy with an extra "m."

16. Edward Jack shared some of Leland's story-gathering methods. In a letter to Leland, Jack explained his arrangement with Acquin—"I usually give

him $1 for an evenings talk" (April 16, 1884, container 373). To put this dollar into some context, here is what anthropologist, Dr. Vincent Erickson, and consultant, Dr. Peter Paul say: "A birchbark canoe brought its maker between $15 and $18 in 1890, and this went a long way to keep a family going through the winter. That year, men loading the wood boats in Fredericton earned $1.50 a day" ("Indian-White Partnership," 13). This kind of exchange is, of course, not unknown in anthropological fieldwork, a fact that invests the usual term for consultants, "informants," with a more malignant connotation.

17. March 12, 1884, container 373, 17.

18. Varesano, in her Ph.D. dissertation on Leland, surmises that Leland limited the size of the stories because he only wanted the outline which he could then work up into a good tale (215–17). She also suggests that Leland's flat rate fee structure might have contributed to stories being shortened or lengthened to fit the 8-page format (216–17).

19. Leland, *Algonquin Legends*, 106–09; Like the Gabriel Thomas version, Acquin's has Kluskap telling his unnamed brother the means of his death only once, although the means are reversed. (Curiously, in a later version, which Jack attributed to Acquin and published in the *Journal of American Folk-Lore*, the means of death agree.) Although Leland usually worked hard to obliterate the distinctive characteristics of different versions, I suspect he found in this case it was worth trading consistency for the support Acquin's story gave his "Of Glooskap's Birth. . . ."

20. Container 373.

21. See the Appendix for a fuller comparison of these texts.

22. "The Algonquin Legends of New England," a review in *The Athenaeum*, January 31, 1885, 6–7; a review in *The Spectator*, "July 25, 1885, 976–78. The latter is an otherwise positive review. A review in *Science* was less discriminating: "The whole work shows the hand of an experienced writer, who is at once practised in the literary art, and alive to the requirements of science."

23. *Algonquin Legends*, 94, 253, nt. 1, 320. For an example of conflating many story versions into one, see pp. 31–35 where he labels a story Micmac, but weaves in Passamaquoddy material, retaining his own voice throughout. In a note appended to a story entitled "The Lazy Indian" in *Algonquin Indian Stories Collected and Written by Lewis Mitchell a Passamaquoddy Indian for Charles G. Leland* (ms., container 372) Leland wrote that the story "forms a part of other [Thunder] legends. It will be a very difficult matter to bring them into harmony."

24. Leland was concerned to make the best story possible out of the data at hand. By "best story" I mean one that read well by late-nineteenth-century

standards. That Leland was considered a raconteur par excellence is without question. Best known in his time for the popular Breitmann Ballads, even his *Memoirs* in two volumes elicited enthusiastic reviews that quoted some of the more "vivacious" passages at length. Walter Lewin, review in *The Academy*, January 27, 1894, 75–76; E.G.J., review in *The Dial*, January 1, 1894, 9–11; and a review in *Book News*, January 1884 (xii, 137: 196–97) which says, "all of this, we must say, is told in a manner so highly engaging as to constitute sufficient excuse for its incessant and flagrant egotism."

There is evidence that Leland was less than honest academically in some other areas of his work as well. Varesano discovered he provided his Romany consultant with story outlines and even confessed to making up "Gypsy" stories himself (89–90). She also suggests Leland may have been "perpetrating a scholarly error of a most despised kind" when he includes in his *Arcadia* a "Gospel of Witches" he claims he recently secured in Italy from his chief consultant who had in fact left for the United States two years earlier (349). For the possible perpetuation of this "error" into the New Age, see *Voices from the Circle*, 28, 78–79.

Finally, there is Leland's remarkable admission about his participation in the exhibition that was part of the Second International Folklore Congress held in London in 1891.

> We all contributed folk-lore articles to our Exhibition. I had only to pick out of one tray in one trunk to get 31 articles, which filled two large glass cases. As Belle [his wife] says, she can't turn over a shirt without having a fetish roll out. And I could n't distinguish between those of my own and those of others. For I am so used to picking up stones with holes in them, and driftwood, and tying red rags round chicken-bones for luck etc., etc., that I consider my own just as powerful as anybody's. (Pennell, II, 352)

Thus the "full galaxy of stars from The Folk-Lore Society" who had planned the Congress, scholars like Lang, Tylor, Frazer, Lubbock, Gaster, and Rhys who examined the items in the exhibit may well have been admiring some of the creative work of Charles G. Leland (Dorson, *The British Folklorists*, 301; cited in Varesano, 402).

    25. Joan Lester explores Tomah Joseph's art throughout *History on Birchbark* and in chapter three of *We're Still Here: Art of Indian New England*, 15–26.

I deduce that the *Century Illustrated* article is the earlier composition based on internal evidence. Toward the end of the article Leland writes,

> I succeeded in awaking in two very intelligent men, one a trader and the other a hunter, a conviction that these stories and songs, which are so rapidly perishing, should be preserved; and they have promised me that

during their travels this winter in the far North they will gather from the old people and write down all that they can collect relative to the olden time. (676)

If Leland is accurate here, the "this winter" would be that of 1882, or perhaps, but less likely, that of 1883. It would appear Leland did not have the Rand manuscript when he wrote this article.

26. That Leland's artifice was not apparent to some reviewers is clear from this in *The Literary World*: "There are about eighty tales in all, with several queer, aboriginal illustrations," (371).

27. Quoted in Pennell, II, 241. A month later he wrote Prince, "I must draw a title page, I don't know whether I can do it now. And a cover and back? Depends on publisher . . ." (245, the ellipsis is Pennell's). By the end of March 1902, he seems to have decided to draw all the pictures for the book himself: "I am very glad that you like my pictures. I could have done *better* had I taken more time, but a kind of devil possessed me to 'hurry, hurry' with all the copy I sent you" (249, emphasis is Leland's). It would seem "honesty" was not of primary importance in either book.

28. Varesano titled her Ph.D. dissertation, *Charles Godfrey Leland: the Eclectic Folklorist.*

29. For a more contemporary look at *Algonquin Legends* see Penobscot scholar, Eunice Baumann Nelson's review in *The Wabanaki: An Annotated Bibliography*, pp. 34–35. She says in part, "the unfortunate ethnocentrism shown in the writer's analyses, interpretations, and evaluations should be recognized for what they are." Neal Salisbury calls *Algonquin Legends* "The most complete . . . collection of tales from northern New England . . . which constitutes a major source for the cultural historian, despite Leland's misguided attempts to find Norse and other external connections for the myths," (*The Indians of New England: A Critical Bibliography*, 55). Folklorist Richard Dorson offers this general assessment: "Texts were not sacred to him; his own stories were at least as good as the ones he collected, and he inserted himself unashamedly into his books. . . . It was Hans Breitmann's fate to be caught between the horns of his belletristic and his scientific impulses," ("American Folklorists in Britain," 202).

30. Powell, 162. Leland's lack of precision seems to have been taken for granted in his time. For his fans it did not detract from the man or his work. See for example the anonymous obituary, one paragraph of which begins, "Although never an accurate scholar . . . ," ("A Wandering Scholar," *The Outlook*, March 28, 1903, 708).

31. Gill, *Mother Earth*, 122.

32. Like all scholars, perhaps more than most—Leland loved discovering things first, being the best. He is never shy about reminding his readers that discovering hitherto unknown "Algonquin" stories among the Roman Catholic Penobscot, Passamaquoddy, and Micmac is a remarkable feat (*Algonquin Legends*, iii–iv, 13). And certainly if people pay attention to his versions of the stories, they pay attention to him. Without denying the immense capacity of Leland's ego, I argue that his writing is story-driven far more than ego-driven. Arguing that Leland did what he did simply for the attention it would bring is belied, as I will show, by the internal logic of his story.

33. A rough draft of a college essay, incomplete, untitled, and undated demonstrates Leland's early fascination with the Norse and their stories. One of a group of similar essays, all dated either 1843 or 1844, found in container 368 of the *Charles Godfrey Leland Papers*, it says in part,

> Our poets have drawn with an unsparing [?] hand from the rich stories of Northern mythology and tradition. Even the bard of Avon—that mighty master of the magic pen stands indebted to a Northern myth for the groundwork of his choicest production.

A diary entry dated June 6, 1844, asks "Can there be doubt that Northmen discovered this continent before Columbus?" Quoted in Ralph Smith, 76. See also Ralph Smith, 404.

34. Leland, "The Mythology, Legends," 70.

35. Leland, "The Mythology, Legends," 74; "The Edda," 224–25; *Algonquin Legends*, 2.

36. *Algonquin Legends*, 132, 133. See also pp. 22–23 where Leland says, "Great stress is laid in the Glooskap legend upon the fact that the last great day of battle with Malsum the Wolf, and the frost-giants, stone-giants, and other powers of evil, shall be announced by an earthquake. . . . Word for word, ash-tree, giantesses, the supreme god fighting with a wolf, and falling hills, are given in the Indian myth. This is not the Christian Day of Judgement, but the Norse."

37. *Algonquin Legends*, 290.

38. *Algonquin Legends*, 9.

39. *Algonquin Legends*, 11–12; see also 3, 335.

40. *Algonquin Legends*, 12.

41. "The Edda," 222.

42. "The Mythology, Legends," 90.

43. *Algonquin Legends*, 5–6.

44. The most stunning evidence that Leland was pushing his consultants for signs of Norse influence is a long questionnaire he sent to Lewy Mitchell. Leland received Mitchell's responses to the twenty-four questions (example: "Question 10th is gluscapp to fight with the wolf at the last day of judgement. I will try to find it out.") in April of 1884, a month after he received the Acquin/Jack version of the story. Eventually he added this comment: "These questions were mostly suggested by the Edda and partly me for the purpose of ascertaining whether Algonkin legends correspond with the Norse." A complete copy of Mitchell's "Answers for your Questions" can be found in Appendix I of Varesano's dissertation, 412–18. From the evidence of the questionnaire, Varesano concludes, "He seemed to intuit a theory, that of diffusion of the Edda to the Algonquins, and let this preconceived notion direct his inquiries," 223.

45. Leland and Prince, 33. Prince is bold enough to call one of Leland's correspondences into question, 36; and to admit that questions of the origins of the Abenaki and Micmac peoples are unknown and unknowable, 39–40.

46. Bailey, 157.

47. While he does not suspect the story of Kluskap and Malsum, Bailey accuses Leland of interpolating material in two other places (163, 173); hints that he added material in another (177); and seems to suggest that he shaped at least one story to fit his thesis. Bailey compares two versions of a Kluskap story involving whale hunting, one in Rand, one in Leland. Apparently Leland, who had the Rand Ms, left out from his version some parts of the story.

> The killing of the wife, the birth of the second son after death, the murder of the father, the origin of flies from the old man's powdered bones, the origin of the markings on the birch-bark, the origin of the bullfrog's crumpled back, and a few succeeding incidents, all of which occur in Rand's version, but not in Leland's, are lacking in the Edda. (162)

48. Bailey, 160.

49. Thompson, 134.

50. Thompson, nt. 1, 133.

51. Thompson, 139. Perhaps the most intriguing aspect of Thompson's study is that he undertook it at all. That the prestigious folklorist would devote so much energy to dismantling Leland's thesis speaks to *Algonquin Legends'* endurance. Thompson admits *The Algonquin Legends of New England* was

"rather famous in its day" and notes its continued recognition as "one of the major sources for the tales and legends of these northeastern tribes" (133–34).

52. Segal, 4, 94–95.

53. Campbell, *Historical Atlas,* 186. Campbell is not entirely alone. E. Tappan Adney, writing in the 1940s from his own experience in New Brunswick, followed Leland, both in his Kluskap-Malsum story and his theory about Norse influence. His notes indicate that he struggled to reconcile what he learned from Leland with his own considerable experience with Maliseet people. Adney never published the results of this study. "Miscellaneous Linguistic Notes," Phillips Library, Peabody Museum, Salem, MA., Box 39.

54. Segal, 139–40.

55. William M. Clements suggests "Leland's focus on Scandinavian analogues to Algonquin folklore reflects the enthusiasm for things Nordic which characterized some aspects of late nineteenth-century American culture" (130).

56. *Algonquin Legends,* 309. See also 337.

57. *Algonquin Legends,* 322.

58. *Algonquin Legends,* 2. Two years later he has honed his thinking on this matter even further. In his conclusion to his London lecture Leland suggests that to understand the Edda, scholars could do no better than study "Algonquin" legends:

> I have spoken of the great number of these Legends. Two years ago I published a collection of them of four hundred pages. . . . And I do most sincerely believe that, since the Edda was discovered, nothing has been found which would cast so much light as these collections. And when we reflect on the immense amount of labour which has been bestowed on explaining and clearing up this wonderful work, which may be called the real Gospel of manliness, and the exponent of the grand Northern spirit of which England inherited the fullest share, it may well be admitted that such work has not been in vain. ("Mythology, Legends," 91)

Chapter 5

1. Pennell, II, 19. In a May 4, 1884 letter Edward Jack writes, "It must be very pleasing to you to receive a notice from so prominent a writer as Max Muller" (container 372).

2. That conversation included Daniel Garrison Brinton, a fellow Philadelphian whose work Leland admired and whose friendship he sought. The outlines of this conversation my be found in Clements, 61–63. For a concise overview of the Aryan conversation and its relationship to racism, see Davies, 21–26.

3. Reither, 11.3.

4. Burke, 110–11. Quoted in Reither, 11.

5. Reither borrows "knowledgeable peers" from Bruffee, 642–46.

6. Schoolcraft dedicates the 1856 edition to Longfellow, p. 1. *Hiawatha* was popular from its publication in 1855, selling out the first run of 4,000 copies on the day it appeared (Pearce, xii).

7. *Algonquin Legends*, 4. It comes as no surprise that Leland was careless quoting Schoolcraft. There is an ellipsis in this quotation that he does not indicate, and, more important, he renders Schoolcraft's ending as "god" rather than "God." Here are Schoolcraft's words with the omission in italics:

> Where the analogies are so general, there is a constant liability to mistakes. Of these foreign analogies of myth lore, the least tangible, it is believed, is that which has been suggested with the Scandinavian mythology. That mythology is of so marked and peculiar a character, that it has not been distinctly traced out of the great circle of tribes of the Indo-Germanic family. Odin, and his terrific pantheon of war-gods and social deities, could only exist in the dreary latitudes of storms and fire, which produce a Heela and a Maelstrom. These latitudes have invariably produced nations, whose influence has been felt in an elevating power over the world; *and whose tracks have everywhere been marked by the highest evidences of inductive intellect, centralizing energy, and practical wisdom and forecast.* From such a source the Indian could have derived none of his vague symbolisms and mental idiosyncrasies, which have left him, as he is found to-day, without a government and without a God. (Schoolcraft, *The Myth of Hiawatha*, xvi)

8. Schoolcraft, "Our Indian Policy . . ." 171. Berkhofer points out that while explaining human behavior by reference to the physical environment is itself an ancient example of human meaning-making, its use in the conversation about Native Americans is "particularly characteristic of Enlightenment thought" (38–44).

9. Bieder, *Science,* 179; Hinsley, *Savages and Scientists,* 21–29.

10. Schoolcraft, *Personal Memoirs,* 343; cited in Bieder, *Science,* 160.

11. Bieder, *Science,* 188–89. The quotation from Schoolcraft is from *Historical and Statistical Information,* 5:87, 15, 44.

12. Bieder, *Science,* 170. The quotation from Schoolcraft is from *Personal Memoirs,* 678–79.

13. There was a political dimension to Schoolcraft's work as well. When he set out in 1847 to undertake a "national study of the Indian" it was not for an academic discourse community but for the War Department. The United States government policy of "removal," that is displacing Native Americans from their lands and moving them to land west of the Mississippi where they would be "safe" had failed: "Settlers were moving onto tribal lands faster than tribes could be removed. By the late 1840s and early 1850s it was apparent that the government's removal policy and the idea of a permanent Indian frontier was bankrupt" (Bieder, *Science,* 184). The Office of Indian Affairs, under the direction of the Secretary of War until 1849, commissioned the survey as a way to gather information on which to base future policies. The repressiveness of those policies is well known.

14. *Algonquin Legends,* 334–35.

15. *Algonquin Legends,* 334.

16. *Algonquin Legends,* 4. Leland may have been emboldened to confront Schoolcraft by Daniel G. Brinton who wrote in 1868, "The government work in the Indians . . . was unfortunate in its editor. It is a monument of American extravagance and superficiality. Mr. Schoolcraft was a man of deficient education and narrow prejudice, pompous in style, and inaccurate in statement" (*The Myths,* 41; quoted in Pearce, 129).

17. *Algonquin Legends,* 5.

18. *Algonquin Legends,* 2, 338; See also pp. 350–51, 78, 113, and 122, nt. 1. Leland has the temerity to suggest that some of the excessive language in the stories Schoolcraft collected are a result of the latter's "florid style" (96, nt. 2).

19. "The Edda," 232. Leland carries on a similar attack against David Cusick's Iroquois creation story. Leland contrasts the *"old* Algonquin" with the "hardly heathen cosmogony, which shows recent Bible influence throughout," noting that compared with the latter, "the Algonquin narrative reads like a song from the Edda," (*Algonquin Legends,* 24–26). It is more likely that Acquin borrowed details of his version from the Mohawk people. Following Speck, Gordon Day notes the story has an "Iroquois flavor." He suggests two points of contact: "a borrowing from the Hurons at Lorette, Quebec in the eighteenth or nineteenth century," and the Wabanaki Confederacy meetings prior to 1850 that included the Maliseets and the Mohawks at Kanawake, Québec ("Western

Abenaki Transformer," 78). More specifically, Nicholas notes that Acquin "may have been the Newell Gov'-leet who was Maliseet wampum keeper at the Wabanaki Confederacy meeting at Old Town, Maine, in 1838" (3).

In a paper from the same period ("Huron Folk-Lore," 1888) Horiatio Hale denigrates the Algonkian and exhalts the Iroquois much as Leland does (with the reverse conclusions). Apparently scholars of the time tended to engage in this kind of arrogant comparing of "their favorite" Native American cultures.

20. Joseph J. Moldenhauer, "Textual Introduction" to Thoreau, 369–70.

21. Thoreau, 172; quoted in *Algonquin Legends*, 65–68, nt. 1. Leland identifies this site as the mouth of Moose River. He gets this quotation right. The tiny disparity of two semicolons for commas could be the work of editors of either author.

22. Thoreau, 172. Compare Schoolcraft: "The Indians are prolix, and attached value to many minutiae in the relation which not only does not help forward the denouement, but is tedious and witless to the last degree" (*Personal Memoirs*, 635; cited in Bieder, *Science*, 170, nt. 53). On the basis of this assessment Schoolcraft decided simply to cut passages from the longer stories.

23. *Algonquin Legends*, 66.

24. Pearce, 242.

25. Pearce, 120.

26. Pearce, 124–25. The emphases are Pearce's. While Leland had little good to say about Schoolcraft, their use of questionnaires is similar.

27. Pearce, 127.

28. Pearce, 74, 169–70.

29. Pearce, 127.

30. Pearce, 146–150, 136. Sayre, following Pearce, says, "But the influence of savagism was not impaired by its inaccuracies. It was a persuasive, universal ideology and mythology, the basis of governmental policy, the material of popular novels and plays, and the assumption of respected historians and antiquarians (15). . . . Savagist prejudices were so strong that the truth was hard to accept" (16).

31. Kehoe, 194. Kehoe cites Homer's *Iliad* (c. 700 B.C.) and the *Europa* of Ephorus in the early fourth century B.C. Primitivism is not just a Western idea. In a "Supplementary Essay" to Lovejoy and Boas's classic study, P.-E. Dumont surveys the idea in the Hindu epics, the *Rāmāyaṇa* and *Mahābhārata*

("Primitivism in Indian Literature," 443–46). This places the idea as early as 400–200 B.C. The stereotyped "savage" roams in twentieth-century North India as well. While attending *Rāmlīlās* in Benares in 1984 I was struck by the portrayal of the nonliterate Niṣādas. The meeting of Rama and the Niṣādas was not a significant event in either the Sanskrit *Rāmāyaṇa* or the popular Hindi *Rāmacaritmānas*, by Tulsidās. Nonetheless their portrayal was often remarkable in this religiodramatic enactment of Rama's story. At the staid Ramnagar *Rāmlīlā* the single Niṣāda looked like a dapper Robin Hood. At another neighborhood, Lat Bhairav, he appeared as a down-at-the-heels king. At the *Rāmlīlā* of the neighborhood that featured the Durgā temple, the Niṣādas were four-strong, all dressed in white T-shirts, yellow (goddess) garlands hanging (improperly) down their backs, plant fronds stuck in their shorts every which way, with long hair, and erratic white face markings. The Niṣādas' performance was very popular. Their stage business consisted of making "offerings," from a green canvas bag, of different vegetables, one by one, each accompanied by a silly name and a little speech that included enough broad humor for the normally semi-attentive crowd to focus fully on the dramatic action. When they left, the Niṣāda "court" of three young men pushed and jostled their way out, while the chief, who heretofore had been undistinguished except by age, strode out purposely. Many of the characteristics underlying savagism and primitivism can be seen in this portrayal of the Niṣādas: they are rude, ritually inept (and thus religiously incompetent), close to nature, and so on.

32. Lovejoy and Boas, 11–12.

33. Lovejoy and Boas, 7. See also Clifton, 15–16.

34. Thoreau, 80–81.

35. The most thorough study of the "Indian" in both "good" and "bad" manifestations is Berkhofer's, *The White Man's Indian*. See also Dippie, *The Vanishing American* and Daniel Francis, *The Imaginary Indian*.

36. Sayre, 6, 63–69.

37. Sayre, 6. The more contemporary equivalent of "doomed to extinction" is "doomed to assimilation," although as we shall see, "extinction" has a following too. Dippie details the policies in the United States intended assimilation (139–96, 243–69).

38. Pearce, 254-55. In fairness to Sayre, Pearce emphasizes this "conflation of all Indians, tribes and subtribes, into one: *the* Indian" only in his 1987 "Postscript" to a new edition of *Savagism and Civilization*. He remarks that he thought this fact was "altogether implicit" in the earlier editions, 254.

39. Berkhofer, xv. See also 26.

40. Simard, 353. Alice Kehoe explores the "invention of an unbridgeable difference" in "Primal Gaia," 198.

41. On an earlier trip in 1846 Thoreau was not guided by Penobscots.

42. Thoreau, 6–7. It is worth noting that Thoreau had difficulty dealing with reports of "Indian" cruelty.

43. Sayre, 161.

44. *Correspondence of Henry David Thoreau,* 504; quoted in Sayre, 119.

45. Sayre, 119. For examples of Thoreau on Polis's accent see *The Maine Woods,* 165, 167, 168–69, 183, 184, etc.

46. *Algonquin Legends,* 13.

47. This timeless characteristic of the "Indian" stereotype has arguably been the most persistent, pervading even the work of anthropologists. Berkhofer states,

> In spite of all the changes in the anthropological profession's theoretical orientations and the increased accumulation of research on Native Americans during the first half of the twentieth century, anthropological monographs and texts continued mainly to describe Indian life in the timeless ethnographic present. Leading texts of the 1950s divided Native Americans into cultural areas and slighted the changes in lifestyle since aboriginal times, as if the only true Indian were a past one. To that extent, these books, so sophisticated in the new scientific approaches to Native Americans, still retained vestiges of the classic idea of the Indian. (67)

48. A fascinating example of this "peculiar logic" is Leland's "official biographer," Elizabeth Pennell who writes of the Passamaquoddy people:

> For, though the Indians of whom he was destined to see most have degenerated into commonplace house-dwellers during the winter, and are civilized to the point of sending representatives to the State Legislature, in the summer, when they pitch their tents under the pines along the coast of New England, they grow very Gypsy-like, while over them always is the mystery of their race and their legends." (II, 229)

"Degenerated into commonplace house-dwellers"? Although the phrase "pitch their tents under the pines along the coast of New England" gives the impression of "old-time Indians" living in wigwams, the less romantic truth is that Passamaquoddies like Tomah Joseph came to Campobello Island from nearby communities because their cash economy was dependent in part on tourism. According to Joan Lester writing in the mid-1980s, "Residents [of Campobello] still remember that during the summer [Joseph] set up a large tent in an open field, led the Indian dances, and sold his work to tourists" (*We're Still Here*, 17). Again, Pennell apparently cannot see this, for it would admit to change and challenge her image of authentic, timeless "Indians."

49. For instances of Leland's conviction that "the Indian" would soon be extinct, see *Algonquin Legends*, 3, 8; and Pennell, II, 420.

50. Leland was, of course, not alone in his sense that those things which belonged to the "Indian" which were useful or salvific needed to be immediately salvaged. The best study of this set of ideas in the United States is Brian W. Dippie's *The Vanishing American*; see especially 222–42.

51. *Algonquin Legends*, 338.

52. Gonzales, 62–65. Gonzales notes that "no [nineteenth-century] Micmac family was committed solely to one economic endeavor" (65). Thomas S. Abler, ("Micmacs and Gypsies") argues that this catalog of economic activities points to a time when Micmacs wandered in small family groups. Abler contends that Micmacs responded to a difficult economic situation by finding a peripatetic niche which by creatively exploiting they could survive the neglect and abuses of the hegemonic culture. Significantly, Abler notes that "writer after writer laments the failure of those Micmac they encountered to duplicate their image of the noble hunters of the past" (7). The wandering Micmacs of the nineteenth century were incongruous with the stereotype of the "Indian."

53. Nicholas, 3. Nicholas chastises Acquin for "abandoning traditional values of conservation" which "contributed also to the demise of the ancient Maliseet way of life" (4) Thoreau, 267.

54. Algonquin Legends, 338–39.

55. Leland was not the first to "internalize the relation between nature and [human beings] and to combine the wildness of [people] in other places with the wildness within all [people]." Berkhofer (80) also notes it was a "French tendency" popularized by Rousseau.

56. Kehoe, 207.

57. It hardly needs to be said that the disparaging use of the stereotype is always benighted and usually combined with the worst prejudice, racism, or both.

58. Pennell, II, 235: "Beautiful days they were [in the "Indian tents" at Campobello], so beautiful that I still regret having gone with Tomah, in his canoe, to the nearest Indian village, treeless, desolate, tragic, where I could see for myself what dreary days were to come when he and his people moved from under the pines."

59. Simard, 359.

60. Simard, 359. See also Day, "The Indian as an Ecological Factor."

61. Simard, 359.

62. Armin W. Geertz, writing about Frank Waters's *Book of the Hopi,* shares these concerns. "My quarrel is with the way native peoples, who have had little or no part in these issues, are used by proponents on both sides of the issues. The overly romanticized and nostalgic view of American Indians as noble savages, born with an environmentalist temperament, is just as harmful as the view propounded by industrialist tyrants laying pipelines on the lands of those same supposedly backward savages" ("Reflections on the Study of Hopi Mythology" in Vecsey ed. *Religion in Native North America,* 132–33). See also Stedman, 248–49.

63. Simard, 360–61.

64. Dorris, 101. I am indebted to Dr. Jennifer S. H. Brown for this reference.

65. *Isinamowin,* 17, 22.

66. Deloria, Jr., *God Is Red,* 32.

67. Rose, 413.

68. See Sayre notes, pp. 3 and 8. By 1988 Pearce is distressed by a "new primitivism, envisaging the Indian once more as noble savage" (255). I would claim that this primitivism is not "new"; the idea has always been with us.

69. For further examples see George; and Hanson and Rouse, 53. James Clifton sees the scholarly replacement of Ignoble Savage by Noble Savage as part of a larger "narrative structure" in which the supporting use of the "Indian" has won out ("Introduction," especially 19–22).

70. Kehoe, 207; Gill, *Native American Religions,* 6–10; Simard, 366–67; Berkhofer, 71.

71. Berkhofer, 31, 71. In different parts of *The White Man's Indian,* Berkhofer apparently contradicts himself. In fact, Hanson and Rouse conclude that their findings are "consistent with Berkhofer's thesis of a more favorable emergent stereotype paradigm" (57). They note that he identifies deficiency as an essential characteristic of the image of the "Indian" (36). This stereotype was struck a blow—this reading goes—by the cultural relativism of the Boasian school in the early twentieth century. I admit Berkhofer can be read this way; see for example, p. 119 where he argues,

> Beneath both the good and bad images used by explorer, settler, missionary, and policy maker alike lay the idea of Indian deficiency that assumed—even demanded—that Whites do something to or for Indians to raise them to European standards, whether for crass or idealistic motives.

Berkhofer has already stated that Boasian anthropology,

> By asserting that each culture could only be described and understood in terms of itself as a total entity and not in relation to other cultures or, worse, to aspects of others cultures ripped from context, these anthropologists pulled the scientific rug out from under the long-time deficiency image of the Indian. (66)

It's no wonder Hanson and Rouse read him as arguing for a progression from bad image to good image.

There are some problems, however. First, Berkhofer admits (p. 67, quoted in an earlier note) that the Boasians are bewitched by the timeless "Indian." Second, it is difficult to see the logic of deficiency in the approving use of the stereotype of the "Indian." Bequeathed from primitivism, this "Indian" stereotype was always a platform from which to criticize the society of the stereotype's user. It was therefore important that the noble savage was assessed as "more than" not "less than" the inhabitants of the criticized society. Finally, there is Berkhofer's own perplexity. How, if the disparaging use was dealt a death blow by the anthropologists of the early twentieth century, can it still be alive and well as Berkhofer writes in 1979?

> What the captivity narrative started the Western novel and movie continued to finish long past the actual events of conquest—as if the American conscience still needed to be reassured about the rightness of past actions and the resulting present times. That the basic conflict over land and lifestyles should be so indelibly engraved upon the White mind so long after the actual events took place would seem to suggest the destruction of Native American cultures and the expropriation of Native American lands still demand justification in White American eyes. (104)

In other places in *The White Man's Indian*, Berkhofer is clear about the persistence of the dual-image stereotype. I have already quoted some of them. Here is another:

> Even if new meaning is given the idea of the Indian, historians of the future will probably chronicle it as part of the recurrent effort of Whites to understand themselves, for the very attraction of the Indian to the White imagination rests upon the contrast that lies at the core of the idea. Thus the debate over "realism" will always be framed in terms of White values and needs, White ideologies and creative uses. (111)

In a more recent study, Rouse and Hanson, as I noted in chapter 1, make a distinction between cultural and personal stereotypes, concluding in part, "Most students . . . tended to share some traditional cultural stereotypes that reflect a pervasive generic 'folk ethnology' promulgated by the media and recreation and leisure industry. Correspondingly, for all three samples, the highest-ranked source of information about American Indians was TV/movies" ("American Indian Stereotyping, Resource Competition, and Status-based Prejudice," 15). I read the conclusions of both these studies, as well as that of Gibbons and Ponting, as supporting the hypothesis that contemporary North Americans can and do use the "Indian" stereotype in both approving and disparaging ways, just as Leland did one hundred years ago.

72. Gill, *Native American Religions,* 13.

Chapter 6

1. Dickason, xiii.

2. Kehoe, 207.

3. Berkhofer, 19–20.

4. Leland, "American Studies of Native Folk-Lore," and "Legends of the Passamaquoddy," 668.

5. *Algonquin Legends,* 338–39.

6. The word Leland usually renders as "magic" is *m'teolin,* a word better left untranslated, but which might be understood as Power. Although the precise word varies, it is a concept central in Abenaki and Micmac religions.

7. *Algonquin Legends,* 338, 67.

8. For the nature of these New England sojourns see Ralph Smith, 24–31. The quotation is from the last words of preface of *Kulóskap the Master,* 18.

9. Schlesinger, 69–72. The other destinations were the manufacturing towns and "the West." Leland's concern for New England also helps explain part of his book's incorrect name. The "Algonquin Legends" were not, as he well knew from Edward Jack's and Silas Rand's addresses, from only New England. The bulk of Leland's stories came from Maliseet and Micmac territory, by then the Canadian provinces of New Brunswick and Nova Scotia.

10. Glaab, 65–79; Pred, 4.

11. Schlesinger, 79.

12. McKelvey; Schlesinger, 87–89; Glaab, 115. The lack of paved roads gave rise to what may be one of the first U.S. urban legends. In many parts of the United States was told a story (cited in Glaab, 115) about a local fellow

stuck up to his neck in a mud hole right in the middle of a city street. Another resident happens by and asks if he needs help. The muddy fellow replies that he is okay; "After all," he says, "I still have my horse under me."

13. Glaab, 115. Larsen notes (244, 247) that although "during the 1850's and 1860's pigs gradually disappeared from the nation's streets," streets were no cleaner for it, perhaps just the opposite.

14. McKelvey, 63–64; Schlesinger, 104, 108–10.

15. Schlesinger, 105–06.

16. Siegel, 18–24.

17. *Philadelphia: Work, Space,* 238.

18. Schlesinger is upbeat about "urban progress"; see for example 120. Adrienne Siegel's careful examination of the literature of popular culture yields another explanation for why people kept coming to the city despite the dangers; for the dangers see 14 and 174; for her analysis of the role "fluff literature" played, see 173–77.

19. That Leland's contemporaries experienced city life in this way is borne out by Adrienne Siegel's study of the image of the city in popular literature of the time.

20. One intriguing response to the problems of urbanization was reform movement to establish parks within cities. New York's immense Central Park opened in the late fifties. Without the support of city governments the movement limped along. Charles N. Glaab claims that "To a large extent this movement represented an attempt to regain the virtues of life in nature lost within the city" (245). Urban life of the period did not lack for nature, only its "virtues." According to Yi-Fu Tuan, gardenlike parks are about nature ordered, about demonstrating power over nature (*Dominance and Affection,* 18–36). Leland's "poetry of nature" did not derive from nature dominated and ordered. Both Leland's ideal and the garden-park, however, derive in part from the same intense everyday nineteenth-century experience of the city as nature that was chaotic and potentially lethal.

21. In a remarkable passage biographer Elizabeth Pennell tells of how the time Leland spent with the Passamaquoddies renewed him for his city life in 1882:

> The hours in their tents by the sea helped to give him courage for the routine of work in Philadelphia. The quiet, industrious, civilized Passamaquoddies danced no war dances with him, led him on no wild chase across the plains. As I saw them, they were tranquillity itself. But

the old fire, the old wildness, the old magic was in their legends, and in each, as he forced it from them by his own spell of sympathy, he drew a fresh breath of life. (II, 120)

Despite this, Leland did not identify himself as part of the intellectual "antiurban" conversation that had hummed and hollered in the United States since its earliest days. See White and White.

22. Pennell, 33–35; Leland, 16–17, 77–78, also cited in Ralph Smith, 41. At Princeton: Ralph Smith, 73. Smith quotes from Leland's diaries on 92. Margery Fee explores the relation of the image of the Native, romanticism, and nationalism in contemporary English-Canadian literature (17–18).

23. Ralph Smith, 119, 121, 123, 124, 132, 144.

24. Varesano argues from the evidence in the 1862 *Sunshine in Thought* that Leland did not approve of "decadent romanticism." This kind of romanticism, typified by melancholy and sentimentality, Leland equated with the outlook of the Southern United States. This he contrasted with the vital wholesomeness of the North (47–60). See also Ralph Smith, 373–85.

25. Mosse, 56–57.

26. Mosse, 34.

27. Mosse, 57. Leland would undoubtedly have also been influenced by the grandfather of German Romanticism, Johann Gottfried von Herder. Writing in the late eighteenth-century, Herder drew together the primitivism of the *Volk,* their stories and songs, and the idea of the nation. Cocchiara, 168–200; Bohlman, 52–54, 112–14.

28. One unexpected voice that resonates with German Romanticism belongs to Vine Deloria, Jr. In *God Is Red* he writes, "Unless the sacred places are discovered and protected and used as religious places, there is no possibility of a nation ever coming to grips with the land itself. Without this basic relationship, national psychic stability is impossible" (287–88).

Although it does not touch directly on our inquiry, it is worth noting that scholars disagree about the importance of this matrix of nature, land, nature, and folklore of the people closest to the land for German nationalism and the development of National Socialism. For an overview, especially of the conversation about nationalism, see Buse and Doerr, 3–15.

29. Leland wrote his collaborator, Prince, about what he intended by *Kulóskap the Master:* "I always had a great desire to make out of the Glusgabe or Glooskap legends, which are really songs, a *real* Indian epic—not a *piece de manufacture* like Hiawatha. So I have *measured* the principal legends and really

made a small epic." He also wrote he wanted this book to be the "perfect flower of his Indian studies." Quoted in Pennell, II, 240.

30. Leland, *Kulóskap*, 14–15.

31. *The Sacred and the Profane*, 140.

32. Tuan, "Geopiety," borrows the term "geopiety" from John K. Wright, 11; the quotation is from 13. Compare D. H. Lawrence: "Every continent has its own great spirit of place. Every people is polarized in some particular locality, which is home, the homeland. Different places on the face of the earth have different vital effluence, different vibration, different chemical exhalation, different polarity with different stars: call it what you like. But the spirit of place is a great reality" (12).

33. Tuan, "Geopiety," 24.

34. Doob, 194; quoted in Tuan, 28.

35. Tuan, "Geopiety," 28.

36. The importance of Place to the religious life of humankind is underscored by the amount of attention paid to it by the "loudest talkers" in the history of religions conversation. Mircea Eliade's work on the sacred center (for example, "Sacred Space and Making the World Sacred" in *The Sacred and the Profane*, 20–65) and Jonathan Z. Smith's reflection on that work come immediately to mind ("The Influence of Symbols on Social Change: A Place on Which to Stand" and "Map Is Not Territory" in *Map is not Territory*, and "In Search of Place" in *To Take Place*, 1–23). For a inquiry on Place that builds on the work of these two scholars see Gill, "Storytracks."

37. For Place in Native American religions, see Gill, *Native American Religions*, 15–36. Robert Sayre uses psychological tools to analyze the same approving use of the "Indian" stereotype. This leads to a different conclusion. Sayre finds that the people of the United States had divided the world between civilized and savage and then identified freely with only one pole, the civilized. This caused an imbalance. Thus, "White Americans also had to turn and cross over into the savage half in order to reunite themselves." Although I am not convinced by his thesis, I find Sayre's final take on the issue a poignant description of the European-American need for Place: "There was no other way, apparently, of having the land, free of the enemy, and becoming a part of the land which still held in it the enemy's ghosts" (*Thoreau*, 18). Making dual or obverse use of the "Indian" stereotype meets this double-bound need.

38. Mosse, 15.

39. Leland, "Indian Impudence," 202. Leland and his brother enlisted as

privates in the First Philadelphia Artillery Home Guard. Ralph Smith documents Leland's Civil War career, 396–402.

40. Hinsley, *Savages and Scientists,* 7.

41. Leland, *Memoirs,* 368–69; Leland wrote his *Memoirs* in 1893.

42. This urgency was compounded by Leland's adherence to the "doomed to extinction" characteristic of the "Indian" stereotype: "When the last Indian shall be in his grave, those who come after us will ask in wonder why we had no curiosity as to the romance of our country, and so much as to that of every other land on earth" (*Algonquin Legends,* 3). Varesano suggests Leland was escaping an unhealthy social and literary climate in order to continue to be creative. Since Leland thought that the "Indian" was becoming extinct, there was some urgency in collecting the stories that held the secrets to this deep-felt relationship.

43. Pennell, II, 376–77; the emphases are Leland's.

44. Nearly fifty years later D. H. Lawrence (59, 54) had another take on this:

> The American landscape has never been at one with the white man. Never. And white men have probably never felt so bitter anywhere, as here in America, where the very landscape, in its very beauty, seems a bit devilish and grinning, opposed to us. . . . America hurts, because it has a powerful disintegrative influence upon the white psyche. It is full of grinning, unappeased aboriginal demons, too, ghosts, and it persecutes the white men, like some Eumenides, until the white men give up their absolute whiteness. . . .
>
> Yet one day the demons of America must be placated, the ghosts must be appeased, the Spirit of the Place atoned for. Then the true passionate love for American Soil will appear. As yet there is too much menace in the landscape.

45. Leland and Prince, 17.

46. Varesano offers an alternative reading of Leland's work. She sees it as a kind of gateway through which the reader might experience another mode of life. "Leland seems to be using folklore as a kind of poetic epic whose central figure is Leland, and whose theme is Nature" (108).

47. Leland was vehemently anti-Irish and therefore anti-immigrant (Ralph Smith, 274, 276). "Whites," "his own people," then, did not include all European-Americans. "Whites" was for Leland (and remains for *Us* and *Them*) a constructed category as stereotypical as "Indian." See Simard's discussion of the *Whiteman,* 360–64.

48. *Algonquin Legends*, 300.

49. See Varesano: "There is the implication that, since he regards himself as having this unusual ability as an 'Indian white man,' his fieldwork may be more than slightly colored by it, and what he reports in his books may be only those stories and events that tend to support this charisma. Then too, as an 'Indian white man,' it is a short step from accepting that he can establish an unusual rapport, to regarding himself as an Indian 'in spirit,' and so capable of reshaping the rough data that he would accumulate into something that he considers more representative of the Indian nature" (155–56).

50. Leland, "Legends of the Passamaquoddy," 676.

51. Varesano claims that Leland felt that "the reader, too, ought to take cognizance of the insights which . . . [his] narratives offer them, and not reject them because it is stated that some were shaped and altered from the original data, in order to produce an effect. The glimpse of 'reality' which they offer the reader, Leland seems to be explaining, is worth it" (150).

52. Pennell, II, 238, 250.

53. Hinsley, *Savages and Scientists*, 190, 192. Another early scholar who fits this pattern is Henry Rowe Schoolcraft. In 1846 in an address to the not-Native organization called "Was-Ah Ho-De-No-Son-Ne" Schoolcraft identified a need to turn to the "now-gone Red traditions." His reasoning was that while the United States had been nurtured by European culture, "No people can bear a true nationality, which does not exfoliate, as it were, from its bosom, something that expresses the peculiarities of its own soil and climate. . . . And where! when we survey the length and breadth of the land, can a more suitable element, for the work be found, than is furnished by the history and antiquities and institutions and love, of the free bold, wild, independent, native hunter race?" (the nonstandard use of exclamation point and commas are the text's; *An Address Delivered*, 6). Schoolcraft's concern for Place is also obvious from this quotation (see also pp. 3–8 and 29–30), although it does not dominate his work. Schoolcraft, as we have seen, had a different agenda.

54. Quoted in Pennell, II, 352–53.

55. Pennell, II, 379.

56. See Varesano: "Folklore was not simply part of the culture of one segment of mankind, nor was it just the poetry which he strove to recreate in his retelling of the legends. It was the very expression in verbal form of Nature, Nature approached in the Romantic sense" (255).

57. Hinsley acknowledges his debt to Slotkin, *Savages and Scientists*, 190. I note not without some irony that Slotkin's work rests on the idea of the hero journey set out by Joseph Campbell.

58. Leland forces a parallel with this aspect of the *Volk* song as an expression of feeling for the land by making much of the conjecture that at one time in the distant past all the "Algonquin" stories he collected were sung. *Algonquin Legends*, 379.

59. Berkhofer, 78. Berkhofer's source is Fred A. Crane who argues in his dissertation, that the approving use of the "Indian" stereotype, which he calls the "glorification of the Indian" was limited to the eastern seaboard. His evidence for the demise of this use is the rise, in the same geographical area, of parodies and satires that ridiculed the same "Indians" who were heralded not so long before.

60. Berkhofer, 95.

61. Berkhofer, 90–92.

62. Berkhofer, 109.

63. Turner, 3–4.

64. Lears (4–7) describes the "crisis of cultural authority" during this period. Lears would have no doubt included Leland as an "antimodernist." He names his biographer, Elizabeth Robins Pennell, quoting some of her essays that sound Lelandesque (163,173–74). Although Lears does not foreground the need for Place, he does explore the religious emptiness of the period.

65. For a discussion of what seems to be another attempt to to establish Place by the approving use of the "Indian" stereotype, see Hinsley, "Zunis and Brahmins," 192–96.

Chapter 7

1. Pohl identifies Kluskap as the Orkney nobleman Henry Sinclair, thus "finding" in Micmac stories evidence of the superiority of British "stock" of which Pohl is not surprisingly a representative (3, 166–67). Charles Godfrey Leland is a significant source for Pohl.

2. None other than Joseph Campbell gives strident voice to this sense of anomie:

> With our old mythologically founded taboos unsettled by our own modern sciences, there is everywhere in the civilized world a rapidly rising incidence of vice and crime, mental disorders, suicides and dope addiction, shattered homes, impudent children, violence, murder, and despair. These are facts; I am not inventing them. (*Myths to Live By*, 8–9)

For a discussion of Campbell as a descendant of the romantics, see Sandler and Reeck, 1–5.

   3. Knudtson and Suzuki, 4, nt. and 9, nt.

   4. See Berkhofer, 110. Evidence that my version of this story is both alive and trivialized in popular culture I take from the March 1994 issue of the *Portland Guide: Discovering Oregon and the Pacific Northwest.* There a company called EcoTours of Oregon list in their "offerings" "Columbia River Gorge/Mt. Hood Tours, Winery Tours in the Countryside (gourmet picnic lunch included), Day Skiing Tours (downhill, alpine and cross country), Scenic and Ancient Forest Day Hikes . . . , Oregon Coast, Whale Watching and Mt. St. Helens Tours, Native American Culture Tours at Warm Springs Indian Reservation and Portland Microbrewery Tours."

   5. Daniel Francis's excellent analysis of this phenomenon locates the "alienation" or Place need in a national (Canadian) context and argues that "non-Native Canadians are trying in a way to become indigenous people themselves" (185–90).

   6. For another, very different critique of Mander's *In the Absence of the Sacred,* see Churchill, *Indians Are Us?*, 154–59. *In the Absence of the Sacred* stands out as a response to the Place-related needs of its readers, but it is not the first. See for example the conclusion of Drinnon's *Facing West* where he says, "By word and example, Native Americans have been reminding Anglo-Americans of their lack of respect for all living things, of their lost communal sanity, and lost wholeness—of how not to see with the eyes and mind only but, as Lame Deer put it, also with 'the eyes of the heart.' With their help, Americans of all colors might just conceivably dance into being a really new period in their history" (467).

   7. Churchill points out some of Mander's more glaring U.S.A.-centered errors. (*Indians Are Us?*, 145–48). Mander's attempts to document injustice to native peoples suffer more the further he strays from the United States. Admittedly the end of the Meech Lake Accord in Canada in 1990 comprised a complicated series of events, but the Newfoundland Micmacs did not have "sufficient political clout in their province" to have an impact on Premier Clyde Wells's decision to stall ratification of the Accord. Nor is the premier of Manitoba "an Indian," although the Member of the Manitoba Legislative Assembly and later Member of Parliament who blocked passage of the bill to ratify the Accord, Elijah Harper, is a Cree (362).

   8. Mander, 202–10; the quotation is on 208.

   9. Most Micmac, Maliseet, Passamaquoddy and Penobscot women do not wear ties, but then neither do most "Western" women. More significantly,

"family" is likely to mean something different to me than to many Micmac and Abenaki people. I am not, however, prepared to generalize on that difference without a careful inquiry into other Canadian understandings of family— Italian-Canadian, Indo-Canadian, and Chinese-Canadian understandings come to mind for comparison.

10. Mander, 384; the emphasis is Mander's.

11. See for example Knudtson and Suzuki, xxxiv, 7–8.

12. Gill, *Native American Religions*, 15–36.

13. Knudtson and Suzuki, 13, 6, 11, 12.

14. Knudtson and Suzuki, xxviii.

15. Knudtson and Suzuki, 185. It is curious that like Leland Knudtson and Suzuki misuse the term "shamanism" (*Algonquin Legends*, 334–35). The difference is that Leland could not have known the "correct" usage of the term for its meaning was still being negotiated. Knudtson and Suzuki, on the other hand, could and do, and yet still improvise on the word. See p. 1, nt.

16. Margary Fee has documented a similar phenomenon in contemporary anglophone Canadian Literature. Examining the role of Native people she identifies a "general pattern" that serves "several ideological functions at once." That general pattern, she says, "allows, through the white character's association with the Native, for a white 'literary land claim,' analogous to the historical territorial take-over, usually implicit or explicit in the text. And it allows for a therapeutic meditation on the evil of technology and the good of a life close to nature, the latter offering a temporary inoculation against the former" (16–17).

17. Berkhofer, 68.

18. Berkhofer, 68.

19. Brown, 1.

20. Brown, 4, 27.

21. Holler points out that Black Elk's statement that he expected Neihardt (and comparably Brown) was part of the proper ritual context for sacred instruction ("Lakota Religion," 22–24). In Brown's case, Black Elk's words were both literally and symbolically true. Neihardt claimed that Brown asked him to arrange with Black Elk for instruction in Oglala rituals. This Neihardt said he did (McCluskey, 239).

22. Brown, 34.

23. Brown, 34–46.

24. See: Sayre, "Vision and Experience"; McCluskey; Castro, 79–97; DeMaillie, ed. *Sixth Grandfather*; Deloria, Jr., "Neihardt"; Holler, "Lakota Religion"; Holler, "Relationship"; Gravely; Powers, "When Black Elk Speaks"; Rice; and Steltenkamp.

25. John G. Neihardt in interview, McCluskey, 238. Neihardt followed Leland in one other way: he subscribed to the theory of Aryanism. "We might liken the ancient Aryan spirit," wrote Neihardt to a pre-Nazi world, "to a prairie fire driven by an east wind." The same "prairie fire," he thought, drove the westward expansion (and attendant conquest) in North America (quoted in Whitney, 86).

26. The most probable explanation is the simplest: Black Elk's conversion to Roman Catholicism was a shift of allegiance, but not a renouncing of his former religious ideas. Although he never performed rituals again (except as demonstrations), he maintained an active appreciation of both. See Holler, "Relationship," and Gravely. That he could hold in some sense to both of these religious traditions at the same time is not an exceptional feat. It is common in the history of religions. Black Elk felt his understanding of Oglala religiousness and especially his vision deserved respect. Neihardt was his vehicle for this.

27. Steltenkamp, 123; DeMaillie, 71.

28. Holler, "Relationship"; Rice, 62–63.

29. Container 373. Holler explores Black Elk's Christianized understanding of the seven rituals, especially the Sun Dance, in "Relationship," 41–47. That Brown withholds the information that Black Elk was a "practising" Roman Catholic shaped the way I read *The Sacred Pipe*. When I first read the following passage from Black Elk's own introduction, for example, I was struck by the elder's openness and generosity. "I am willing to accept that *your* Christian way has validity," he seemed to be saying, "Why can't you accept that *my* way also has validity?"

> We have been told by the white men, or at least by those who are Christian, that God sent to men His son, who would restore order and peace upon the earth; and we have been told that Jesus the Christ was crucified, but that he shall come again at the Last Judgement, the end of this world or cycle. This I understand and know that it is true, but the white men should know that for the red people too, it was the will of *Wakan-Tanka*, the Great Spirit, that an animal turn itself into the two-legged person in order to bring the most holy pipe to His people; and we too were taught that this White Buffalo Cow Woman who brought our sacred pipe will appear again at the end of this "world," a coming which we Indians know is now not very far off. (*The Sacred Pipe*, xix–xx)

Knowing Black Elk was a Christian changed my reading of this passage completely. Now I take it to mean, "I understand the Christian way to be true, but I also understand the way of the sacred pipe to be true." Gone, in other words, are the "your" and "my." Both are Black Elk's. By 1948, Black Elk had found a series of correspondences between Christianity and his older Oglala religion. Holler notes Black Elk's equation of Christ and White Buffalo Cow Woman in this passage ("Relationship," 42) calling him a "'Lakota catechist'" (43) and a "creative theologian" (47). It seems to me he had begun to articulate an Oglala Catholicism.

30. Brown, 57, 48, 49

31. For another discussion of Black Elk tinged with righteous anger, see Powers, "When Black Elk Speaks."

32. Brown, 49 (the emphasis is Brown's), 52.

33. Brown, 51. See also pp. xvi and 4.

34. For Brown's approving use of the "Indian doomed to extinction" see his affirming of John Collier's words with which he ends *The Spiritual Legacy of the American Indian*, 129.

35. That some scholars held this hope at about the same time is evidenced in McCluskey, 242.

36. Kehoe, 197. The weight of Brown's editorial hand has been an issue since the book's publication (LaFarge).

37. Kehoe, 194–95.

38. Vecsey, "Introduction," xiv–xv.

39. Kehoe, 194–95.

40. For more recent evidence that Hultkrantz is sometimes bewitched by the generic "Indian," see the (singular) "Indian" worldview in his *Native Religions*, 21; and the "Native American ideology" in his *Shamanic Healing*, 4. For more on this latter work see Thomas Parkhill, "Booknote."

41. Hultkrantz, "Feelings," 123, 119, 122.

42. Hultkrantz, "Feelings," 122, 127.

43. Hultkrantz, "Feelings," 128, 134.

44. Morrison, "Ritual Work, critiques Hultkrantz's use of the "supernatural." "Sharing the Flower" demonstrates the elaborate Yaqui understanding and appropriation of Roman Catholicism on their terms. Closer to Leland's timeless "Indians," Morrison has shown the complexity of the religious

alliances between Abenaki, Micmac, and Europeans (*The Embattled Northeast*). It seems to me that if Black Elk teaches us nothing else, his example of creative religious appropriation following upon a military defeat typified by unrelenting inhumanity should put to rest the image of the passive "Indian" brainwashed by clever missionaries.

45. Morrison, "Montagnais Missionization," 16.

46. Hultkrantz apparently runs up against his own timeless "Indian" stereotype when he tries to explain the "plastic trash, fractured glass bottles, old tires, and wrecked cars" found "on many Indian reservations in North America." Incredibly, rather than cite poverty, social problems, and corresponding byproducts of colonialism, Hultkrantz treats this pollution as a cultural survival of the "Indian's" closeness to nature.

> The reason for their behavior is quite simple: once all used material could be thrown out from the tent, lodge, or house to decay in nature; today this custom still prevails, but unfortunately the modern material is more permanent and consequently remains on the spot. ("Feelings," 124)

47. Hultkrantz, "Feelings," 134.

48. It is clear Hultkrantz is personally moved by the connection of "Indians" and nature. Vecsey tells us that "the romantic image of Indians as lovers of nature, as people at harmony with their world, has persisted through his works. His first publication . . . surveyed Indians and other `nature-folk'; his latest article (in a book entitled—in Swedish—*They Took Our Land*), published by a Swedish 'Indian Club' to which he belongs, is on the topic of 'Indians as Nature-protectors'" ("Introduction," x–xi).

49. Mooney, 716; cited in Gill, *Mother Earth*, 40.

50. Cited in Gill, *Mother Earth*, 8.

51. Gill, *Mother Earth*, 121.

52. Cited in Gill, *Mother Earth*, 114.

53. "Feelings," 128–29.

54. Hultkrantz makes the same generalization and quotes the same speech of Smohalla in *The Religions*, 54.

55. The volatile power of Gill's thesis requires that I stress that neither he nor I intend to distract from the power of Mother Earth by setting forth her history and stories. All important deities—eg. Indra, Kālī, Kuan-yin, Jesus— have histories. See *Mother Earth*, 157.

56. Paper, "Through the Earth Darkly"; Paper, Book Review of *Mother*

Earth; Vecsey, Book Review of *Mother Earth;* Churchill, "A Little Matter of Genocide," *Bloomsbury Review;* Churchill, "Sam Gill's *Mother Earth"*; Churchill, "A Little Matter of Genocide," *Fantasies;* Deloria, Jr., "On Teaching Native American Religions," 3.36; Grimes, "Teaching Native American Religions"; and Hultkrantz, Book Review of *Mother Earth.* Gill responds directly to Churchill's reviews in "The Power of Story." In addition, see Tony Swain, "The Mother Earth Conspiracy."

57. Gill uses the word "heresy" in "An American Myth," 141, and "heretical" in *Mother Earth,* 156.

58. Hultkrantz, *The Religions,* 54.

59. Gill, "An American Myth," 137, 139, *Mother Earth,* 63–66.

60. Hultkrantz, "The Goddess."

61. Hultkrantz, "The Goddess," 202, 215.

62. Gill, *Mother Earth,* 125.

63. Vecsey, "Introduction," xi–xii. McIntosh in his work on Thoreau notes the ongoing power of the romantic idea of nature, 19.

64. Vecsey, "Introduction," xi.

65. In his "Reply to [Thomas] Buckley's Review of *Belief and Worship in Native North America"* Hultkrantz acknowledges and contextualizes his use of words like "primitive"; he also apologizes.

> As other reviewers have told me, terms like "heathenism," "squaw" and "redskin" have a pejorative sense in American linguistic usage. In my own native country, Sweden, they are romantic, but not depreciating. I am sorry about this mistake. (86)

66. Dorris, 102.

67. *"Isinamowin,"* Transcript, 22.

68. Dorris, 103.

69. From 1815 to 1860 in the Northeastern United States was such a time, as was the mid- to late 1960s among counterculture North Americans. See Crane; Brand, 570.

70. Yi-Fu Tuan, *Dominance and Affection,* 1–2.

71. For example, Jack to Leland, March 18, 1884, container 373; Jack to Leland, April 16, 1884, container 373; Jack to Leland, May, 4, 1884, container 373. The next time you come across the phrase, "our native people" or a vari-

ant, attend to the genuine affection that is probably there. But there are other things going on as well. Here is an example of good intentions gone awry from the *StoryFest Day Program*, February 22, 1992, Fredericton, NB. Under the subheading, "Whispering Leaves" it says, "Pat Polchies shares wonderful stories from the world of our aboriginal peoples" (4).

72. For instance, "There is a very intelligent Wabenaki residing opposite Fredericton he is generally known as 'Gabe' he speaks good English and knows more of the Indian traditions than any man I know of" (December 17, 1883, container 373). Or this: "Every body knows Gabe here he is probably not far from 70 years of age 65 at least Very obliging with a powerful memory is a good hunter and speaks English remarkably well" (April 16, 1884, container 373, the underlining is Jack's).

73. Gordon, 9.

74. For another example of how a well-intentioned scholar can skew ethnographic findings, especially in the context of colonialization, see Harvey A. Feit's description of Frank Speck's story in "The Construction of Algonquian Hunting Territories."

Chapter 8

1. I have cataloged the popularity of the story in not-Native contexts. The story's absence from a number of collections of Abenaki and Micmac stories in which it ought to appear, but does not is significant. The Kluskap-Malsum story does not appear in the collections of Alger; Hagar, "Micmac Customs"; Hagar, "Micmac Magic"; Wallis and Wallis. (Although Ruth and Wilson Wallis gathered some stories in 1953, Wilson Wallis collected most of the stories in *Micmac Indians* in 1911–1912.) Mechling, *Malecite Tales*; Michelson, "Micmac Tales"; Speck, "Some Micmac Tales;" Speck, "Malecite Tales." Fisher reports (229) that the story is not known at all to the Penobscot people. The story does not occur anywhere in the immense 655 Maliseet story collection which Laszlo Szabo recorded between 1971 and 1984 (*Malecite Stories*).

2. De Mille, *Castaneda's Journey;* De Mille, ed. *The Don Juan Papers;* Kehoe, 203–05.

3. Michael William Francis, interview.

4. Michelson, "Micmac Tales," 51–53.

5. Ives, 6–7.

6. Ives, 16–17.

7. For example, Mechling, *Malecite Tales*, 3–4; and these stories in the Szabo collection: Margaret Polchies, Oromocto/Kingsclear, vol. IV, pp. 89–100; John Sacobie, vol. VIII, pp. 462–67; Frank Tomah, Peter Dana Point, vol. VIII, pp. 536–39.

8. Day ("Western Abenaki Transformer," 78) wonders just the opposite: "Was this a genuine old Malecite motif coming to the surface again or was it derived at some point from a literate informant who knew the printed versions of Leland and Prince?"

9. When "traditionalists" refer to themselves as "the Wabanaki, the people of the dawn," or the "Four Tribes," they mean Micmac, Maliseet, Passamaquoddy, and Penobscot. These more generic names seem to be a kind of midpoint between "Indians" or "Native People" and the individual nation's name.

For an eloquent explication of some of the tenets of neotraditionalism, see gkisedtanamoogk, *Anoqcou*.

10. George Paul interview.

11. Knockwood insisted on using Malsumsis, correcting me when I used Malsum. He said he did not know what the word "malsumsis" meant. Knockwood is a Micmac speaker; malsum(sis) is a Maliseet word. Of the easily available texts of the story, only Leland's uses Malsumsis.

12. Noel Knockwood, interview.

13. Noel Knockwood, interview.

14. Isabelle Knockwood.

15. Both Knockwood's mother and the other elder are now deceased.

16. Powers, "When Black Elk Speaks," 149.

17. Berkhofer noted in 1978 that this was already happening in the political sphere (195). This self-understanding of Native Americans as "Indians" who share a common oppressor and who therefore deserve justice continues.

18. Dorris, 100.

19. Berkhofer, 111.

20. The impulse to direct this dual usage of the stereotype is clear in the recent film career of Lakota AIM activist, Russell Means. Described as "unhappy with what he considered the stereotypical portrayals in more recent [movie] offerings such as 'Black Robe,' 'Geronimo,' and even 'Dances with Wolves,'" Means "vowed to work from within" (Dutka, "Can a Revolutionary"). Consequently he took roles in *The Last of the Mohicans, Natural Born Killers,* and

as Powhatan's voice in *Pocahontas*. Defending his role in Disney's *Pocahontas* from "'scholastic, linear-thinking, nit-pickers' fixated on the movie's historical inaccuracies," Means describes this paean to the "Indian" stereotype—approvingly used—as "the finest feature film on American Indians Hollywood has turned out." Looking to Means's explanation for this assessment of *Pocahontas*, we can see a conscious effort to fix the oscillating "Indian" stereotype so that it might be used primarily in an approving fashion. Says Means, "'Pocahontas' is the first time Eurocentric male society has admitted its historical deceit. . . . It makes the stunning admission that the British came over here to kill Indians and rape and pillage the land" (Dutka, "Can a Revolutionary"). In another article Means is quoted as saying, "'Pocahontas' presents a host of lousy settlers . . . and there's not a bad Indian is sight. . . . But there's nothing wrong with telling the truth'" (Dutka, "Disney's").

21. The image of the "Indian" close to nature appears in Rita Joe (30).

22. Bruchac is described as "a storyteller and writer of Abenaki, English and Slovak ancestry. He is an enrolled member (Band No. 3312) of the Abenaki Nation/Vermont." Kluskap, according to Bruchac, is a "Trickster," who "contains both the Good Mind, which can benefit the people and help the Earth, and that other Twisted Mind, a mind governed by selfish thoughts that can destroy a natural balance and bring disaster" (5). I have not seen elsewhere this collapsing of Malsum's characteristics into Kluskap. The Good Mind/Twisted Mind dichotomy is, of course, reminiscent of Iroquois teachings.

23. For some powerful neotraditional statements of the relationship of "Indians" to Mother Earth that appropriate the approving use the stereotype, see Mander, 222–24. Kehoe (200) traces the introduction of the Medicine Wheel into neotraditionalism to Hyemeyohsts Storm's *Seven Arrows*. She suspects Storm's source to be "Grinnell's classic ethnographic study of the nineteenth century Cheyenne," in which the wheels are a "minor item in Cheyenne life." See also Townsend, especially nt. 9.

24. Winowna Stevenson uses the phrase in *"Isinamowin,"* 14. To be fair, her usage is more generous than some I have heard.

25. *On Teaching Native American Religions*, 3.36.

26. Badone, 518.

27. Badone, 529, 528.

28. Although Brown is a proponent of the gulf between the *Them* of the Plains "Indians" and the *Us* of his reading audience, the *Us* most affected by his *Sacred Pipe* has, ironically, been the neotraditional *Thems*.

29. This "purist preference" is Joel W. Martin's springboard for his

assessment of the "disappearing Indian" in the study of religions (678).

30. Badone, 535, 536. Badone is quoting Clifford's "Introduction: Partial Truths," in *Writing Culture* (22).

31. Morrison, T*he Embattled Northeast,* 42–101.

32. Martin, 686.

33. I am thinking of the attacks by sacred specialists on alcohol consumption, land cessions, as well as economic and political dependency on not-Native society. See Martin, 686.

34. Eliade, 140.

35. Isocrates, 1,133; cited in Tuan, "Geopiety," 25.

36. Deloria, Jr., 60; see also 274.

37. Daniel Francis, 190.

Appendix

1. David Russell Jack, "The Indians of Acadia," 190–91; I. Allen Jack, 532–34; I. Allen Jack's biography of his uncle notes he was a bachelor and an abstainer, and ends "A man of profound religious belief, he met his end calmly and fearlessly, going down to the valley of the shadow of death in the sure and certain hope of a glorious resurrection."

BIBLIOGRAPHY

Abler, Thomas S. "Micmacs and Gypsies: Occupation of the Peripatetic Niche."
    Papers of the Twenty-First Algonquian Conference, Ottawa: Carleton
    University, 1990.
Adney, Edwin Tappan. *Edwin Tappan Adney Papers*. Ms. Box 39. Philips Library,
    Peabody Museum, Salem, MA.
Albanese, Catherine L. *Nature Religion in America: From the Algonkian Indians to
    the New Age*. Chicago: Chicago University Press, 1990.
Alger, Abby Langdon. *In Indian Tents: Stories Told by Penobscot, Passamaquoddy
    and Micmac Indians to Abby L. Alger*. Boston: Roberts, 1897.
Anderson, *George K. The Saga of the Volsungs, Together with Excerpts from the
    Nornageststhattr and Three Chapters from the Prose Edda*, translated and
    annotated by George K. Anderson. Newark: University of Delaware
    Press, 1982.
Anonymous, "A Wandering Scholar." *The Outlook*. Obituary Notice of Charles
    Leland, March 28, 1903, 708–10.
Anonymous. Book Review. "Indian Folk-Lore and Ethnology: *The Algonquin
    Legends of New England . . .*" *Science*, 4;95 (Nov 28, 1884): 499–500.
Anonymous. Book Review. "Indian Legends of New England" (a review of *The
    Algonquin Legends of New England*). *The Literary World*, 1884, 371.
Anonymous. Book Review. "*The Algonquin Legends of New England*." *The
    Spectator*, July 25, 1885, 976–78.
Anonymous. Book Review. "*The Algonquin Legends of New England*. By Charles
    G. Leland." *The Athenaeum*, No. 2988, January 31, 1885, 6–7.
Anonymous. Book Review. "*The Algonquin Legends of New England . . .*" *The
    American Antiquarian*, 6(1884): 428.
Badone, Ellen. "Ethnology, Fiction, and the Meanings of the Past in Brittany."
    American Ethnologist, 18(3), August 1991, 518–45.
Bailey, Alfred Goldsworthy. *The Conflict of European and Eastern Algonkian
    Cultures*, 1504–1700. Toronto: University of Toronto Press, 1969 [1937].
Barbeau, Marius. "Comparison between 'The Micmacs: Their Life and Legends'
    by Cyrus Macmillan and 'Legends of the Micmacs' by S. T. Rand as well

as 'Algonquin Legends' by Leland." Ms. Canadian Museum of Civilization (III-F-29M).

Bataille, Gretchen M. "Black Elk—New World Prophet," in *A Sender of Words: Essays in Memory of John G. Neihardt*. ed. Vine Deloria, Jr. Salt Lake City: Howe Brothers, 1984, 135–42.

The Bear Tribe Directory. Devon, PA: The Bear Tribe, East Coast Office, January, 1993.

Beck, Horace P. *Gluskap the Liar and Other Indian Tales.* Freeport, ME: Bond Wheelwright, 1966.

Beckwourth, James P. *The Life and Adventures of James P. Beckwourth, Mountaineer, Scout, Pioneer, and Chief of the Crow Nation of Indians. Written from His Own Dictation by T. D. Bonner,* ed. Charles Godfrey Leland, with Preface. New York: Macmillan & Co. 1892 [1856].

Berkhofer, Robert F., Jr. *The White Man's Indian: Images of the American Indian from Columbus to the Present.* New York: Alfred A. Knopf, 1978.

Bertolino, Daniel and Diane Bertolino. *Indian Legends of Canada:* "Glooscap Country." Video, 1982.

Bieder, Robert E. *Science Encounters the Indian, 1820–1880: The Early Years of American Ethnology.* Norman, OK: The University of Oklahoma Press, 1986.

Bieder, Robert E. and Tax, Thomas G. "From Ethnologists to Anthropologists." *American Anthropology: The Early Years, 1974 Proceedings of the American Ethnological Society.* John V. Murra, ed. St. Paul: West Publishing Co., 1976.

Black Elk, Nicholas. *The Sacred Pipe: Black Elk's Account of the Seven Rites of the Oglala Sioux.* Recorded and Edited by Joseph Epes Brown. New York: Penguin Books, 1971 [1953].

Bohlman, Philip V. *The Study of Folk Music in the Modern World,* Bloomington: Indiana University Press, 1988.

Brand, Steward. "Indians and the Counterculture, 1960s–1970s." *Handbook of North American Indians, vol. 4 History of Indian-White Relations.* Washington, Smithsonian Institution, 1988, 4, 570–72.

Bremer, Richard G. "Henry Rowe Schoolcraft: Explorer in the Mississipi Valley, 1818–1832." *Wisconsin Magazine of History,* 66 (Autumn, 1962): 40–59.

Brinton, Daniel G. "The Hero-God of the Algonkins as a Cheat and Liar." *Essays of an Americanist.* Philadelphia: Porter & Coates, 1890, reprinted 1970, Johnson Reprint Corporation, 130–34.

Brinton, Daniel G. *The Myths of the New World.* New York, 1876 [1868].

Brown, Joseph Epes. *The Spiritual Legacy of the American Indian.* New York: Crossroad, 1986 [1982].

Brown, Mrs. W. Wallace (Louise). "Some Indoor and Outdoor Games of the Wabanaki Indians." *Transactions of the Royal Society of Canada.* Section II. 1988, 41–46.

Browne, G. "Indian Legends of Acadia." *Acadiensis,* 1902, 2: 54–64.

Bruchac, Joseph. "The Circle Is the Way to See," in *Story Earth: Native Voices on the Environment*, compiled by Inter Press Service. San Francisco: Mercury House, 1993.

Bruffee, Kenneth A. "Collaborative Learning and the 'Conversation of Mankind.'" *College English* 46:7 (November, 1984), 635–52.

Buckley, Thomas. "Book Review of *Belief and Worship in Native North America.*" *Ethnohistory*, 31(2): 139–41.

Burke, Kenneth. *The Philosophy of Literary Form: Studies in Symbolic Action.* Berkeley: University of California Press, 1973.

Buse, Dieter K. and Juergen C. Doerr. *German Nationalisms: A Bibliographic Approach.* New York: Garland Publishing, 1985.

Butler, Eva M. and Wendell A. Hadlock. "Dogs of the Northeastern Woodland Indians." *Massachusetts Archaeological Society Bulletin*, 10:2 (1949) 17–35.

Campbell, Joseph. *Historical Atlas of World Mythology, Vol. II: The Way of the Seeded Earth; Part 2: Mythologies of the Primitive Planters: The Northern Americas.* New York: Harper & Row, 1989.

Campbell, Joseph. *Myths to Live By.* New York: The Viking Press, 1972.

Castro, Michael. *Interpreting the Indian: Twentieth Century Poets and the Native American.* Albuquerque: University of New Mexico Press, 1983.

Chamberlain, A. F. "Nanibozhu Amongst the Otchipwe, Mississagas, and Other Algonkian Tribes." *Journal of American Folklore*, IV: XIV (July-September, 1891), 193–213.

Chamberlain, Alex F. "In Memoriam: Daniel Garrison Brinton." *Journal of American Folklore*, 12: 215–25 (1899).

Chapman, J. K. *The Career of Arthur Hamilton Gordon, First Lord Stanmore, 1829–1912.* Toronto: University of Toronto Press, 1964.

Churchill, Ward. *Indians Are Us?: Culture and Genocide in Native North America.* Toronto: Between the Lines, 1994.

Churchill, Ward. "A Little Matter of Genocide: Native American Spirituality and New Age Hucksterism." *The Bloomsbury Review*, Sept/Oct 1988: 23–26.

Churchill, Ward. "A Little Matter of Genocide: Sam Gill's *Mother Earth*, Colonialism and the Expropriation of Indigenous Spiritual Tradition in Academia," in *Fantasies of the Master Race: Literature, Cinema and the Colonization of American Indians*, ed. M. Annette Jaimes. Monroe, ME: Common Courage Press, 1992, 187–213.

Churchill, Ward. "Sam Gill's *Mother Earth*: Colonialism, Genocide and the Expropriation of Indigenous Spiritual Tradition in Contemporary Academia." *American Indian Culture and Research Journal*, 12:3(1988) 49–67.

Ciklamini, Marlene. *Snorri Sturluson.* Boston: Twayne Publishers, 1978.

Clark, Jeremiah S. *Rand and the Micmacs: The Life Story of our Maritime Indian Missionary.* Charlottetown: The Examiner Office, 1899.

Clements, William M. *Native American Folklore in the Nineteenth-Century Periodicals*. Athens, Ohio: Swallow Press/Ohio University Press, 1986.

Clifford, J. "On Ethnographic Authority." *Representations* 2 (1983): 118–46.

Clifford, J. and G. Marcus, eds. *Writing Culture: the Poetics and Politics of Ethnography*. Berkeley: np, 1986.

Clifton, James A. "Introduction, Memoir, Exegesis," in *The Invented Indian: Cultural Fictions and Government Policies*, ed. James A. Clifton. New Brunswick NJ: Transaction Publishers, 1990, 1–28.

Cocchiara, Giuseppe. *The History of Folklore in Europe*, translated by John N. McDaniel. Philadelphia: The Institute for the Study of Human Issues, 1981 [1952].

Conrad, Rudolf. "Mutual Fascination: Indians in Dresden and Leipzig," in *Indians and Europe: An Interdisciplinary Collection of Essays*, ed. Christian F. Feest. Aachen, Germany: Ed. Heordot, Rader-Verl., 1987, 455–71.

The Correspondence of Henry David Thoreau. Walter Harding and Carl Bode, eds. New York, 1958.

Crane, Fred A. *The Noble Savage in America, 1815–1860: Concepts of the Indian, with Special Reference to the Writers of the Northeast*. Unpublished doctoral thesis, Yale University, 1952.

Cro, Stelio. *The Noble Savage: Allegory of Freedom*. Waterloo: Wilfrid Laurier Press, 1990.

Cronon, William. *Changes in the Land: Indians, Colonists, and the Ecology of New England*. New York: Hill and Wang: 1983.

Darnell, Regna. "Daniel Brinton and the Professionalization of American Anthropology." *American Anthropology: The Early Years*. 1974 Proceedings of the American Ethnological Society. John V. Murra, ed. St. Paul: West Publishing 1976, 69–98.

Davidson, H.R. Ellis. *Gods and Myths of Northern Europe*. Middlesex, England: Penguin Books, 1964.

Davidson, Hilda R. Ellis. "Eddas," in *Encyclopedia of Religion*, ed. Mircea Eliade. New York: MacMillan, 1987. Vol. 5, pp. 27–29.

Davies, Alan. *Infected Christianity: A Study of Modern Racism*. Montreal: McGill-Queen's University Press, 1988.

Day, Gordon M. "The Indian as an Ecological Factor in the Northeastern Forest." *Ecology*, 34:2, April 1953, 329–46.

Day, Gordon M. "The Western Abenaki Transformer." *Journal of the Folklore Institute* 13 (1976): 75–89.

De Mille, Richard. *Castaneda's Journey: The Power and the Allegory*. Santa Barbara: Capra Press, 1978 [1976].

De Mille, Richard, ed. *The Don Juan Papers: Further Castaneda Controversies*. Santa Barbara: Ross-Erikson Publishers, 1980.

Deloria, Vine, Jr., ed., *A Sender of Words: Essays in Memory of John G. Neihardt*. Salt Lake City: Howe Brothers, 1984.

Deloria, Vine, Jr. "American Fantasy," forward to Gretchen M. Batialle and Charles L. P. Silet, eds. *The Pretend Indians: Images of Native Americans in the Movies*. Ames, Iowa: Iowa State University Press, 1980.

Deloria, Vine, Jr. *God Is Red: A Native View of Religion*, 2nd ed. Golden, CO: Fulcrum Publishing, 1994.

Deloria, Vine, Jr. "Neihardt and the Western Landscape," in *A Sender of Words: Essays in Memory of John G. Neihardt*, ed. Vine Deloria, Jr. Salt Lake City: Howe Brothers, 1984, 85–99.

Demaillie, Raymond J. "John G. Neihardt's Lakota Legacy," in *A Sender of Words: Essays in Memory of John G. Neihardt*, ed. Vine Deloria, Jr. Salt Lake City: Howe Brothers, 1984, 110–34.

Demaillie, Raymond J., ed. *The Sixth Grandfather: Black Elk's Teachings Given to John G. Neihardt*. Lincoln: University of Nebraska Press, 1984.

Detwiler, Fritz. "'All My Relations': Persons in Oglala Religion." *Religion* 22(1992): 235–46.

Dickason, Olive Patricia. *The Myth of the Savage and the Beginnings of French Colonialism in the Americas*. Edmonton: University of Alberta Press, 1984.

Dippie, Brian W. *The Vanishing American: White Attitudes and U.S. Indian Policy*. Middletown, CN: Wesleyan University Press, 1982.

Dixon, Roland Burrage. "The Mythology of the Central and Eastern Algonkins." *Journal of American Folklore*, 22(1909): 1–9.

Doob, Leonard. *Patriotism and Nationalism: Their Psychological Foundations*. New Haven: Yale University Press, 1964.

Dorris, Michael. "Indians on the Shelf," in *The American Indian and the Problem of History*, ed. Calvin Martin. New York: Oxford University Press, 1987, 98–105.

Dorson, Richard M. "American Folklorists in Britain." *Journal of the Folklore Institute* 7 (1970): 187–219.

Dorson, Richard. *The British Folklorists: A History*. Chicago: Chicago University Press, 1968.

Doxtator, Deborah. *Fluffs and Feathers; An Exhibit on the Symbols of Indianness: A Resource Guide*, rev. ed. Brantford, ON, Canada: Woodland Cultural Centre, 1992.

Drinnon, Richard. Facing West: *The Metaphysics of Indian-Hating and Empire-Building*. Minneapolis: University of Minnesota Press, 1980.

Dumezil, Georges. *Gods of the Ancient Northmen*. Berkeley: University of California Press, 1973.

Dunsmore, Roger. "Nicolaus Black Elk: Holy Man in History," in *A Sender of Words: Essays in Memory of John G. Neihardt*, ed. Vine Deloria, Jr. Salt Lake City: Howe Brothers, 1984, 143–58.

Dutka, Elaine. "Can a Revolutionary Co-exist with 'Pocahontas'?" *Los Angeles Times*, June 11, 1995.

Dutka, Elaine. "Disney's History Lesson: 'Pocahontas' has its share of supporters, detractors." *Los Angeles Times,* Calendar Section, part F, 1:2, February 9, 1995.

Eckstorm, Fanny Hardy. *Old John Neptune and Other Maine Indian Shamans.* Portland, ME: Southworth-Anthoensen Press, 1945. Orono: University of Maine: Marsh Island Reprint, 1980.

Eliade, Mircea. *The Sacred and the Profane: the Nature of Religion.* Willard R. Trask, tr. New York: Harper & Row, 1961 [1957].

Erickson, Vincent and Peter Paul. "Indian-White Partnership Recalled." *The Daily Gleaner* (Fredericton, NB, Canada), Saturday, March 23, 1974, 13.

Erickson, Vincent O. "Maliseet-Passamaquoddy," *Handbook of North American Indians.* vol. 15. *Northeast.* Washington: Smithsonian Institution, 1978, 123–36.

Ewers, John C. "The Emergence of the Plains Indian as the Symbol of the North American Indian," in Arlene B. Hirschfelder, ed. *American Indian Stereotypes in the World of Children.* Metuchen, NJ: The Scarecrow Press, 1982, 16–32.

Ewing, Juliana Horatia. *Canada Home: Juliana Horatia Ewing's Fredericton Letters, 1867–1869,* ed. Margaret Howard Blom and Thomas E. Blom. Vancouver: University of British Columbia Press, 1983.

Fauset, Arthur Huff. "Folklore from the Halfbreeds in Nova Scotia." *Journal of American Folklore* 38 (1925): 300–15.

Fee, Margery. "Romantic Nationalism and the Image of Native People in Contemporary English-Canadian Literature," in *The Native in Literature: Canadian and Comparative Perspectives,* ed. Thomas King, Cheryl Calver, and Helen Roy. Oakville, ON, Canada: ECW Press, 1987, 15–33.

Feit, Harvey A. "The Construction of Algonquian Hunting Territories: Private Property as Moral Lesson, Policy Advocacy, and Ethnographic Error," in *Colonial Situations: Essays on the Contextualization of Ethnographic Knowledge,* ed. George W. Stocking, Jr. Madison: University of Wisconsin Press, 1991, 109–34.

Fenton, William A. "The Present Status of Anthropology in Northeastern North America." *American Anthropologist,* 50 (1948): 494–514.

Fewkes, J. Walter. "A Contribution to Passamaquoddy Folklore." *Journal of American Folklore,* 3 (1890): 257–80.

Fisher, Margaret W. "The Mythology of Northern and Northeastern Algonkians in Reference to Algonkian Mythology as a Whole," in *Man in Northeastern America,* ed. Frederick Johnson. Papers of the Robert S. Peabody Foundation for Archeology, vol. 3. Andover, MA, 1946.

Flannery, Regina. "Algonquian Indian Folklore." *American Journal of Folklore,* 60 (1947): 397–401.

Francis, Daniel. *The Imaginary Indian: The Image of the Indian in Canadian Culture.* Vancouver: Arsenal Pulp Press, 1992.

Francis, Michael William. Interview. March 26, 1992. Big Cove, NB, Canada.

Francis, Michael William. *Jipuktewik Sipu, River of Fire: Nuji-atukwet Mi'kmawa'j, Micmac Storyteller.* Video. Big Cove, NB, Canada, 1991.

Freeman, John Finley. "Religion and Personality in the Anthropology of Henry Schoolcraft." *Journal of the History of the Behavioral Sciences,* 1 (October, 1965): 301–12.

Frost, Helen Keith. "Two Abenaki Legends." *Journal of American Folklore,* 25 (1912): 188–90.

Frye, Northrup. "Haunted by Lack of Ghosts," in *The Canadian Imagination,* ed. D. Staines. Cambridge: Harvard University Press, 1977.

Geertz, Armin W. "Reflections on the Study of Hopi Mythology," in Christopher Vecsey ed., *Religion in Native North America.* Moscow, ID: University of Idaho Press, 1990, 132–33.

Geertz, Clifford. "The Cerebral Savage," in Clifford Geertz, *The Interpretation of Cultures.* New York: np, 1973, pp. 345–513.

Geertz, Clifford. *Works and Lives: The Anthropologist as Author.* Stanford, CA: Stanford University Press, 1988.

George, Katherine. "The Civilized West Looks at Primitive Africa: 1400–1800, a Study in Ethnocentrism," in Ashley Montagu, ed. *The Concept of the Primitive.* New York: The Free Press, 1968, 175–93.

Gibbons, Roger and J. Rick Ponting. "Contemporary Perceptions of Canada's Native Peoples." *Prairie Forum,* 2:1 (1977): 57–81.

Gill, Sam D. "Mother Earth: An American Myth," in *The Invented Indian: Cultural Fictions and Government Policies,* ed. James A. Clifton. New Brunswick NJ: Transaction Publishers, 1990, 129–43.

Gill, Sam D. *Mother Earth: An American Story.* Chicago: Chicago University Press, 1987.

Gill, Sam D. *Native American Religions: An Introduction.* Belmont, CA: Wadsworth Publishing Company, 1982.

Gill, Sam. "The Power of Story." *American Indian Culture and Research Journal,* 12:3 (1988), 69–84.

Gill, Sam D. "Storytracks: Australia and the Academic Study of Religion." Paper presented at the 1992 International Congress for the Study of Religion, Melbourne, Australia.

gkisedtanamoogk, and Frances Hancock. *Anoqcou: Ceremony Is Life Itself.* Portland, ME: Astarte Shell Press, 1993.

Glaab, Charles N. *The American City: A Documentary History.* Homewood, IL: The Dorsey Press, 1963.

Gonzales, Ellice B. *Changing Economic Roles for Micmac Men and Women: An Ethnohistorical Analysis.* Canadian Ethnology Service Paper No. 72. Ottawa: National Museums of Canada, 1981.

Gordon, Arthur Hamilton. [Baron Stanmore]. *Wilderness Journeys in New Brunswick in 1862–63.* Saint John, NB, Canada: J.&A. McMillan Publishers, 1864.

Gordon, Robert J. *The Bushman Myth: The Making of a Namibian Underclass.* Boulder: Westview Press, 1992.

Gravely, Will. "New Perspectives on Nicholas Black Elk, Oglala Sioux Holy Man." *The Iliff Review,* Winter, 1987, 3–19.

Gray, Viviane, ed. *TAWOW: Micmac People.* 5:2 (April, 1977). TAWOW was a periodical published in Ottawa.

Green, Rayna Diane. *The Only Good Indian: The Image of the Indian in American Vernacular Culture.* Unpublished doctoral thesis, Folklore, Indiana University, 1973.

Grimes, Ronald L. *Ritual Criticism: Case Studies in Its Practice, Essays on Its Theory.* Columbia, SC: University of South Carolina Press, 1990.

Grimes, Ronald L. "Teaching Native American Religions." *Spotlight on Teaching.* American Academy of Religion and the Society of Biblical Literature (on press).

Guillemin, Jeanne. *Urban Renegades: The Cultural Strategy of American Indians.* New York: 1975.

Gyles, John. *Nine Years a Captive, or John Gyles' Experience Among the Malicite Indians from 1689–1698 with an Introduction and Historical Notes by James Hannay.* Saint John, NB, Canada: 1875, pp. 1–37.

Hagar, Stanley. "Micmac Customs and Traditions." *American Anthropologist,* 8,1 (1895 [OS]):31–42.

Hagar, Stanley. "Micmac Magic and Medicine." *Journal of American Folk-Lore,* 9,34 (1896): 170–77.

Hale, Horatio. "Huron Folk-Lore." *The Journal of American Folk-Lore,* I;3 (October-December 1888):177–83.

Hallowell, A. Irving. "The Backwash of the Frontier: The Impact of the Indian on American Culture," in *Contributions to Anthropology: Selected Papers of A. Irving Hallowell.* Chicago: University of Chicago Press, 1976.

Handlin, Oscar and Lilian Handlin. *Liberty in Expansion, 1760–1850.* Harper & Row, 1989.

Hannay, James. *History of New Brunswick.* Saint John: John Bowes, 1909.

Hanson, Jeffery R and Linda P. Rouse. "Dimensions of Native American Stereotyping." *American Indian Culture and Research Journal,*11:4(1987): 33–58.

Hardy, Campbell. "In Evangeline's Land." Ms., Nova Scotia Museum Printed Matter File. *ca.* 1910.

Hardy, Campbell. *Forest Life in Acadia: Sketches of Sport and Natural History in the Lower Provinces of the Canadian Dominion.* London: Chapman & Hall, 1869.

Hardy, Campbell. *Sporting Adventures in the New World.* 2 vols. London: Hurst and Blackett, 1855.

Heckewelder, John. *History, Manners, and Customs of the Indian Nations Who Once Inhabited Pennsylvania and the Neighboring States.* New York: Arno Press and the New York Times, 1971 [1819].

Hill, Kay. *Glooscap and His Magic: Legends of the Wabanaki Indians,* read by Rita Moreno. New York: Caedmon, 1979 (CDL 5 1607). Cassette.

Hill, Kay. *Glooscap and His Magic: Legends of the Wabanaki Indians.* Toronto: McClelland and Stewart, 1973 [1963].

Hill, Kay. Interview, November 14, 1992, Ketch Harbor, NS, Canada.

Hill, Kay. *More Glooscap Stories: Legends of the Wabanaki Indians.* Toronto: McClelland and Stewart, 1978 [1970].

Hinsley, Curtis M., Jr. *Savages and Scientists: The Smithsonian Institution and the Development of American Anthropology, 1846–1910.* Washington, D.C.: Smithsonian Institution Press, 1981.

Hinsley, Curtis M., Jr. "Zunis and Brahmins: Cultural Ambivalence in the Gilded Age," in *Romantic Motives: Essays in Anthropological Sensibility,* ed. George W. Stocking, Jr. Madison: University of Wisconsin Press, 1989.

Hoffman, Bernard Gilbert. *Historical Ethnography of the Micmac of the Sixteenth and Seventeenth Centuries.* Unpublished doctoral thesis. University of California, Berkeley, 1955, 839 pages.

Holler, Clyde. "Black Elk's Relationship to Christianity." *American Indian Quarterly,* Winter, 1984, 37–47.

Holler, Clyde. "Lakota Religion and Tragedy: The Theology of *Black Elk Speaks.*" *Journal of the Amerian Academy of Religion,* 52 (March, 1984), 19–45.

Hultkrantz, Åke. *Belief and Worship in Native North America,* ed. Christopher Vecsey. Syracuse: Syracuse University Press, 1981.

Hultkrantz, Åke. Book Review of Sam D. Gill's *Mother Earth: An American Story. Ethnohistory,* 37:1 (Winter 1990): 73–74.

Hultkrantz, Åke. "Feelings for Nature among North American Indians," in *Belief and Worship in Native North America,* ed. Christopher Vecsey. Syracuse: Syracuse University Press, 1981.

Hultkrantz, Åke. "The Goddess in North America," in *The Book of the Goddess Past and Present: An Introduction to Her Religion,* ed. Carl Olson. New York: Crossroad, 1983, 202–16.

Hultkrantz, Åke. *Native Religions of North America : The Power of Visions and Fertility.* San Francisco: Harper & Row, 1987.

Hultkrantz, Åke. *The Religions of the American Indians.* Berkeley: University of California Press, 1979.

Hultkrantz, Åke. "Reply to [Thomas] Buckley's Review of *Belief and Worship in Native North America.*" *Ethnohistory,* 33 (1986).

Hultkrantz, Åke. *Shamanic Healing and Ritual Drama: Health and Medicine in Native North American Religious Traditions.* New York: The Crossroad Publishing Company, 1992.

Hyde, Douglas. "Letter to U.N.B. Graduates," in *Up the Hill* (yearbook). Fredericton, NB, Canada: The Students' Representative Council of the University of New Brunswick, 1939.

Hymes, Del, ed. *Reinventing Anthropology*. New York: np, 1974.

Indian Island School 1992 Animations, "Kluscap and His People" (6th grade). Video. Old Town, ME: Indian Island School, 1992.

Isocrates. *Panegyricus*, trans. George Norlin. Cambridge: Harvard University Press, 1928, pp. 23-26.

Iverson, Peter. "Neihardt, Collier and the Continuity of Indian Life," in *A Sender of Words: Essays in Memory of John G. Neihardt*, ed. Vine Deloria, Jr. Salt Lake City: Howe Brothers, 1984, pp. 100–09.

Ives, Edward D. "Malecite and Passamaquoddy Tales." *Northeast Folklore*, VI (1964): 5–81.

Jack, David Russell. "Gabe Aquin." *Acadiensis*, 1:4 (October, 1901): 250–52.

Jack, David Russell. "The Indians of Acadia." *Acadiensis*, 1:4 (October, 1901), 187–201.

Jack, Edward. "An Expedition to the Head-Waters of the Little South-West Mirimichi," ed. W. F. Ganong. *Acadiensis*, 5 (1905): 116.

Jack, Edward. "From Stanley to the Miramichi." *Maritime Monthly*, 5 (March 1875): 224–35.

Jack, Edward. "Glooscap." *University Monthly*, 16 (March 1897): 146–48.

Jack, Edward. "Grand Manan and Its Early History." Ms. Typescript, 3, nd. [c. 1905] New Brunswick Provincial Museum, checklist, p. 51.

Jack, Edward. "Heroic Deeds of Glooscap." *Journal of American Folklore*, 1 (1888): 85

Jack, Edward. "Kulloo and Glooscap." *University Monthly*, 16 (March 1897): 148–49.

Jack, Edward. "Lost in the Forests of Acadia in 1677." *Acadiensis*, II (1902): 107.

Jack, Edward. "Maliseet Legends." *Journal of American Folklore*, 8 (1895): 193–208.

Jack, Edward. "Martins Head." 3, Ms. Typescript, nd. New Brunswick Provincial Museum.

Jack, Edward. "The Mohawks on the War-path . . ." *University Monthly*, 16 (Feb. 1897): 125–27.

Jack, Edward. "Passamaquoddy." Ms. Typescript 4, nd. [c. 1905]. New Brunswick Provincial Museum, checklist, p. 44.

Jack, I. Allen, ed. *Biographical Review*. Boston: Biographical Review, 1900.

Jaenen, Cornelius J. "Concepts of America: Amerindians and Acculturation." Ms. pp. 1–31, unpublished paper, presented in Ottawa, 1977.

Jagendorf, Moritz. "Charles Godfrey Leland—Neglected Folklorist," in *New York Folklore Quarterly*, 1963, 19: 211–19.

Jameson, Anna B. *Winter Studies and Summer Rambles in Canada*. London: Saunders & Otley, 1838.

Joe, Rita. *Lnu and Indians We're Called*. Charlottetown, PEI, Canada: Ragweed Press, 1991.

Johnson, Frederick. "Notes on Micmac Shamanism." *Primitive Man,* 16 (1943): 53–80.

Johnston, Angus Anthony. *A History of the Catholic Church in Eastern Nova Scotia.* 2 vol. Antigonish: St. Francis Xavier University Press, 1960, 1971.

Jones, Prudence and Caitlin Matthews, eds. *Voices from the Circle: The Heritage of Western Paganism.* Wellingborough, England: The Aquarian Press, 1990.

Jung, Carl G. "The Complications of American Psychology," in *Collected Works* vol. 10, *Civilization in Transition.* New York: Bollingen Foundation, 1964, 502–14.

Kaiser, Rudolf. "'A Fifth Gospel, Almost' Chief Seattle's Speech(es): American Origins and European Reception," in *Recovering the Word: Essays on Native American Literature,* ed. Arnold Krupat and Brian Swann. University of California Press, 1987.

Kehoe, Alice B. "Primal Gaia: Primitivists and Plastic Medicine Men," in James A. Clifton, ed. *The Invented Indian: Cultural Fictions and Government Policies.* New Brunswick, NJ: Transaction Publishers, 1990.

Knockwood, Isabelle with Gillian Thomas. *Out of the Depths: The Experiences of Mi'kmaw Children at the Indian Residential School at Shubenacadie, Nova Scotia.* Lockeport, NS, Canada: Roseway Publishing, 1992.

Knockwood, Noel. Interview. February 13, 1992, Ottawa, Ontario.

Knudtson, Peter and David Suzuki. *Wisdom of the Elders.* Toronto: Stoddart Publishing, 1992.

Lafarge, Oliver. "Wakan Tanka and the Seven Rituals of the Sioux." *The New York Times Book Review,* November 22, 1953, 6.

Larsen, Lawrence H. "Nineteenth Century Sanitation: A Story of Filth and Frustration." *Wisconsin Magazine of History,* 52 (Spring 1969).

Lawrence, D. H. *Studies in Classic American Literature.* London: Martin Secker, 1924.

Lears, T. J. Jackson. *No Place of Grace: Antimodernism and the Transformation of American Culture, 1880–1920.* New York: Pantheon Books, 1981.

Leland, Charles Godfrey and John Dyneley Prince. *Kulóskap the Master: And Other Algonkin Poems.* New York: Funk & Wagnalls, 1902.

Leland, Charles Godfrey. *The Algonquin Legends of New England.* Boston: Houghton Mifflin & Co., 1884, reprinted Singing Tree Press, 1968, and Dover Press, 1992.

Leland, Charles Godfrey. "American Studies of Native Folk-Lore," a letter to the editor of *The Critic,* 12:225 (1888), 194.

Leland, Charles Godfrey. *Charles Godfrey Leland Papers.* Ms. Pennell-Whistler Collection of the Papers of Joseph and Elizabeth Robins Pennell and James A. Whistler. Washington, D.C.: Library of Congress, containers 365–73.

Leland, Charles Godfrey. "The Edda among the Algonquin Indians." *Atlantic*

Monthly, vol. 54, August, 1884, 222–34. This is reprinted in Clements, Native American Folklore, 129–54.

Leland, Charles Godfrey. *Fusang; or, The Discovery of America by Chinese Buddhist Priests in the Fifth Century.* London: Truber & Co., 1875.

Leland, Charles Godfrey. "Indian Impudence." *Temple Bar,* 48(1877): 189–205.

Leland, Charles Godfrey. "Legends of the Passamaquoddy; With Drawings on Birch Bark by a Quādi Indian." *The Century Illustrated Monthly Magazine,* 6 (September, 1884): 668–77.

Leland, Charles Godfrey. *Memoirs,* 2 vol. London: William Heinemann, 1893.

Leland, Charles Godfrey. "The Mythology, Legends, and Folk-Lore of the Algonkins," in *Royal Society of Literature of the United Kingdom Transactions,* series 2, vol. 14, pp. 69–91. (Paper was read in June 1886.)

Leland, Charles Godfrey. *The Union Pacific Railway, or Three Thousand Miles in a Railway Car.* Philadelphia: Ringwalt & Brown, 1867.

Lester, Joan A. "The American Indian: A Museum's Eye View." *Indian Historian.* 5 (Summer, 1972).

Lester, Joan A. *History on Birchbark: The Art of Tomah Joseph, Passamaquoddy.* Providence, RI: Haffenreffer Museum of Anthropology, Brown University, 1993.

Lester, Joan A. *We're Still Here: Art of Indian New England, The Children's Museum Collection.* Boston: The Children's Museum, 1987.

Lovejoy, Arthur O. and George Boas. *Primitivism and Related Ideas in Antiquity.* New York: Octagon Books, 1973 [1935].

Lovesey, Dorothy May. *To Be a Pilgrim: A Biography of Silas Tertius Rand, 1810–1889; Nineteeth Century Protestant Missionary to the Micmac.* Hantsport, NS, Canada: Lancelot Press, 1992.

Macmillan, Cyrus. *Canadian Wonder Tales.* London: The Bodley Head, 1974 [1918].

Macmillan, Cyrus. *Glooskap's Country and Other Indian Tales.* Toronto: Oxford University Press, 1962 [1918].

Macmillan, Cyrus. *The Micmacs: Their Life and Legends.* Ms., Canadian Museum of Civilization: III-F-6M, 1911–1913.

Maillard, l'Abbé Antoine Simon. *An Account of the Customs and Manners of the Micmakis and Maricheets.* London: np, 1758.

Mander, Jerry. *In the Absence of the Sacred: The Failure of Technology and the Survival of the Indian Nations.* San Francisco: Sierra Club Books, 1991.

Manfred, Frederick. "Those Western American Darks," in *A Sender of Words: Essays in Memory of John G. Neihardt,* ed. Vine Deloria, Jr. Salt Lake City: Howe Brothers, 1984, 39–45.

Marcus, G. and D. Cushman. "Ethnographies as Texts," in *Annual Review of Anthropology,* ed. B. Siegel. vol. II. Palo Alto: np, 1982, pp. 25–69.

Marcus, G. and M. Fisher. *Anthropology as Cultural Critique: An Experimental Moment in the Human Sciences.* Chicago: np, 1986.

Mark, Joan. *Four Anthropologists: And American Science in its Early Years.* New York: Science Publications, 1980.

Martin, Joel W. "Before and Beyond the Sioux Ghost Dance: Native American Prophetic Movements and the Study of Religion." *Journal of the American Academy of Religion,* LIX:4 (Winter, 1991): 677–701.

Martin, John. Interview. January 6, 1994. Gesgapegiag.

Matthews, Maureen. "*Isinamowin:* The White Man's Indian," on Canadian Broadcasting Corporation *Ideas* (radio program). Originally broadcast December 11 and 12, 1991. Transcript.

McBride, Bunny, "A Penobscot in Paris." *Down East,* August, 1989: 63–84.

McCluskey, Sally. "Black Elk Speaks, and So Does John G. Neihardt." *Western Literature of America,* 6:4 (1972): 231–42.

McGregor, Gaile. *The Noble Savage in the New World Garden: Notes Toward a Syntactics of Place.* Toronto: Toronto University Press, 1988.

McIntosh, James. *Thoreau as Romantic Naturalist.* Ithaca, NY: 1974.

McKelvey, Blake. *The City in American History.* London: George Allen and Unwin, 1969.

Mechling, William H. "The Malecite Indians with Notes on the Micmacs." *Anthropologica,* (OS) 7 and 8 (1958–59): 1–275.

Mechling, William H. "Maliseet Tales." *Journal of American Folklore,* 26 (1913): 219–58.

Mechling, William H. *The Social and Religious Life of the Malecites and Micmacs.* Unpublished doctoral thesis, Harvard, 1917.

Mechling, William. "Malecite Tales." *Memoir.* Ottawa: Department of Mines, 1914, 49: 1–133.

Medicine, Bea. "The Anthropologist as the Indian's Image-Maker." *Indian Historian,* 4;3 (1971): 27–37.

Michelson, Truman. "Micmac Tales." *Journal of American Folklore,* 38; 147 (Jan.-Mar. 1925): 33–54.

Michelson, Truman. "Review of *Penobscot Transformer Tales* by F. G. Speck." *American Journal of Philology,* 41 (1920): 305–06.

Momaday, N. Scott. "To Save a Great Vision," in *A Sender of Words: Essays in Memory of John G. Neihardt,* ed. Vine Deloria, Jr. Salt Lake City: Howe Brothers, 1984, 30–38.

Mooney, James. "The Ghost Dance Religion and the Sioux Outbreak of 1890," in *Fourteenth Annual Report of the Bureau of Ethnology, 1892–1893,* Washington, D.C.

Morrison, Ann. "Voces Cantantes in Vestro: History of Research on Music among the Wabanaki," in *Papers of the Twenty-Second Algonquian Conference,* ed. William Cowan. Ottawa: Carleton University Press, 1991.

Morrison, Kenneth M. "Discourse and the Accommodation of Values: Towards a Revision of Mission History." *Journal of the American Academy of Religion,* 53 (Sept. 1985) 365–82.

Morrison, Kenneth M. *The Embattled Northeast: The Elusive Ideal of Alliance in Abenaki-Euramerican Relations.* Berkeley: University of California Press, 1984.

Morrison, Kenneth M. "Montagnais Missionization in Early New France: The Syncretic Imperative." *American Indian Culture and Research Journal,* 10:3 (1986) 1–23.

Morrison, Kenneth M. "Ritual Work in Many Dimensions: The Supernatural Versus the Yaqui and Ojibwa Idea of the Person." Ms. October, 1992.

Morrison, Kenneth M. "Sharing the Flower: A Non-Supernaturalistic Theory of Grace." *Religion,* 22 (1992): 207–19.

Mosse, George L. *The Culture of Western Europe: Nineteenth and Twentieth Centuries,* 3rd ed. Boulder, CO: Westview Press, 1988 [1961].

Murray, David. *Forked Tongues: Speech, Writing and Representation in North American Indian Texts.* Bloomington: Indiana University Press, 1991.

Nash, Roderick. *Wilderness and the American Mind.* New Haven: Yale University Press, 1967.

Nelson, Eunice Baumann. *The Wabanaki: An Annotated Bibliography.* Cambridge, Massachusetts: American Friends Service Committee, 1982.

Nicolar, Joseph. *Life and Traditions of the Red Man.* Fredericton NB, Canada: St. Anne Point Press, 1979. [Bangor: self-published, 1893.]

Nicholas, Andrea Bear. "Acquin (Atwin, Decoine, Dequine, Equin, Echikewen), Gabriel (Kobleah, Gobliel)," in the *Dictionary of Canadian Biography,* XIII, 1901–1910. Toronto: University of Toronto Press, 1994, 3–4.

"On Teaching Native American Religions," compiled by Ron Grimes. e-Ms. The compilation is from three electronic discussion groups: Religion, a discussion group on religious studies (religion@harvarda.harvard.edu); Anthro-L, whose focus is anthropology (listserv@ubvm.cc.buffalo.edu); and Natchat, a discussion group on native issues (natchat@tamvm1.bitnet). It is available from the listserver at Harvard [listserv@harvarda.harvard.edu] by asking in a single line message, **get religion log9306;** "On Teaching Native American Religions" is contained in five messages from Tim Bryson, beginning with one dated Friday, June 11. One could retrieve the whole (uncompiled) conversation by using similar commands to "get" the religion list logs from April through August (log9304 –log9308) of 1993.

Ortiz, Alfonso. "Some Concerns Central to the Writing of 'Indian' History." *The Indian Historian,* x (1977): 17–22.

Osborn, Chase S. and Stellanova Osborn. *Schoolcraft-Longfellow-Hiawatha.* Lancaster, PA: Jacques Cattell Press, 1942.

Pandey, T. N. "Anthropologists at Zuni." *Proceedings of the American Philosophical Society,* 116 (Aug. 1972): 321–37.

Paper, Jordon. Book Review of Sam D. Gill's *Mother Earth: An American Story. Studies in Religion,* 17 (1988): 488–89.

Paper, Jordon. "Réponse/Rejoinder: Methodological Controversies in the Study of Native American Religions." *Studies in Religion/Sciences Religieuses,* 22:3 (1993): 365–77.

Paper, Jordon. "Through the Earth Darkly: The Female Spirit in Native American Religions," in *Religion in Native North America,* Christopher Vecsey, ed. Moscow, ID: University of Idaho Press, 1990, 3–19.

Parkhill, Thomas. "Book Review of Åke Hultkrantz, *Shamanic Healing and Ritual Drama: Health and Medicine in Native North American Religious Traditions." Studies in Religion/Sciences Religieuses,* 23:3 (1994): 375–76.

Parkhill, Thomas. "Book Review of Jordan Paper, *Offering Smoke: The Sacred Pipe and Native American Religion." Studies in Religion/Sciences Religieuses,* 20 (1991): 119–21.

Parkhill, Thomas. "'Of Glooskap's Birth, and of His Brother Malsum, the Wolf': the Story of Charles Godfrey Leland's 'Purely American Creation.'" *American Indian Culture and Research Journal,* 16:1 (1992): 45–69.

Parsons, Elsie Clews. "Micmac Folklore." *Journal of American Folklore,* 38 (1925): 55–133.

Parsons, Elsie Clews. "Micmac Notes." *Journal of American Folklore,* 39 (1926): 460–85.

Partridge, Emelyn Newcomb. *Glooscap the Great Chief and Other Stories: Legends of the Micmacs.* New York: Sturgis and Walton, 1913.

Paul, George. Interview. April 9, 1992. Lennox Island, Prince Edward Island.

Pearce, Roy Harvey. *Savagism and Civilization: A Study of the Indian and the American Mind.* Berkeley: University of California Press, 1988, [1953].

Pennell, Elizabeth Robins. *Charles Godfrey Leland: A Biography.* New York: Houghton Mifflin, 1906. 2 vol.

Philadelphia: Work, Space, Family, and Group Experience in the Nineteenth Century; Essays Toward an Interdisciplinary History of the City. Theodore Hershberg, ed. New York: Oxford University Press, 1981.

Pohl, Frederick J. *Prince Henry Sinclair: His Expedition to the New World in 1398.* New York: Clarkson N. Potter, Inc., 1974.

Powell, F. York. "In Memoriam," obituary of Charles Godfrey Leland. *Folk-lore.* 14 (1903): 162–64.

Powers, William K. "The Indian Hobbyist Movement in North America." *Handbook of North American Indians,* vol. 4 *History of Indian-White Relations.* Washington, D.C.: Smithsonian Institution, 1988, 557–61.

Powers, William K. "When Black Elk Speaks, Everybody Listens," in *Religion in Native North America,* Christopher Vecsey, ed. Moscow, ID: Idaho University Press, 1990, 136–51.

Pratt, M.L. "Fieldwork in Common Places," in J. Clifford and G.E. Marcus, eds, *Writing Culture: The Poetics and Politics of Ethnography.* Berkeley: University of California Press, 1986.

Pred, Allan. *Urban Growth and City-Systems in the United States, 1840–1860.* Cambridge: Harvard University Press, 1980.

Prince, John Dyneley. "A Passamaquoddy Aviator." *American Anthropology.* (NS). XI (1909): 628–50.

Prince, John Dyneley. "A Passamaquoddy Tobacco Famine." *International Journal of American Linguistics.* 1 (1917–1920); [Kraus reprints. New York: 1965, 58–64].

Prince, John Dyneley. "Algonkians (Eastern)." *Encyclopedia of Religion and Ethics.* 1 (1908): 319–21.

Prince, John Dyneley. *Passamaquoddy Texts; Publications of the American Ethnological Society,* vol. 10. ed, Franz Boaz. New York: np, 1921, 1–85.

Prince, John Dyneley. "The Passamaquoddy Wampum Records." *New York State Museum Bulletin,* 184 (1916): 119–25.

Prince, John Dyneley. "Some Passamaquoddy Witchcraft Tales." *Proceedings of the American Philosophical Society.* 38 (1899): 181–89.

Rabinow, P. *Reflections on Fieldwork.* Berkeley: np, 1977.

Rand, Silas Tertius. "The Beautiful Bride." *American Antiquarian (and Oriental Journal).* 12 (1890): 156–59.

Rand, Silas Tertius. *Diary,* vol. 7 (1870), Rand Papers. Atlantic Baptist Historical Collection. Acadia University. Wolfville, NS, Canada, 1–45.

Rand, Silas Tertius. "Glooscap, Cuhkw and Coolpurjot." *American Antiquarian (and Oriental Journal),* 12 (1890): 283–86.

Rand, Silas Tertius. *Legends of the Micmac.* New York: Longnass, Green & Co., 1894.

Rand, Silas Tertius. "The Legends of the Micmacs." *American Antiquarian (and Oriental Journal),* 12 (1890): 3–14.

Rand, Silas Tertius. "The Micmac Indians: Their Legends." Ms. Public Archives of Nova Scotia, no date.

Rand, Silas Tertius. "Relation of a Visit to St. John . . ." *Ninth Annual Report of the Committee of the Micmac Missionary Society, from Sept. 30, 1857 to Sept. 30, 1858.* Halifax, NS, Canada: 1858, 11–12.

Rand, Silas Tertius. "Terms of Relationship of the Micmac, and Etchemin or Malisete, collected by Rev. S. T. Rand, Missionary, Hantsport, N.S." *Systems of Consanguinity and Affinity of the Human Family.* Lewis Henry Morgan. Washington, D.C.: 1871. 293–382.

Reither, James A. "Voices: Academic Discourse Communities, Invention and Learning to Write." Paper presented at the Conference on College Composition and Communication, New Orleans, March, 1986. (ERIC ED 270 815.)

Rice, Julian. *Black Elk's Story: Distinguishing Its Lakota Purpose.* Albuquerque: University of New Mexico Press, 1991.

Robertson, Marion. *Red Earth: Tales of the Micmacs; With an Introduction to the*

Customs and Beliefs of the Micmac Indians. Halifax, NS, Canada: Nova Scotia Museum, 1969.

Rose, Wendy. "The Great Pretenders: Further Reflections on Whiteshamanism," in *The State of Native America: Genocide, Colonization, and Resistance,* ed. M. Annette Jaimes. Boston: South End Press, 1992, 403–21.

Rosenthal, Bernard. *City of Nature: Journeys to Nature in the Age of American Romanticism.* Newark: University of Delaware Press, 1980.

Roth, D. Luther. *Acadie and the Acadians.* Utica, NY: L.C. Childs, 1891. Philadelphia: Lutheran Publication Society, 1890.

Rouse, Linda P. and Jeffery R. Hanson. "American Indian Stereotyping, Resource Competition, and Status-based Prejudice." *American Indian Culture and Research Journal,* 15:3(1991):1–17.

Salisbury, Neal. *The Indians of New England: A Critical Bibliography.* Bloomington: Indiana University Press, 1982.

Sandler, Florence and Darrell Reeck. "The Masks of Joseph Campbell." *Religion,* 11 (1981) 1–20.

Sapir, Edward. *Edward Sapir's Correspondence.* Ms. folder: MacMillan Cyrus, 1911–1915. Canadian Museum of Civilization: I-A-236M.

Sark, John Joe. *Micmac Legends of Prince Edward Island.* Illustrations by Michael Francis and George Paul. Lennox Island, PEI, Canada: Lennox Island Band Council, 1988.

Sauer, Carl O. *Sixteenth Century North America: The Land and the People as Seen by the Europeans.* Berkeley: University of California Press, 1975.

Sayre, Robert F. *Thoreau and the American Indians.* Princeton: Princeton University Press, 1977.

Sayre, Robert F. "Vison and Experience in *Black Elk Speaks.*" *College English,* 32:5 (February 1971): 509–35.

Schedule of Indian Bands, Reserves and Settlements Including—Membership and Population Location and Area in Hectares, Indian and Northern Affairs Canada, Ottawa: Minister of Supply and Services Canada, 1990.

Schlesinger, Arthur M. *The Rise of the City, 1878–1898.* New York: Macmillan, 1933.

Schoolcraft, Henry R. *Historical and Statistical Information respecting the History, Condition and Prospects of the Indians Tribes of the United States,* 6 vols. Philadelphia: Lippincott, Grambo & Co., 1851–1857.

Schoolcraft, Henry R. *The Myth of Hiawatha, and Other Oral Legends, Mythologic and Allegoric, of the North American Indians.* Philadelphia: J. B. Lippincott & Co., 1856. Originally published as *Algic Researches, Comprising Inquiries Respecting the Mental Characteristics of the North American Indians.* 2 vols. New York: Harper & Row, 1839; with a new preface and dedication.

Schoolcraft, Henry Rowe. *An Address Delivered Before the Was-Ah Ho-De-No-Son-Ne or New Confederacy of the Iroquois by Henry R Schoolcraft, A Member at its Third Annual Council, August 14, 1846.* Rochester, Jerome & Brother, 1846.

Schoolcraft, Henry Rowe. "Our Indian Policy." *Democratic Review,* 14 (Feb. 1844): 169–84.

Schoolcraft, Henry Rowe. *Personal Memoirs of a Residence of Thirty Years with the Indian Tribes on the American Frontiers.* Philadelphia: Lippincott & Grambo, 1851.

Segal, Robert A. *Joseph Campbell: An Introduction.* New York: Garland Publishing, 1987.

Siegel, Adrenne. *The Image of the American City in Popular Literature, 1820–1870.* Port Washington, NY: Kennikat Press, 1981.

Silverberg, Robert. *Mound Builders of Ancient America: The Archaeology of a Myth.* Greenwich, CT: New York Graphic Society Ltd., 1968.

Simard, Jean-Jacques. "White Ghosts, Red Shadows: The Reduction of North American Natives," in James A. Clifton. ed. *The Invented Indian: Cultural Fictions and Government Policies.* New Brunswick NJ: Transaction Publishers, 1990.

Slotkin, Richard L. *Regeneration Through Violence: The Mythology of the American Frontier, 1600–1860.* Middletown, CT: Wesleyan University Press, 1974.

Smethurst, Gamaliel. *A Narrative of an Extraordinary Escape out of the Hands of the Indians in the Gulph of St. Lawrence.* London: privately printed, 1774.

Smith, Jonathan Z. *Map Is Not Territory. Studies in Judaism of Late Antiquity,* vol. 23. Leiden: E. J. Brill, 1978.

Smith, Jonathan Z. *To Take Place: Toward Theory in Ritual.* Chicago: The University of Chicago Press, 1987.

Smith, Marion Whitney. *Strange Tales of Abenaki Shamanism.* Lewiston, ME: Central Maine Press, 1963.

Smith, Ralph Carlisle. *Charles Godfrey Leland: The American Years, 1824–1869.* Unpublished doctoral thesis. University of New Mexico, 1961.

Snow, Dean R. "Eastern Abenaki," in *Handbook of North American Indians,* vol. 15, Northeast. Washington: Smithsonian Institution, 1978, 137.

Speck, Frank G. "Eastern Algonkian Wabanaki Confederacy." *American Anthropologist,* new series, 17 (1915): 492–508.

Speck, Frank G. "Malecite Tales." *Journal of American Folk-Lore,* 30 (1917): 479–85.

Speck, Frank G. "Some Micmac Tales from Cape Breton Island." *Journal of American Folk-Lore,* 28 (1915): 59–69.

Spray, Carole. *Will O' The Wisp: Folk Tales and Legends of New Brunswick.* Fredericton, NB, Canada: Brunswick Press, 1979.

Spence, Lewis. *The Myths of the North American Indians.* New York: Frederick A. Stokes, 1914. Most recently published as *North American Indians: Myths and Legends.* London: Senate, an imprint of Studio Editions Ltd., 1994; and New York: Dover, 1989.

Squires, Austin. "The Great Sagamore of the Maliseets." *Atlantic Advocate.* 59;3 (1968): 49; 51–52.

Squires, Mrs Susan K. "Reminiscences of the St. Mary's Indian Reserve and It's Inhabitants Fifty Years Ago." Ms. Read before the York-Sunbury Historical Society Ltd., January 1937. MC 300 MS2 128, Archives of the Province of New Brunswick.

Starkloff, Carl J., S. J. "Renewing the Sacred Hoop," in *A Sender of Words: Essays in Memory of John G. Neihardt*, ed. Vine Deloria, Jr. Salt Lake City: Howe Brothers, 1984, 159–72.

Statistics Canada. *Age and Sex*. Ottawa: Industry, Science and Technology Canada, 1993. 1991 Census of Canada, Catalogue number 94–327.

Steager, Peter. "The Child Who Was Not Born Naturally," in *Papers of the Seventh Algonquian Conference*, edited by William Cowan. Ottawa: Carleton University Press, 1976.

Stedman, Raymond William. *Shadows of the Indian: Stereotypes in American Culture*. Norman: University of Oklahoma Press, 1982.

Steltenkamp, Michael F. *Black Elk: Holy Man of the Oglala*. Norman: University of Oklahoma Press, 1993.

Stocking, George W. Jr. *Victorian Anthropology*. New York: The Free Press, 1987.

Sturluson, Snorri. *Edda: Prologue and Gylfaginning*, ed. Anthony Faulkes. Oxford: Clarendon Press, 1982.

Sundel, Alfred. "Joseph Campbell's Quest for the Grail." *The Sewanee Review*, 78 (1970) 211–16.

Swain, Tony. "The Mother Earth Conspiracy: An Australian Episode." *Numen*. XXXVIII, Fasc. 1, June 1991, 3–26.

Sweetser, Moses Foster. *The Maritime Provinces: Handbook for Travellers; A Guide to the Chief Cities, Coasts, and Islands of the Maritime Provinces of Canada, and to Their Scenery and Historic Attractions; with the Gulf and River of St. Lawrence to Quebec and Montreal; also, Newfoundland and the Labrador Coast. With Four Maps and Four Plans*. 3rd ed. Boston: James R. Osgood and Company, 1883.

Szabo, Laszlo. *Malecite Stories*. vols. 1–12. Canadian Museum of Civilization, (III-E-(It)47M), 1971–1984.

Szabo, Laszlo. "Malecite Stories: Contents, Characters, Motifs." *Studies in Canadian Literature*, 13:2; 1988, 157–65.

Szabo, Laszlo. "Maliseet: The Language of the Saint John River Indians," in *A Literary and Linguistic History of New Brunswick*, ed. Reavley Gair. Fredericton: Fiddlehead & Goose Lane, 1985, 29–40.

Taylor, Colin F. "The Indian Hobbyist Movement in Europe," in *Handbook of North American Indians*, vol. 4, *History of Indian-White Relations*. Washington, D.C.: Smithsonian Institution, 1988, 562–69.

Therien, Gilles. "L'Indien Imaginaire: Une Hypothese." *Recherches Amerindiennes au Quebec*, 17:3 (1987); 3–21.

Thompson, Stith. "Icelandic Parallels Among the Algonquians: A

Reconsideration," in *Nordica et Anglica: Studies in Honor of Stefán Einarsson*, Allan H. Orrick, ed. The Hague: Mouton, 1968, 133–39.

Thoreau, Henry D. *The Maine Woods*, edited with afterword by Joseph J. Moldenhauer. Princeton: Princeton University Press, 1972 [1864].

Torgovnick, Marianna. *Gone Primitive: Savage Intellects, Modern Lives*. Chicago: University of Chicago Press, 1990.

Townsend, Joan. "Shamanic Spirituality: Core Shamanism and Neo-Shamanism in Contemporary Western Society," in *Anthropology of Religion: a Handbook in Theory and Method*, ed. Stephen Glazier. Westport, CT: Greenwood Publishing, 1994.

Trigger, Bruce. "The Historians' Indian: Native American in Canadian Historical Writing from Charlevoix to the Present." *Canadian Historical Review*, LXVII, 3 (Sept. 1986), 316–21.

Tuan, Yi Fu. *Dominance and Affection: The Making of Pets*. New Haven: Yale University Press, 1984.

Tuan, Yi Fu. "Geopiety: A Theme in Man's Attachment to Nature and to Place," in *Geographies of the Mind: Essays in Historical Geosophy; In Honor of John Kirkland Wright*. David Lowenthal and Martyn J. Bowden, eds. New York: Oxford University Press, 1976.

Tuan, Yi-Fu. *Space and Place: The Perspective of Experience*. Minneapolis: University of Minnesota Press, 1977.

Turner, Frederick Jackson. "The Significance of the Frontier in American History," in *The Frontier in American History*. New York: Holt, Rinehart and Winston, 1962 [1920].

Turville-Petre, E.O.G. *Myth and Religion of the North: The Religion of Ancient Scandinavia*. London: Weidenfeld and Nicolson, 1964.

Varesano, Angela-Marie Joanna. *Charles Godfrey Leland: The Eclectic Folklorist*. Unpublished doctoral thesis, University of Pennsylvania, 1979.

Vecsey, Christopher. Book Review of Sam D. Gill's *Native American Religious Action and Mother Earth: An American Story*. *American Indian Quarterly*. 12:3 (Summer, 1988): 254–56.

Vecsey, Christopher. "Introduction," *Belief and Worship in Native North America*, ed. Christopher Vecsey. Syracuse: Syracuse University Press, 1981.

Vecsey, Christopher. *Traditional Ojibwa Religion and Its Historical Changes*. Philadelphia: The American Philosophical Society, 1983.

Vermette, Michael E. Telephone interview. July 9, 1992.

Voices from the Circle: The Heritage of Western Paganism, ed. Prudence Jones and Caitlin Matthews. Northamptonshire, England: The Aquarian Press, 1990.

The Wabanakis of Maine and the Maritimes: A Resource Book about Penobscot, Passamaquoddy, Maliseet, Micmac and Abenaki Indians, with lesson plans for grades 4 through 8. Prepared and published by The Maine Indian Program of The New England Office of the American Friends Service Committee. Bath, ME; Maine Indian Program, 1989.

Walker, Willard, Robert Conkling, and Gregory Buesing. "A Chronological Account of the Wabanaki Confederacy." *Political Organization of Native North Americans*, ed. Ernest L. Schusky. Washington, D.C.: University Press of America, 1980, 41–84.

Walker, Willard. "Gabriel Tomah's Journal." *Man in the Northeast*, 21 (1981): 87–101.

Wallis, Wilson D. and Ruth S. Wallis. *The Micmac Indians of Eastern Canada.* Minneapolis: University of Minnesota Press, 1955.

Washburn, Wilcomb E. "Introduction," *Handbook of North American Indians*, vol. 4. *History of Indian-White Relations.* Washington: Smithsonian Institution, 1988, 2–4.

Waters, Frank. "Neihardt and the Vision of Black Elk," in *A Sender of Words: Essays in Memory of John G. Neihardt*, ed. Vine Deloria, Jr. Salt Lake City: Howe Brothers, 1984, 12–24.

White, Morton and Lucia White. *The Intellectual Versus the City: From Thomas Jefferson to Frank Lloyd Wright.* Cambridge, MA: Harvard University Press, 1962.

Whitehead, Ruth Holmes, and Ronald Kaplan. "A Visit with Max Basque, Whycocomagh." *Cape Breton's Magazine*, 1989; 51: 15–29.

Whitehead, Ruth Holmes and Ronald Kaplan. "Max Basque, Whycocomagh— Conclusion." *Cape Breton's Magazine*, 1989, 52: 53–65.

Whitehead, Ruth Holmes. *Old Man Told Us: Excerpts from Micmac History 1500–1950.* Halifax: Nimbus, 1991.

Whitehead, Ruth Holmes. *Stories from the Six Worlds: Micmac Legends.* Halifax, NS, Canada: Nimbus , 1988.

Whitney, Blair. *John G. Neihardt.* Boston: Twayne Publishers, 1976.

Wright, John K. "Geopiety: A Theme in Man's Attachment to Nature and to Place," in *Geographies of the Mind: Essays in Historical Geosophy*, ed. David Lowenthal and Martyn J. Bowden. New York: Oxford University Press, 1976.

INDEX